People Out of Place

Globalization, Human Rights, and the Citizenship Gap

Alison Brysk and Gershon Shafir, Editors

Routledge
Taylor & Francis Group

NEW YORK AND LONDON

Published in 2004 by
Routledge
29 West 35th Street
New York, NY 10001
www.routledge-ny.com

Published in Great Britain by
Routledge
11 New Fetter Lane
London EC4P 4EE
www.routledge.co.uk

Printed in the United Stated of America on acid-free paper.

10 9 8 7 6 5 4 3 2 1

Library of Congress Cataloging-in-Publication Data

People out of place : globalization, human rights, and the citizenship
gap / Alison Brysk and Gershon Shafir, editors.
    p. cm.
Includes bibliographical references and index.
  ISBN 0-415-93584-9 (HC : alk. paper) -- ISBN 0-415-93585-7 (PB : alk.
paper)
1. Citizenship. 2. Human rights. 3. Globalization--Social aspects.
4. Globalization--Political aspects. I. Brysk, Alison, 1960- II.
Shafir, Gershon.
 JF801.P43 2004
 323--dc22
                          2003015085

Contents

Part V. Reconstructing Citizenship

Acknowledgments

We are grateful to all of this project's participants and supporters. A generous grant from the University of California's Institute for Global Conflict and Cooperation, through its director, Peter Cowhey, enabled us to host two workshops that provided the basis for this book. The October 2001 workshop was hosted by UCSD's sociology department, and attended by Nina Berkovitch, David Jacobson, Ronnie Lipschutz, Aihwa Ong, and Peter Spiro. Invaluable logistical assistance was provided by UCI doctoral student Sharon Lean and UCSD Ph.D. candidate Caroline Lee. The second workshop, in April 2002, also took place at UCSD. Richard Falk, Kristen Maher, and Gay Seidman presented, while UCSD's John Skrentny provided insightful commentary. Saskia Sassen defied geographic challenges to contribute to this book. Sociology student Grischa Metlay assisted greatly in the preparation of the book manuscript. Professor Tom Farer and two peer reviewers from Routledge gave constructive and incisive suggestions for revision. Our editor at Routledge, Eric Nelson, encouraged and guided this project from its inception. Many thanks to Human Rights Quarterly for permission to reprint a revised version of Jacobson and Ruffer's chapter. Both of us acknowledge most of all our families, the people who help us to find our place. To all of these, we owe gratitude for their contributions, and apologies for any remaining flaws.

Jacobson, David and Gayla Benarieh Ruffer, Courts Across Borders: The Implications of Judicial Agency for Human Rights and Democracy. Human Rights Quarterly 25:1 (2003), Excerpts from pp. 74–92. © The Johns Hopkins University Press. Reprinted with permission of The Johns Hopkins University Press.

I
Framework

1
Introduction
Globalization and the Citizenship Gap

ALISON BRYSK AND GERSHON SHAFIR

Citizenship is a mechanism for allocating rights and claims through political membership. In the past two centuries or so, citizenship has been nested in nation-states. Globalization is a package of transnational flows—of people, production, investment, information, ideas, and authority. As exchange intensifies across borders, such globalization changes the nature of citizenship. Globalization has put some flows out of the reach of states, putting rights at risk, but also created new levels of membership and rights claims. Among the changes it has wrought, globalization coincides with a universal, deterritorialized, and postnational human rights regime.

We critically analyze the interaction of two traditions of rights: citizenship and human rights. While citizenship has come to signify full membership in the polity on the basis of broad claims and entitlements, human rights are more universal in coverage but encompass a more modest set of rights and are institutionally less settled. This book will consider how globalization has created a "citizenship gap" (Brysk 2002), which puts noncitizens and "second-class citizens" at risk. We will discuss the key concepts of citizenship, human rights, and globalization, the nature of the citizenship gap, and our approach to analyzing—and reducing or closing—the gap.

In an era of globalization, how do these traditions affect the provision of rights in response to global migration, markets, and transnational ties? How do these flows affect the state—the site of citizenship—in its ability to sustain existing citizenship rights and provide new forms of membership? How does globalization affect those most marginalized by the state—second-class citizens—and how does it impact noncitizens who fall between the cracks of a state-based membership system? This book is an attempt to address those questions. Finally, we will ask what steps would be necessary to provide citizenship on a global scale?

Though we identify citizenship with the nation-state, its origins are ancient. They lay in the Greek polis as privileged participatory membership in the polity. In between the polis and the modern national state, citizenship has been transformed and overlaid with new content through its association with the Roman imperial framework and the medieval city-states. Social struggle in modern industrial society often took the form of, or was diverted to, aspirations for equal citizenship. Whereas in antiquity citizenship was most clearly associated with military service, even with freedom from laboring, nowadays many of the rights of citizenship are accessed through labor market participation. Modern struggles, either through the mobilization of trade unions, workers' parties, and social movements or through preemptive concessions, led to the extension of citizenship to workers and later to women and minorities. Eventually, this led to the expansion of citizenship rights themselves, spanning from civil through political and social rights and now, perhaps, to cultural ones as well. Though citizenship rights are now universally accorded, they are available only to members of political communities of limited size and particular characteristics, leaving out those devoid of membership.

While it is customary to point to the Magna Carta and the English or American Bill of Rights as early human rights documents, the recipients of these rights were privileged and members of specific political communities (Orend 2002: 101–6). Only with the universalization of rights—that is, with the endowment of individuals with rights by virtue of their common humanity—does an alternative tradition, that of human rights, commence. Its legacy is derived from natural law and is associated with the Enlightenment's individualistic and anti-hierarchical perspective, and finds its first clear expression in the French Revolution's constitutive document, the Declaration of the Rights of Man and Citizen, though here the two rights traditions appear interlinked. Since the Second World War, and in an accelerated fashion in the globalizing decade of the 1990s, human rights have been gaining on citizenship as the main purveyor of rights (Leary 1999). This ongoing transition from citizenship rights to human rights is partial. Even as the political framework within which these rights are exercised seems to be changing again, this time becoming transnational or global, the sovereign nation-state still remains the primary institution that administers and enforces rights, even those conceived to be universally held (Soysal 1994; Shafir 1998).

Citizenship has evolved into a full complement of rights, as T. H. Marshall first argued (1963). Human rights have not yet developed such coherence, and their social and especially political dimensions are being intensely questioned and debated. Universal human rights (as was citizenship earlier) were first laid down in regard to a small number of civil rights. But will they be arrested there, or will they follow the evolution of modern citizenship, which commenced in the eighteenth century with civil citizenship, to be followed by political and social rights (and recently, in some cases, by a modicum of group-based cultural rights), all of which ensure effective implementation of an earlier layer of civic citizenship?

At the same time, the universalism of human rights promises more than nation-state citizenship. Implicitly, and sometimes explicitly, it suggests not only the possibility of an international order, which a well-ordered state sovereignty system also promises, but a global community. But the enforcement of human rights has suffered from the lack of robust institutional underpinning. Modern state institutions have been among the most effective enforcers and enablers of citizenship rights (Tilly 1996), but even human rights accords rely on the very same states they call into question to enforce those accords.

One important consequence of the link between citizenship and state sovereignty is the state's determination regarding the interpretation and enforcement of citizenship. Different states, and different types of states, historically have held distinct standards for membership, based on combinations of birth, descent or blood, residence, identity, achievement, and even characteristics of migrants' states of origin. Globalization intensifies the impact of these disparities and the numbers of people in dual or overlapping status, at the same time as it pressures states to harmonize their standards with international norms.

Globalization is a new concept that was developed with the expectation that a new world economic, political, and cultural order was emerging. While this hope has been frequently overstated, for our project the central question is which elements of the era of globalization impact citizenship and how?

What are the crucial elements of the era of globalization? In Barrie Axford's opinion (1995), globalization is the very defining concept of our age, while Paul Hirst and Grahame Thompson (1996) find that claims for both its centrality and its novelty have been exaggerated. While some analysts treat globalization as a predominantly economic process of commodification or the spread of global capitalism (Greider 1997; Korten 1995), others focus on the growth of international institutions and organizations; that is, on cosmopolitanism (Ruggie 1998; Meyer et al. 1997). Some scholars emphasize the impact of transnational demographic, environmental, and cultural connections (Sassen 1996), while others plot the emergence of cross-border networks and communication that may constitute a "global civil society" (Lipschutz 1996; Wapner 1996; Castells 1997) or a Western cultural hegemony (Latouche 1996). Globalization is all this and more, and it would be a mistake to claim to exhaust the meaning of globalization with one favored element.

The underlying dynamic of globalization is cosmopolitan: it is a simultaneous but increasingly differentiated growth of world markets, interstate institutions, and global civil society and norms (Brysk 2000). While this process is catalyzed by U.S. hegemony, the dynamic, once unleashed, has diverse consequences. Thus, while the political economy of hegemony dictates an unequal distribution of resources among and within states and a general weakening of state citizenship, the resulting dynamic is more complex: power is moving from weak states to strong states, from states to markets, and away from state authority entirely in certain domains and functions (Strange 1998).

We hold that the current wave of globalization does surpass previous eras in the breadth, scope, and intensity of the *combination* of connection, cosmopolitanism, commodification, and communication. *Connection* is a functional parameter of globalization, involving increasing numbers, volumes, and salience of transnational flows of bodies, business, and information, as well as norms. The *cosmopolitan* dimension is structural and implies the evolution of multiple, linked, and overlapping centers of power above and below the state. Commodification highlights the distinctive characteristics of expanding world markets. The underlying causal dynamic that catalyzed and intensified each of these dimensions of the current wave of globalization is enhanced *communication* (Brysk 2002). The process of communication creates and strengthens transnational social networks of various kinds, while the content of communication introduces new norms—including rights—which facilitate but also structure and sometimes constrain the process of globalization altogether. Globalization creates a citizenship gap, but also furthers the import and spread of the rights that potentially may close the gap.

The first characteristic manifestation of the citizenship gap is the growing number of residents in increasing numbers of states who are *noncitizens* (or ambiguous citizens), whose lives are subject to global markets and mobility without secure membership in a national community. Migrants, refugees, and undocumented residents all lack basic membership in the state; certain ethnic groups, rural residents, and laborers are often granted a lesser, conditional, or ambiguous status. This means that they may be ineligible for rights of political participation, social services, and sometimes even international recognition of their status. Their presence in a specific locale is often a result of the current globalization, and the difficulties of meeting their needs also flow from factors such as global patterns of investment, international immigration law, and transborder community ties. Today more than 25 million people are international refugees. Tens of millions more are international economic migrants—mostly undocumented and generally lacking civil rights (Mills 1998: 97–124). In China alone, an estimated 100 million people are unregistered domestic migrant workers (Solinger 1995). Women governed by "family law"—which frequently directly denies full citizenship or nationality, and generally violates international human rights standards (Chinkin 1999)—are doubly disadvantaged as migrants: they may lack permission to migrate unaccompanied, be tied to their husband's status or nationality, or lose status in the host state. Within many countries, internally displaced persons, rural-urban migrants, and isolated peasants (often illiterate) are also undocumented, and also lack rights and civil status.

But formal, *legal citizens* are also at risk from the deflation of citizenship rights by global influences. Welfare entitlements are removed at the behest of international lenders, labor rights are curtailed, and trade agreements are concluded with little or no citizen participation. The lives of more and more legal citizens depend on distant decisions over which they cannot exert effective political influence. Institutions such as the WTO and regional trade accords may displace local and national institutions formerly subject to citizen debate, leaving citizens at the mercy of unaccountable global managers. The unevenness of regional integration further adds to the deepening of the divide between residents of richly institutionalized regions such as Europe, which thereby gain a new layer of rights and protections, and their poorer cousins, cut adrift by thinning states and cast aside by wobbly and depoliticized regional bodies. Even within global institutions seeking to enhance citizen participation and control, residents of rich and powerful states are overrepresented; thus their national citizenship transfers more readily to decisions and debates at the global level.

Second-class citizens historically granted lower rights of membership—the informal sector, women, children, ethnic minorities, and sometimes labor—also suffer from globalization. Overall, there are ample signs of the thinning of citizenship rights. Frequently, the state becomes divided between local and global institutional factions, with some agencies, such as central banks and supreme courts, supporting globalization, while others, like legislatures, oppose it. Observers of states undergoing not only economic but also political liberalization decry the emergence of "low-intensity citizenship" (Stahler-Sholk 1994).

Yet globalization also creates new opportunities and multiple venues in which to claim rights in other states and global institutions. Kosovars can claim accountability from Slobodan Milosevic at the Hague, while Rwandan victims of genocide could potentially approach courts in their own state, Belgium, the United States, or the International Tribunal in Tanzania. Export-zone laborers denied social rights in Mexico could seek relief through appeals to a NAFTA labor panel, a transnational boycott with U.S. activists, cross-border union organizing with the U.S. or Central America, or complaints to the International Labor Organization.

Attention to human rights is accompanied by the judicialization of international relations and the spread of liberal legal norms of the right of judicial review, a greater autonomy given to courts, and constitutional expansion as well as the enforcement of long dormant international conventions of human rights, greater enforcement of punishment for crimes against humanity, and the creation of an international criminal court. While participatory citizenship seems to decline, NGOs and networks represent a new activist thrust with a clear global dimension, sometimes referred to as "globalization from below." Civil society organizations have the potential to restore political participation, but in the process they may be transferring the effective arena of debate from national elections and competition for individual voters to a "new aristocracy" of global activists. Furthermore, these new opportunities tend to propose new rights without the membership or responsibility provided by citizenship. New mechanisms do not sufficiently address the range of rights deflated by globalization, and they are often less available to those most excluded by their own states. We would like to analyze the global impact of legal liberalism and the balance between "citizenship deficit," due to the contraction of political democracy, and "citizenship surplus," created by new venues of political influence.

In this volume we will, finally, inquire how far human rights are likely to evolve as a distinct tradition apart from citizenship, and, whether thick human rights can become a reality without turning into global citizenship, namely becoming embedded in global governance and its institutions.

Our Analysis

The chapter that follows, by Gershon Shafir, will trace some of the stops along the way in the historical evolution of citizenship and human rights, in order to provide a background and context for measuring globalization's effects on citizenship rights. This section concludes that globalizing rights are superceding territorial citizenship, but without providing the defined membership, institutional accountability, or social aspirations of the citizenship construct.

The next section, "Producing Citizenship," argues in different ways that the economic aspects of globalization determine the shape and scope of citizenship rights. Ronnie D. Lipschutz contends that globalization, as the highest stage of Lockean liberalism, constitutes a political space that inherently limits our ability to construct meaningful political community. Aihwa Ong analyzes a different dynamic: the construction of citizenship packages across national states, in accordance with the requirements of globalized relations of production. For Ong, globalization is what pushes people out of place (physically and socially), while for Lipschutz, liberalism denies everyone a place.

In the third section, "Constructing Rights," contributors focus on the institutional and normative aspects of globalization. Both of these chapters show that international law and understandings produce new rights for people out of place—migrants and aliens. David Jacobson and Galya Benarieh Ruffer argue that globalization has generated international institutions, norms, and models of "agency"—individual capacity to contest rights on the basis of rules. They show that this transnational judicialization can be gauged in the hard case of migrants, who can assert rights despite their lack of citizenship. Peter J. Spiro's contribution focuses on conflicts over citizenship and nationality generated by migration. His analysis of international law shows an increasing influence of international treaties and norms even on states' ultimate prerogative of allocating citizenship rights, which increasingly favor the individual over the collective.

Next, we directly consider the contradictory impacts of globalization on vulnerable sectors of people out of place. Gay W. Seidman analyzes the deflation of social citizenship rights for labor movements in response to global market pressures, and the shifting political role of labor in democratizing but underdeveloped states. Kristen Hill Maher's essay shows how women migrants are excluded from public citizenship at home and abroad, and isolated from transnational rights. Alison Brysk treats a case of double displacement—children possessing ambiguous citizenship who are also migrants. In this case, economic migration generates effects like those seen by Ong and Lipschutz, but refugee status brings in a debate on rights, while a third type of identity-based movement—adoption—reconstructs citizenship across state lines. Thus, we return to the issues of globalizing norms, not just of rights but of identities.

In the concluding section of the book, Richard Falk lays out the alternative models of global citizenship that may supplement—or eventually supplant—the nation-state tradition. His analysis shows how the reemergence of geopolitics as a factor in globalization may limit the potential of transnational rights and norms. Saskia Sassen rethinks the shifting domain of citizenship, and at the same time returns citizenship to its roots—the city—reconstructed across borders. Overall, we hope to establish a better understanding of the sources, reach, and remedies of the citizenship gap. In this way, our project may contribute to the study and amelioration of globalization.

2

Citizenship and Human Rights in an Era of Globalization

GERSHON SHAFIR

In one of the most influential studies on contemporary immigration, *The Limits of Citizenship*, Yasemin Soysal (1994) found that guest-workers-turned-immigrants in western Europe have been incorporated into their host societies not as citizens but through a new model of membership—universal personhood. The new incorporation regime emerges as universal human rights are replacing national rights, and universal personhood is supplanting nation-hood as the defining focus of citizenship. And yet, the sovereign nation-state still remains the sole institution that administers and enforces rights, even those conceived to be universally held. Soysal cautiously calls hers a "*postnational*" model of citizenship, one in which state sovereignty is contested but not yet replaced. While she is undoubtedly correct in describing this partial transformation as the sign of a transitional era, by treating universal personhood itself as a form of citizenship she obscures an important distinction and its implications for her thesis. Christian Joppke further criticizes her for ignoring the notion that "national citizenship remains indispensable for immigrant integration," especially for second- and third-generation immigrants who would otherwise remain excluded from the national community as members of stigmatized minorities (Joppke 1999: 645). Soysal's study leaves the nature of the relationship between national membership and postnational identity open: Is, in this view, universal personhood an attack on or an extension of citizenship? Do these types of incorporation overlap or clash? The way these questions are answered also has implications for judging whether the incorporation of immigrants eclipses or reinforces nation-states.

As a more productive way of addressing these questions, I wish to argue that we are faced with two alternative traditions—citizenship and human rights—that, however, have interacted in crucial ways. These traditions have been propelled by conflicting aims: anchoring rights in membership versus disconnecting them from membership and thus universalizing them. Nevertheless, though human rights emerged from autonomous intellectual sources, they were predicated on the legacy of political citizenship. In this chapter I will distinguish between the two traditions' origins, assumptions, and characteristics.

My questions are, first: What is the relationship between the citizenship and human rights traditions; is their interaction mostly one of mutual enabling or constraining? And, second, under present conditions of globalization, what combination can best protect the rights of current second-class citizens and "people out of place"?

The Two Rights Traditions: Citizenship and Human Rights

Citizenship is a broad legal and social framework for membership in a political community. It is based in and has been a central axis of Western political philosophy. The long tradition of citizenship is a bridge between antiquity and the modern era, linking the civic and political self-conception of the Greek *polis* and the Roman Empire with the French Revolution and Enlightenment emphasis on the equal moral worth of all individuals. As an intellectual and political tradition, citizenship has been repeatedly revisited and updated as the political framework—which was the site of membership—changed. There have been, roughly speaking, four transitions in the site of citizenship: from the *polis* to the Roman Empire, to the medieval city, and to the nation-state. Now, its purview seems to be changing again, and it has been suggested that it might become transnational or global (Soysal 1994; Shafir 1998).

The notion of citizenship originated in the Greek polis with the intention of liberating a portion of humanity from tribal loyalties and fusing it into a voluntary civic community. Citizenship was founded on the definition of the human being as "a creature formed by nature to live a political life," and, in J. G. A. Pocock's words, this emphasis on practicing freedom through political participation is "one of the great Western definitions of what it is to be human" (Pocock 1992). As Max Weber demonstrated, the foundation for this ancient freedom was military service (Weber 1981). Reenactments of the identity of soldier and citizen appear in subsequent revolutionary moments. But citizenship that begins with the acquisition of political rights did not remain linked to politics and military service and limited to it. In the Roman Empire, citizenship was linked to legal protection of property, in the medieval polis it was linked to guild membership, and in the modern era it was for the first time tied to the freedom to chose one's employment, and, later, linked to employment in general.

Citizenship, thus is a tradition that changed as its political basis was transformed. The main venues of change were the *expansion* of citizenship by coining new rights, sometimes referred to as generations of rights, and through the *transformation* of privileges into rights and subsequently through the *extension* of existing rights to new groups, thus broadening the body politic—the community of members. New rights make the possession and wielding of previous rights more effective, and the accession to such rights removes fences between groups previously separated by laws or social customs. Each time citizenship was expanded or extended it became stronger and richer.

During the Enlightenment, another tradition—human rights—emerges out of natural law philosophy. Human rights, as Lynn Hunt points out, gain their effectiveness and poignancy from their universal, equal, and natural character. Human rights are universal and equal because they are anchored in a person by virtue of his or her humanity and not by virtue of his or her status in the body politic (Hunt 2001: 3–5).

The first step in universalizing rights was taken by Hugo Grotius, who in 1625, during the Dutch revolution for independence from Spain, defined natural rights as "something self-possessed and conceivable separately from God's will" that could be used "to establish the contractual foundations for social life" (Hunt 2001: 6). They were first given a practical dimension by the Levellers during the English Civil War of the 1640s. As part of both the American and the French revolutions, rights were universalized. The French approach to rights as the rights of man was particularly radical, since until then these rights were a form of privilege (Hunt 2001: 7). It is during the Enlightenment that this tradition of human rights coalesces as a legal framework.

The notion that individuals are endowed by nature with inalienable rights *apart from their bonds to a state* has a complex relationship with the citizenship idea, which posits that rights are *contingent on membership in a political entity*. Human rights were for the first time laid down in August 1789 in the French Revolution's Declaration of the Rights of Man and Citizen, thus initially tethering the new tradition to the older one. Human rights and citizens' rights were not yet separated, and their respective domains remained unmarked, but they included liberty, property, security, and resistance to oppression. As soon as the Declaration of the Rights and Man and Citizen had been promulgated, its applicability began to grow. It was immediately extended to Protestants, in September 1791 to Jews, and in February 1794 it led to the abolition of slavery in French colonies (Hunt 2001: 11).

The proponents of the citizenship and human rights traditions sometimes used each other's accomplishments as starting blocks, and at other times viewed them as stumbling blocks or limits to be leapfrogged. Though growing in depth and reach, both traditions were and still are limited in their ambitions. I will now examine how these affected the two traditions differently and the steps through which they evolved. I will examine four such limits by seeking answers to these questions: How far do the backers of the two traditions seek to equalize social conditions? How far do they seek to universalize the rights they advocate? How robust do they wish to make these rights? And, finally, from an institutional point of view, how effectively can these rights be enforced?

Equality and Amelioration

Both citizen and human rights institutionalize the ethical and political principle of formal equality by depoliticizing and decommodifying access to rights and resources. Rights lie outside of or above partisan or state politics and, in Ronald Dworkin's terms, are recognizable by their ability "to trump" all appeals, even ones to collective goods (Dworkin 1977: xi; Sarat and Kearns 2001: 9). At the same time, they were conceived of and evolved within certain parameters: granting citizenship was intended to ameliorate economic inequality, i.e. to enhance social solidarity among selected individuals in the face of continued inequality—not to equalize social and economic conditions. Human rights were to provide basic protections against arbitrariness—not to equalize access to power.

Weber located the sociological foundation of citizenship in the military dimension of the Greek *polis*. The city-state was based on the association of those who could afford to purchase their own weapons and military equipment, first for the protection of the city and later for conquest and the acquisition of land and booty (a venture Weber termed political or military capitalism). Equal access to arms led to the demand for the granting of effective citizenship rights to the armed plebeians. The democratic character of the *polis* reflected the further desire to ensure that growing economic inequality would not undermine the ability of free men to participate in the military; that is, to ensure the survival of the partnership of soldiers (called by Weber a soldiers' guild). The identity of soldier and citizen was firmly established in the *polis*, and participation in the military became the foundation for ancient freedoms. Though in the Roman Empire citizenship was extended to ever larger populations, it became stratified among groups and regions, thus preserving its status as privilege. Finally, medieval cities, like the *polis*, also legislated their own law, and their citizens, mostly guild members and therefore still only a fraction of the inhabitants, elected their own officials (Weber 1981).

Even in the modern state, where universal citizenship becomes the norm, its evolution is driven by the goal of ensuring solidarity in the face of inequality. Significantly, the question that led to T. H. Marshall's classical inquiry was: To what extent can the reduction of class in equality, through the expansion of citizenship rights, reconcile people to the remaining inequality? He argued that social citizenship and capitalism are at war, and that the exercise of citizenship rights will always generate social conflict. At the same time, Marshall concluded that citizenship and social class are compatible in our society, "so much so that citizenship has itself become ... the architect of legitimate social inequality" (Marshall 1977: 70).

Early human rights demands and documents were even less ambitious than citizenship. The desired equalization was to take place wholly outside the economic realm, and we find no manifestation of any intention to reduce social gaps in order to maintain social solidarity. Negative freedoms—life and liberty, expressed through religious freedom and freedom of expression and property—were the main goals, even in revolutionary eras.

The one clear exception, of course, is Marx, who opposed the formalism of individual natural rights because they seemed to enshrine inequalities; in their place, he demanded the kinds of communal entitlements we more closely associate with citizenship. Rights, he stated in *The Jewish Question*, were degraded by offering protection not to the man as citizen—that is, as a member of the political community—but to a bourgeois—that is, a presocial, egoistic . . . man. Marx thought that human rights were the antithesis of citizenship and, therefore, could not be enlarged in pursuit of social equality. Marx, of course, is never invoked in the context of human rights debates, though the study of citizenship has become the new abode of some of the Marxian preoccupations with conflict, oppression, resistance, and equality. Consequently, Marx's class analysis has not been dismissed but rather, ironically, it has been subsumed within the citizenship tradition—for example, through Marshall's critique that views citizenship as continuing to coexist with the class structure while reducing class struggle and legitimating inequality. As we shall see later, the major human rights organizations are in the process of incorporating more equitable access to health care and other resources into their demands but only as a safety net, not as a way of abolishing economic stratification. Neither citizenship nor human rights has become the language of social equality, and when invoked to oppose unequal access they have been used for nothing more than the reduction of market-generated inequality and, above all, discrimination. In this sense they seem to have been constrained by their origins in the visions of the propertied classes of the *polis* and the French Revolution.

Privilege and Universalism

The Greek concept of citizenship enshrined freedom, but only for a portion of mankind. The elevation of the public domain of political life over the private sphere of the family and economic life signaled the emancipation of free male citizens at the expense of women and slaves, who remained excluded from citizenship. The purview of Greek citizenship was limited and never amounted to more than a participatory aristocracy. The legacy of Greek citizenship, consequently, remained contradictory. With the growth of citizenship from a local to a state-wide institution in the modern era, the freedoms conferred on citizens in the *polis* and the medieval towns were radically expanded, and freedom itself was converted from privilege into right.

The expansion of rights, argues Marshall, was part and parcel of the process of democratization, of the attainment by the lower classes, specifically the working class, of the privileges originally fashioned by the upper classes for themselves. Even when the reach of citizenship is nearly universal, in Iris Young's and many other feminists' and multiculturalists' view, it still retains part of its character as privilege for those who fall within its implicit criterion of adhering to the elusive common good. Consequently, they hold that citizenship's transformation from privilege to right has not yet been, and maybe never can be, completed. The ideal citizen was defined according to the dominant group's characteristics (for example, leaving the private sphere of necessity behind in order to enter the disembodied rationality of the realm of freedom). Even when it was expanded and extended, the putative universalism of citizenship didn't keep up with the characteristics of the new populations brought under its umbrella (see, for example, Kymlicka 1995; Young 1989).

The restrictive application of human rights appears all the crueler against the background of their *prima facie* universality. In spite of their lofty promise, human rights were for a long time not viewed as inherent in every individual; they were "about the achievement of a status and the attainment of qualities that would admit one to political society, to civil society, and, indeed, full humanity." Human rights debates revolved around the question of whether "large groups of people had the maturity, however defined, to share in political power" (Kotsonis 2001: 101). Maturity itself was connected with another eighteenth-century term, *progress*, and its counterpart, *backwardness* (Kotsonis 2001: 101). Those assigned to the latter category were to remain under permanent or temporary tutelage, paternalism, or coverture—that is, subsumed under the legal personality of those whose human rights were taken for granted. As European ambitions proceeded from the abolition of slavery to the colonial dismemberment of Africa, "human rights became a philosophical basis for racial hierarchy" (Bernault 2001: 128).

The universalism of the Enlightenment, and the eighteenth-, nineteenth-, and twentieth-century revolutions that invoked it, was constrained by a triple equation: rights were available to human beings, but humans were defined through the responsibilities of the citizen; hence the parameters of humanity coincided not with humankind but with particular membership. To ascend to human rights one had to become a citizen, and to be a citizen one had to assume the mantle of rationality. "If we look at 'human' in these terms—the possession of rationality and enlightenment—then it appears that the Enlightenment did not give us universal human rights" (Kotsonis 2001: 101).

> The question of who was deserving of human rights and liberation depended in part on who was considered mature enough to accept the responsibilities of the citizen. In this sense, the Enlightenment did not tell us all people were human; it gave us universal standards for deciding who was human, and much of the history of Europe ever since has entailed a struggle to decide where to set the boundaries. (Kotosnis 2001: 99)

Consequently, "human rights were absolute . . . but it was . . . a long time before the boundaries of humanity were expanded to include all people" (Kotsonis 2001: 100).

Just as citizenship commenced as participatory aristocracy, so the Enlightenment, and therefore the human rights tradition, started as an exclusionary humanism. In most cases, since personhood was yoked to property, human rights hinged on property ownership. Only with the "emancipation" of human rights from reliance on citizenship did their universal character come to assume its proper place. At the same time, the very universalism of human rights makes it all the more difficult to expand their purview.

Thin and Robust Rights

It was the strength of Marshall's and of the social-democratic approach in general that, in search of full membership, they went beyond the conventional idea that membership in a community is predominantly a civil and political matter. Marshall's theory is at once legal, political, and socioeconomic, and being historical it introduces into the study of citizenship the element of social change that was missing from the more one-dimensional and static normative approaches. Marshall surveys and analyzes the *expansion* of the rights of citizens as a process of extending them to a new group—the English working classes—in order to incorporate them into the modern nation-state. Marshall distinguishes between three sets, or what in the legal idiom we might term three "generations," of citizenship rights: civil, political, and social. *Civil rights* are the bundle of rights necessary for individual freedom that emerged in the eighteenth century. *Political rights* originated in the nineteenth century and guaranteed individuals participation in the exercise of political power as voters or representatives. Finally, in the twentieth century, *social rights* of citizenship—Marshall's original conceptual contribution to the theory of citizenship—make possible the attainment of a measure of economic welfare and security or, as gracefully expressed by Marshall, "the right to share to the full in the social heritage and to live the life of a civilized being according to the standards prevailing in society." Marshall's emphasis on the common standard of civilization allows us to avoid the common mistake of conflating welfare rights with social citizenship: the former are means-based and single out vulnerable individuals as needing protection; the latter is extended to all citizens of the political community.

A novel citizenship right is currently under debate. As articulated eloquently by Will Kymlicka, multiculturalism calls for reforming social institutions in a way that will allow the accommodation of the cultural distinctiveness of multiple ethnic groups in a single state through a novel concept of citizenship. Such an approach requires that rights be bestowed not only on individuals, as is done in the liberal mold, but on groups as well, thus leading to "*differentiated citizenship.*" Kymlicka's illustrations demonstrate that most democracies already confer rights on distinct groups when their members live in territorial proximity and, in fact, the claims of homogeneity made by nation-states had never been fully met and are in the process of rapid erosion. Multiculturalists would like to go further by instituting rights for groups that are not concentrated territorially; theirs is a novel goal for a new era of diversity. This would be attained by awarding what we might characterize, following Marshall's sequencing, as a *fourth citizenship right* (or fourth "generation" right), by adding cultural citizenship rights to the congeries of civil, political, and social citizenship rights.

In contrast to citizenship, human rights have not undergone such progressive expansion and have remained much thinner in the way they have been conceived. An enduring liberal articulation of human rights is offered in the last chapter of the second of Locke's *Two Treatises of Government*, in which he links property and personhood through a notion of equality according to which everyone has property in his own person (Minogue 1979: 9). Locke himself listed "the rights to life, liberty, and property" as the fundamental human rights.

A survey of the evolution of human rights in the international arena will demonstrate that the safeguarding of human rights was predicated on citizenship status and remains most closely associated with civil rights. Historically, international law was confined to interstate relations, and shielded states by guaranteeing their privileges and immunities. Before the Second World War, the protection of rights fell within the domain of domestic jurisdiction and national law. In only four areas had an international legal framework requiring the protection of human rights by states evolved: the treatment of aliens, the abolition of the slave trade, the establishment of common employment conditions, and the protection of minorities. But even among these, legislation was not justified by reference to human rights as such.

Aliens were viewed as "citizens abroad," and, consequently, the violation of their rights was viewed as an affront to their state of origin, which, consequently, was to be the beneficiary of compensation (Borchard 1970).

The second area was the abolition of slavery; after 1814, the practical instrument chosen was the abolition of the slave trade, mostly through binational treaties initiated by Great Britain. One of the main reasons for this initiative was the complaint that slave labor provided an "unfair advantage" vis-à-vis other colonial competitors in international trade (Henkin 1990: 15). Only in 1926 did states commit themselves, through the Slavery Convention, to bringing about the complete abolition of slavery itself. By then, it seems that slavery had become so odious that no state was allowed to sanction it within its own boundaries. This sequence, of course, is suggestive of the pattern of other reforms.

A significant, though anomalous and ambiguous, example of an early international human rights institution is the International Labor Organization. The ILO was established after the First World War in response to the influence of the socialist movements of the era. Through the promulgation of international conventions, the ILO sought to promote basic common standards of employment and social welfare. It might also be, as has been suggested, that the ILO served as a tool of reducing competition from countries with dismal labor conditions (Henkin 1990: 15).

Finally, in the wake of the First World War, the League of Nations promised minorities in successor states of the dismantled multiethnic empires to protect their collective cultural, linguistic, and religious rights simultaneously with the protection of their members from discrimination. One of the conditions of admission of new or enlarged states (but not previously existing states) to the League was a pledge to uphold such obligations (Driscoll 1979: 42–43). This regimen was as flawed as the League of Nations itself.

Since the Second World War, and in accelerated fashion in the globalizing decade of the 1990s, human rights have been upheld through international (as well as national) law and, simultaneously, they have been gaining on citizenship as the main purveyor of rights (Leary 1999). In the legal arena, the new ascendence of human rights is accomplished through the incorporation of international law on human rights (and other issues) into domestic law and the consequent transformation of national law. It is in this new normative and legal context that the possibility for the expansion of human rights beyond civil rights seems to lie.

A recent manual on human rights, published under the auspices of UNESCO, surveys the cutting-edge areas of human rights debate and legislation. Some of the topics examined are: the right to peace, democracy as a condition for other rights, the right to development, environmental protection, the right to good health, workers' rights and women workers' rights, and the rights of indigenous people (Symonides 1998). In spite of this long and expanding list of human rights, starting with the Universal Declaration and the International Covenant on Economic, Social, and Cultural Rights, in a recent survey of the internalization of the international human rights norms, Thomas Risse and Kathryn Sikkink tellingly narrow their study to the "central core of rights: the right to life (. . . define[d] as the right to be free from extrajudicial execution and disappearance) and the freedom from arbitrary arrest and detention," because these alone "have been most accepted as universal rights and not simply associated with a particular political ideology or system" (Risse and Sikkink 1999: 2).

The "rights" enumerated in the Covenant on Economic, Social, and Cultural Rights have been routinely ignored, and most human rights organizations have rarely sought to demand their implementation. Still, a radical change might be taking place in the thinking of some of these bodies. Human Rights Watch adopted Amartya Sen's conclusion that "in the terrible history of famines in the world, no substantial famine has ever occurred in any independent and democratic country with a relatively free press." The Charter of the Center for Economic and Social Rights in Brooklyn requires it "to challenge economic injustice in violation of international human rights law." Oxfam's current program seeks to pursue "rights to a sustainable livelihood," but also the much vaguer goal of "the rights and capacities to participate in societies and make positive changes to people's lives." Since 1998, the UN's WHO has demanded the recognition of health as a human right. Another UN body, the Human Rights Commission, called for the harmonization of international trade law with international human rights legislation. In 2000, the UN Commission on Economic, Social, and Cultural Rights held that a government's "core obligations" include the provision of equal access to health services, and enough food, potable water, sanitation, and essential drugs (*Economist*, August 28, 2001).

Finally, the International Council Meeting, the policy-making body of Amnesty International—the largest and most important such body—debated in its meeting in Dakar in August 2001 a resolution that would place social and economic rights on par with civil and political rights. A compromise was reached between those who wished to concentrate on a "core concept" and those who preferred to pursue a "full spectrum" of goals by finding a middle ground, in new areas; for example, the right to education and good health where their attainment is impaired by discrimination *(International Issues News* 79, September 2001; "Question and Answer: Outcomes of the 2001 International Council Meeting," POL 21/004/2001). The abuse of such rights is now expected to fall within Amnesty International's mandate (*Economist*, August 28, 2001). Initially, Amnesty International suggested that women's right to education in Afghanistan and the struggle against the spread of HIV and AIDS in Africa be the first campaigns within the expanded mandate. Though both goals are new ones for the organization, they are still viewed as resulting from discrimination and therefore as justified through reference to the protection of human rights from discrimination. With the indirect resolution of the former issue, Amnesty International's National Week of Student Action in 2003 was focused on the latter, and, in the process, this educational project broadened the purview of the traditional understanding the human rights. AI describes the rationale as follows: "The AIDS pandemic is a human rights crisis. The spread of HIV/AIDS is exacerbated by systematic abuses of the right to be free from discrimination, the right to prevention and treatment, the rights to physical and mental integrity, and the right to freely receive and impart information" (AI, *Out Front*, winter 2002–03). Amnesty International's new mission, which "encompasses grave abuses of economic, social, and cultural rights," signals that the organization holds that "all human rights are interdependent and indivisible." The highest attainable level of health from this perspective "is dependent upon respect for human dignity" (AI, *Out Front*, winter 2002–3). This list of initiatives and expanded rationales indicate a desire to expand human rights with the goal, in effect, of having them coincide with citizenship rights.

The opposition to this approach is formidable. The U.S. ambassador to the UN's Human Rights Commission, George Mosse, expressed "concern" about the advent of international legal norms and the adoption of laws that "would lead in the direction of the creation of legal, enforceable entitlements to economic, social, and cultural rights," because that would enable citizens "[to] sue their governments for enforcement of rights" (*Economist*, August 18, 2001).

Enforcement

Conservative critics, like Edmund Burke, rejected the eighteenth-century attempts to extend the purview of rights by elevating them to an abstraction, and continued to favor a particular citizenship—"the rights of Englishmen." Indeed, for a long time the narrow bundle of existing human rights was termed in Great Britain civil liberties. But even Jeremy Bentham, a radical in his day, held that positive law alone guaranteed rights. With the flair for the dramatic, Bentham wrote, in"Anarchical Fallacies," "Right is the child of the law; from real laws come real rights, but from imaginary laws, from 'laws of nature' come imaginary rights. . . . Natural rights is simply nonsense" (quoted in Cranston 1979: 18). Though Burke was troubled by the propagandistic value of natural law in fostering revolution, while Bentham worried that it might forestall substantive legislation (Cranston 1979: 18), the concurrence of their visions indicates the existence of a common English vantage point for their criticism: the historical legacy of the rights of Englishmen, a citizenship tradition as it was articulated in England. After all, the English Bill of Rights of 1689, in the wake of the 1688 revolution, sought to reaffirm "ancient rights and liberties" established by English law (Hunt 2001: 6–7).

As Burke, Bentham, and their followers recognized, the crucial trade-off is between the extension of human rights and their enforcement. The UN's December 10, 1948, Universal Declaration of Human Rights moved far beyond traditional civil and political rights and, under the influence of its communist member states, included as human rights entitlements that until then were more likely to be associated with citizenship rights outside liberal societies. Among these was the right to an adequate standard of living (article 26) and to social security (22), the right to work and to equal pay for equal work (23) (Glendon 2001). But this "international bill of rights" did not guarantee or protect these rights; it merely demanded that member states "strive . . . to promote them [and] to secure them." The December 1966 International Covenant on Civil and Political Rights and the International Covenant on Economic, Social, and Cultural Rights not only articulated these rights but also made an attempt to ensure compliance by establishing a self-reporting procedure (imitating the ILO) and a weak interstate complaints procedure. These procedures fall far short of international enforcement.

The UN possesses no independent enforcement machinery and so is restricted to the monitoring rather than to the enforcement of human rights enumerated in its covenants. Its powers of suasion are great, but limited. Some of its commissions publish reports; others are only allowed to submit questions to member states (Beetham 1998: 62; Donnelly 1992: 252).

Some of what is missing on the international level is made up for on the regional one, where there is a network of human rights bodies; however, their enforcement capacities vary widely. Effective regional human rights jurisdiction and real enforcement capacity exist in Europe: individuals might appeal to the European Court of Human Rights, which is the final enforcement authority of the European Convention of Human Rights, against domestic courts. The European Court plays a similar role for employment-related complaints. In general, the EU established the principles of "direct effect," namely that EU laws must be applied by national courts without their adoption by national parliaments, and "supremacy," signaling that relevant EU law always prevails over conflicting national laws (Preuss 1998: 138). The institutional key to the effectiveness of human rights implementation in Europe lies in the "existence of an independent supranational body alongside intergovernmental ones" (Beetham 1998: 67). The Conference on Security and Cooperation in Europe (CSCE) created in 1973 another quasi-regional human rights regime, which came to be known as the "Helsinki process." It was, subsequently, vested with investigation and conciliation procedures but still lacks enforcement powers. The Organization of American States' Inter-American Commission of Human Rights played a crucial role in exposing the brutality of Argentina's and Chile's military governments in the 1970s, but its considerable investigative and reporting powers are not matched by real enforcement powers. The Inter-American Court of Human Rights may, in principle, issue legally binding judgements but has done so only in the most cursory fashion. The African Commission on Human and People's Rights has only modest powers of investigation. There are no intergovernmental regional human rights organizations in either Asia or the Middle East (Donnelly 1992: 251–53; Beetham 1998: 61–66). Finally, in the United States no human rights reports are issued to international monitoring institutions, leaving one with the impression that homelessness and lack of health insurance for millions are just matters of policy priorities rather than human rights violations.

The transition from citizenship rights to human rights, Soysal warns us, is partial: nation-states are declining but not disappearing (Soysal 1994). No new structure has emerged to replace the nation-state. The sovereign nation-state still remains the main institution that administers and enforces rights, even those conceived to be universally held. In fact, EU citizens exercising their "European rights" almost invariably do so through the agencies of the state in which they reside, and "the European character of the rights conferred by the [EU] is rarely visible" (Preuss 1998: 146).

Since human rights have been internationalized, their enforcement, by and large, has remained national; however an informal international network of activists has come to fill the gap. NGOs—from Amnesty International to the parallel forums at the UN World Conferences on women's rights in Vienna and Beijing—are playing an increasing role in monitoring state compliance, offering suggestions, and bringing pressure to bear on offending states. While it is customary to celebrate the NGOs' growing impact, it is equally true that their existence reflects limited formal state-based enforcement capacities. A yet embryonic challenge is the attempt of a number of UN agencies in the fields of economic, health, and social rights, such as the WHO and the Commission on Economic, Social, and Cultural Rights, to redefine their mandate from the alleviation of hunger and the reduction of disease, child mortality, and so on to the pursuit of human rights. In effect, they seek to remake themselves from what one might call international social welfare agencies into international human rights bodies—that is, to transform welfare born of sympathy into binding rights.

In contrast to the lax enforcement of human rights, in democratic regimes citizenship rights have been characterized by relatively effective implementation. Political communities, and especially modern nation-state institutions, have been among the most effective enforcers and enablers of such rights (Tilly 1996). Many theorists have pointed to the crucial significance of the nation-state as a vehicle for winning rights in the modern world, but Hannah Arendt has probably done so most forcefully. The aspiration for a nation-state of one's own was based on the authoritative illustration by the French Revolution of the far-reaching success of "combin[ing] the declaration of the Rights of Man with national sovereignty." The tight interdependence of sovereignty and rights was manifested with special clarity after the First World War, when the Minority Treaties at once placed nonsovereign peoples under the governments of the national majorities and charged the League of Nations with the duty of safeguarding their rights. This, in effect, was an admission that the majority nations could not be trusted to uphold minority rights. In Arendt's words,

> the worst factor in this situation was not even that it became a matter of course for the nationalities to be disloyal to their imposed government and for the governments to oppress their nationalities as efficiently as possible, but that the nationally frustrated population was firmly convinced—as was everybody else—that true freedom, true emancipation, and true popular sovereignty could be attained only with full national emancipation, that people without their own national government were deprived of human rights. (Arendt 1951: 272)

Arendt highlights the fundamental paradox of modern citizenship: since the sovereign nation-state was the primary enforcer of the "inalienable" and, therefore, universal human rights, individuals not enjoyed rights not by virtue of their humanity, but by virtue of their membership in the major political institution of the day—a particular, territorially based nation-state. "Because the sovereign state had become the vehicle for claiming rights, members of nations who had not achieved sovereignty had no effective rights" (Klusmeyer 1996: 71). As John Torpey has pointed out, even today the nation-state remains the main guarantor of rights, be they citizen or human rights (Torpey 2000).

Globalization and Rights

My analysis of the two traditions has illustrated that neither citizenship nor human rights has been used to justify social equality as a goal in itself. When their advocates are confronted with the adverse effects of unequal access to resources, their demand is usually limited to securing sufficient resources to enable the exercise of the rights by their bearers. It is not in these spheres that the two traditions' major differences lie.

In the Greek *polis* and in the long tradition ensuing from it, citizenship gained an enduring inclusionary dimension by superseding prepolitical identities based on narrow tribal or parochial identities. Citizenship that had emerged as political membership was no longer restricted to the sphere of politics (Preuss 1998: 142–43). To ensure fuller membership, citizenship has been expanded to include ever newer rights, from negative, through enabling, to positive. Citizenship rights have been cumulative and relatively robust, and they continue to benefit from the enforcement capacities of nation-states. At the same time, once they reach the border of the national community the limits of their universalism become obvious: citizenship cannot be extended to outsiders without restructuring the political units within which they are embedded. Today, in comparison with what had evolved as the human rights tradition, the particularism of citizenship, confined to members of political units, its exclusionary aspect, looms larger.

We live through an exciting period of extension in human rights that protect the individual and, on occasion, groups facing extreme cruelty. Attention to human rights is accompanied by the judicalization of international relations and the spread of liberal legal norms of the right of judicial review, greater autonomy to courts, and constitutional expansion, as well as the enforcement of long dormant international conventions of human rights, greater enforcement of punishment for crimes against humanity, and the creation of an International Court of Justice. At the same time, the exponential growth in international trade, homogenization of property laws, and the marketization of public goods from welfare to health care have further enhanced the influence of capital markets and movements. Efforts to ensure global competitiveness and the fear of "capital flight" threaten to undermine the social citizenship rights of various groups, especially labor and women, embedded in national welfare states and institutions. For example, in both Britain and the United States social citizenship rights and welfare rights that seemed secure for decades have been recently abrogated.

Citizenship has evolved into a robust complement of rights, in which later political and social citizenship ensure effective access to the earlier civic citizenship, as Marshall has demonstrated. But human rights have remained thinner, they have yet to develop such coherence, and their social and especially political dimensions are still debated. A trade-off is at work: citizenship rights are thicker but available only to members of a particular state, human rights are universal and, as such, thinner. The same applies to the protection of rights: the more universal rights are, the more difficult it becomes to enforce them.

Universal human rights were first defined, as was modern citizenship earlier, in regard to civil rights. But will they be arrested there, or will they follow the course of modern citizenship, which commenced in the eighteenth century with civic citizenship rights, to be followed by political and social rights, and, more recently, by the possibility of collective cultural rights? Our analysis of the relationship of the two traditions leads us now to ask: Can human rights evolve further without, in effect, becoming citizenship rights, and can human rights turn into citizenship without the enforcement capacities of global governance and its institutions?

The blurring of human and citizenship rights has not weakened states: international regimes of enhanced human rights are more likely to continue strengthening states' enforcement capacities. But if social and economic rights are progressively adopted as human rights, the inherent limits of citizenship as membership will likely reduce its appeal and concurrently the influence of nation-states. Human rights have made great strides in the past 250 years, but to be truly effective in a globalizing era they would have to be transformed into citizenship—namely, membership in a global political community that has its own distributive and enforcing institutions. (In our conclusion, we discuss alternative interim situations in which human rights and citizenship may coexist and reinforce each other.) The contemplation of such possibilities indicates the fluidity of frameworks of citizenship and the corresponding notions of state sovereignty.

II
Producing Citizenship

3

Constituting Political Community

Globalization, Citizenship, and Human Rights

RONNIE D. LIPSCHUTZ

State, sovereignty, citizenship, and rights have never been what we conventionally assume them to be. A genealogical examination of the intersection of these concepts would illustrate their contingency and contextuality, even as their meanings and associated practices have been frozen over and over. When we speak of these concepts, therefore, we invoke understandings fixed in time and space, even as those concepts and practices about which we speak are constantly changing and shifting.[1]

As a consequence of globalization,[2] the four concepts and practices have changed from what we imagine them to have been, but never were. Thus, the changes in political community and membership that have been so remarked on during the past ten years (for example, Brysk and Shafir, this volume; Lipschutz 2000) are not so much about changes from some mythic originary condition as the contradictions and changes in the tensions inherent in maintaining particular fictions of state, sovereignty, citizenship, and rights in the face of globalization. It is fair to ask, therefore, if the idealized condition has never existed—is, at best, a kind of Lockean myth of contract—why be concerned about how citizenship is changing, how these changes affect people on the ground, and how our conceptions and practices of membership, belonging, and political community might be altered?[3]

That something is mythical does not mean that it has no social meaning or political significance. I use the term *mythical* to denote a story that purports to explain very real phenomena and conditions, to account for things whose origins and causes are something of a mystery. Our accounts of state, sovereignty, citizenship, and rights have this quality, for, although we can point to places and times important in their realization—such as Westphalia, 1648—we can never locate the places and times of their origins. Moreover, our creation myths not only elide the sheer complexity of the process, they also completely disregard other forms of state, sovereignty, citizenship, and rights whose successes have been lost to memory under the swords and tank treads of geopolitics.[4]

A genealogy of these four concepts, especially human rights, does not delegitimize their very important functions in global politics, nor does it imply their rejection. Rather, as Foucault put it, "the search for descent . . . disturbs what was previously considered immobile; it fragments what was thought unified; it shows the heterogeneity of what was imagined consistent with itself" (Foucault 1984: 87, cited in Brown 2001: 103). Understanding how these concepts and practices came to be what we think they are also illuminates the ways in which they are responses to conditions and contradictions in particular times and places. As we conceive of them today, all four concepts are contingent artifacts of the play of power, and hence politics, arising out of the fifty-year history of contemporary globalization. To put this another way, the constitution and distribution of citizenship and rights by the state and through institutions such as the human rights regimes should be seen not as a natural outcome of some sort of progressive political process but, rather, as one that is as much about the exigencies of particular historical moments as it is about ethics or social welfare.

Under conditions of globalization, the contemporary state is a facilitator of open markets, which rely on flows of capital, goods, and labor across borders as part of the process of continual accumulation. If sovereignty is understood as the prerogative of the state to prevent, restrict, or permit activities that challenge its authority and jurisdiction, two consequences (at least) become evident. First, the state cannot fully choke off labor mobility, even though it may engage in some restrictive actions for political purposes. Indeed, a certain degree of labor mobility and flexibility is essential to the state's maintenance of its authority, and if this cannot be supplied from within, it must come from without. Second, the market does not recognize or reward "national citizenship," here understood as membership in a limited polity (a point once made by Robert Reich about capital and industry; see Reich 1991). Capital selects investment opportunities only on the basis of costs, and citizens are less costly than migrants only if the latter are unavailable (and under those circumstances, capital may choose to relocate elsewhere). One of the costs of globalization, it would appear, is this tension. To put the point more bluntly, it is not "citizenship" that needs to be reconceptualized; citizenship is a variable dependent on the state, so to speak. What needs to be rethought and deployed is political community and the nature of membership therein.

In this chapter, therefore, I examine the continually emergent contradictions between the mythical condition of citizenship and the reality, under the pressures of globalization, as it is expressed today, especially in Europe and the United States. I do not seek to achieve definitional closure in our conceptualizations of the four concepts, thereby foreclosing alternatives. Rather, I address some of the ways in which changes in the global political economy are generating different (and not always new) types of relations between individuals, groups, and states. These changes are, in part, the result of the movement of people, but they are also a consequence of the shifting and reconfiguration of loci of political authority that is one effect of globalization (Lipschutz 2000).

In the first part of this chapter, I offer a theoretical perspective on the relationship between citizenship and the state, with a particular focus on citizenship as a "scarce" property right granted by the state to selected members of the political community who meet specified qualifying conditions. Globalization has had peculiar impacts on property, in particular, especially with respect to intellectual property and its commodification, with consequent ramifications for the Lockean conception of the producing, consuming, propertied citizen. I next discuss how recent changes in the global economy have created a contradiction—and not for the first time, I might note—between spaces of political membership (national citizenship) and spaces of market participation (economic citizenship).

I then examine the framework offered by Yasemin Soysal (1994). In particular, she has noted the divergence between the constitutional foundation of "postnational citizenship," based in "transnational discourse and structures celebrating human rights as a world-level organizing principle" (1994: 3), and the necessity for implementation of such rights within national contexts, a consequence of the sovereignty principle. I argue here that Soysal disregards the roots of individual(ized) human rights in economic liberalism and, therefore, comes to more optimistic conclusions than might be warranted where incorporation of noncitizens into the body politic is concerned.

In the second part of the chapter, I consider the cosmopolitan alternative—that is, "global citizenship"—as it is discussed by a growing number of commentators, such as David Held (1995b, 1996). Drawing, in particular, on observations by R.B.J. Walker (1999), I argue that global citizenship, as understood by the devotees of cosmopolitanism, is not much more than a thin version of the national variety, projected into the transnational realm. Given, moreover, that "global political space" is organized along the lines of the American domestic system, the former is strongly characterized by liberal beliefs and practices and therefore subject to the same tensions and contradictions that are found within U.S. politics (as well as in the politics of other liberal states). Therefore, without the existence of a strong and well-enforced framework of rights, obligations, and entitlements at the global level, and an authority to instantiate them, there is nothing for the individual to be a citizen in "relation to." One is left only with a kind of global economic citizen, whose material manifestations are consumption, credit, and property.

In the final section of my chapter, I ask whether there are any alternatives and, indeed, whether the very concept of citizenship, as we understand it, as a contingent and contextual product of the era of the nation-state, must be replaced by or subsumed into some other relational construct. I examine several possibilities and find them wanting. A complete reconceptualization of citizenship will, I conclude, require a reexamination of what we understand as "politics" and the spaces of political action (Arendt 1958; Wolin 1996). Contemporary citizenship is an artifact of what we might call distributive politics, in the sense that the constitutional bases for the use of power have been inscribed in beliefs, documents, and practices. The several common definitions of politics—authoritative allocation of values; who gets what, when, where, and so on—presume that the citizen is interested only in how resources are distributed and in periodic ratification of that distribution. When, however, distribution becomes disassociated from those constitutional bases that comprise and legitimate the use of power within and by the state, as is the case under globalization, distribution and ratification are no longer related to citizenship. Any effort to restore the accustomed concordance will necessitate a change in our understanding and practices of politics with, in particular, a focus on how power is to be used and within what form of political community it is to be applied.

A Brief Genealogy of Citizenship

Under the theoretical conditions of international anarchy with no world government, the exclusiveness of the state, maintained by law and force, is supposed to be tempered by economic and cultural interdependence. But this very interdependence results in the much-noted contradiction between the function of borders in demarcating zones of exclusiveness (and exclusive citizenship) and the growing permeability of those borders to all sorts of transnational flows. Government and police power are problematic where the fiction of closed borders clash with the realities of open economies (Lipschutz 2002).

Borderlands become an especially vexing matter, inasmuch as national sovereignty and individual citizenship and rights may operate at cross-purposes in them. But borderlands are no longer restricted to border areas; they can be anywhere. If, historically, borders marked the extent of citizenship and associated rights, political, social, and economic, emanating from a particular political center, today those markers have lost their discursive and practical standing, as diasporas create new "homelands" far away from the old ones, and binational migrants confound the political economies of liberal states. Who then is a bona fide citizen? Who is not? Why does it matter?

Constitutionally and legally, of course, states and governments have long established standard requirements for citizenship as well as the conditions under which it might be obtained by those who are alien and not "national," but even these rules change over time in response to the exigencies of everyday life. A century ago, one's home state could place limits on the right to leave, but passports were not required to enter a host state. Today, with the exception of parts of the European Union, one cannot leave one country or enter another without a passport. A decade ago, there were no "citizens of Europe." Today, there are. As Kathy Ferguson has put it, "A state or society is never a simple or static thing; it is always a process of becoming" (Ferguson 1996: 436). Similarly, even as there may be fundamental rights, privileges, and obligations associated with citizenship in any given state, these are always in a "process of becoming" something different. Those changes are better explained by the interplay of politics and economics than by concerns about ethics, justice, or abstract rights.

Hence, contemporary struggles to limit citizenship cannot be explained by either the widespread abjuring of traditional values and historical conventions, or effects arising from social mixing and immigrant cultures. If there is a problem here, it may be attributable more to a "crisis of the nation-state," and the relationship of the individual to that crisis, than to the individual herself (Lipschutz 2000). It follows, therefore, that, absent the advent of a world state, any displacement of citizenship and rights to the global level will not resolve the contradictions or instantiate a fixed resolution of the dilemma.[5]

The very concept of "citizen" as a contractual relation between the propertied individual and the sovereign state is not much more than two hundred years old, in spite of the fact that "citizen" was not an invention of nineteenth-century nationalists but, rather, an inheritance from feudalism. Prior to the emergence of the modern nation-state and the associated concepts and practices of citizenship, most people were literally property, bound to the land via feudal relationships with their lord. Changes in the character of political community in Europe from an aristocratic hierarchy under God to a more polyarchic form under the state were paralleled by the gradual transformation of subjects into citizens. This process took several centuries and was closely linked to the rise of capitalism.

The delinking of labor from land inherent in the demise of feudalism and the transition to capitalism raised a dilemma for rulers and states alike: What was to bind the free (bourgeois) individual to the state, if ties to the land no longer kept them imprisoned? John Locke provided one part of the answer; G.W.F. Hegel, the other. Locke argued that it was private property that "made" the citizen and provided the foundation for civil society (Locke 1988: II, 122–24, 138). John Stuart Mill made similar arguments, insisting that it was property that created both wealth and nationhood (Mill 1962: 52). Locke, of course, was referring to more than just material possessions. Nonetheless, in the democratic societies of the nineteenth and twentieth centuries, and even as late as the 1960s in parts of the United States, only possession of material property in the form of real estate qualified certain, for the most part, male individuals to full citizenship and associated rights (I return to this point below).

Hegel argued that property was essential to identity. As he put it, property was central to the (re)production of selfhood, and selfhood related to the establishment of individual social existence. Recognition of the functioning individual rested, therefore, on property (Hegel 1821: sec. 1.1; Avineri 1972). The differentiation of individuals and their interests from the more collective concepts of feudalism was central to the rise of liberalism, as it was, indeed, to the very notion of citizenship as an individualized attribute conferred on the person, rather than an ascriptive characteristic inherited from one's ancestors or arising from physical location.

Industrialization and enclosure of common lands between the seventeenth and nineteenth centuries, especially in Great Britain, further dispossessed many who had never been citizens in any contemporary sense of the word, but who had certainly been members of communities, albeit with few "rights" as we conceptualize them today (Polanyi 1944). Contrary to the claims of Garrett Hardin (1968), the "tragedy of the commons" was not ecological but social (as is the case with enclosures taking place today). Community membership rested heavily on reciprocal bonds of obligation and extensive kinship ties—what anthropologists used to regard as the "customs" of so-called traditional societies. Today, such bonds have acquired new legitimacy and respect under the rubric "social capital" (Putnam 2000), even as this represents another move to transmogrify personal relations into semimonetized values.[6]

I do not mean to reify or romanticize these arrangements; such kin- and land-based communities were closed, parochial, exclusivist, and often un-friendly to "outsiders." They were also, for the most part, excluded from the elite political life of a country. Nevertheless, enclosure and the penetration of markets and industry into these communities disrupted long-established social ties and devalued those forms of social capital so important to house-holds and communities (Berman 1982). As a result, the material bases neces-sary for the survival of these "ur-citizens" went into decline or were stolen outright. Left without livelihoods, people began to leave the countryside and migrate to the cities. (This process is almost identical to that which we see today around the world, most noticeably in less-developed countries; see, for example, Sassen 1994, 1998). Once in the cities, migrants owned little or nothing, thereby failing to qualify for citizenship defined in terms of posses-sions. The more fortunate became members of the working class and began to accumulate things, if not actual real property. The less fortunate became members of a disenfranchised lumpen proletariat.[7]

In time, these new urban residents became too numerous to ignore. Governments were compelled to acknowledge them as bona fide members of the nation, if only to give them a stake in the defense of the state and to protect governments from the domestic instability. But for decades, citizen-ship, nationality, and rights were restricted to small numbers, defined in fairly narrow terms—by blood, as in Germany, or language, as in France—and limited to men. With time, these legal requirements were linked less and less to masculinity or ownership of real property and in their place an often tacit link to the individual's property rights in the self, in the form of alienable labor, became the basis for citizenship (Stanley 1998). As testified to by con-temporary debates over welfare and employment, liberal societies continue to regard those who do not work for a wage as less than full members of the political community, and sometimes impose restrictions on their liberty and rights (as is the case with workfare schemes; see also Arendt 1958: chs. 3–4).

The political turmoil of the century and a half between 1800 and 1945 resulted in the consolidation of European nation-states even as it created vast numbers of stateless refugees, who found themselves without passport or papers.[8] But many of these were, eventually, able to acquire citizenship. At the same time, as seen in the case of Nazi Germany, what was granted by the state could also be confiscated by it. After World War II, enfranchisement of previously marginalized minorities, as through the Civil Rights movement in the United States, and the integration in Europe and Britain of immigrants from former colonial possessions seemed to indicate a universal trend toward a more inclusive conception of citizenship. But this trend may have been an illusory one. As we have seen in more recent decades in the United States, Germany, France, the United Kingdom, and most of Europe and Asia, with new patterns of migration and immigration and growing fiscal stringencies, full inclusion has become very controversial.

In simplified terms, citizenship can be understood as an individual's entitlement to participate in some aspects of the state's establishment and maintenance of authority (this participation is what we conventionally call "politics"), and to receive protection for one's self and property, in return for an obligation to commit one's body, property, and taxes to the state in times of national need. Prior to the French Revolution, the typical member of political society was a propertied gentleman—often of the aristocracy—with an interest in preserving his title to property and his status. With the French Revolution, property became less central to the grant of citizenship (as member of political society), and property in the self became more important (and, eventually, the only requirement, albeit only so long as no other state had a "lien" on a person's body). In keeping with its role in creating and legitimizing property rights, only the state was authorized to grant such title to property in the self (as happened with abolition in the United States), and only those who met a set of sometimes arcane and complicated criteria were deemed qualified to receive such title.

While it is often assumed (as I have above) that the earliest forms of citizenship were merely political—that is, they encompassed only political rights of membership (Arendt 1958)—in fact, citizenship has always been better understood as part of an industrializing state's political economy. In the late-nineteenth-century United States, for example, citizenship was, in many instances, a prerequisite for acquiring title to property, on the one hand, and confiscating it from those who held or occupied land under other forms of customary or usufruct title (which was rarely inscribed in documents recognized by the United States or the individual states). By binding certain people to territory via citizenship, and using citizens to lay claims to territory on its behalf, the American state was able to extend its national sovereignty to parts of the continent in which initially it had no legitimate claim or title other than "Manifest Destiny" (for example, Texas, California, the Southwest).

European struggles for land had a similar character. Disputes over control of Alsace-Lorraine, for example, revolved around the national character of its inhabitants, and which group—French or German—were dominant both numerically and economically. Prior to the Second World War, Germany asserted its right to sovereignty over many of those areas in which ethnic Germans lived, claiming them as "property" of the Nazi Reich and, by implication, the land they occupied as territory of the Reich. While such revanchist claims no longer carry much weight in most of Europe—unlike in other parts of the world, such as Israel/Palestine or Kashmir—the emergence of the European Union seems, nonetheless, to have generated a sense of unease regarding the relationship between citizenship in its member states and "citizenship" in the EU.

There also exists a critical but mostly unremarked parallel between private property and sovereign territory. (Indeed, there is a not-accidental relationship between the self-interested individual of liberal political theory and the self-interested state of both realism and neoliberalism, a point discussed in Onuf 1989.) Not only does the nation-state grant property rights and protect property, it can also define who is permitted to own property and where. While the spread of capitalist ideology and practice has served to eliminate many restrictions on property ownership throughout the world, one can still find countries where only citizens are permitted to own land, and places where only property owners are permitted to vote. These parallels are especially apparent in the case of Israel, in which almost 95 percent of the land was and is held by the state or other national institutions as the "collective property" of the Jewish people. Among other things, such national property prevents non-Jews from taking title to land—that is, the national territory—and, therefore, maintains the "Jewish" character of both citizenry and land.

What do these arguments and observations have to do with contemporary citizenship and rights? First, only the individual who puts labor (or money, a proxy for labor) into land is entitled to call it his or her property, and only the individual who owns property or exercises rights to property in the self (that is, through wage labor) is, even today, considered a full member of the national political community. Second, since the state exists to preserve property, among other things, only those who have property are believed to have an interest in preserving the state (Locke 1988: II, 138). Note that those who put labor into land but lack title to it (that is, hold property in themselves), whether peasants or squatters, can never be fully rational or full citizens, according to Locke (1958: 252), even with the extension of suffrage and other accoutrements of citizenship (McPherson 1962: 221–29). Finally, because of these links between citizen, property/sovereignty, and state, the extension of suffrage and other rights to those who do not hold property has happened only very slowly. Because citizenship and the rights associated with it can be understood as grants of privilege or property in the self, authorized by the state, the incorporation of "outsiders" into the political economy can be seen as constituting a major change in the status and practices of state sovereignty. This happens, of course, frequently and continuously, even as it creates internal tensions and contradictions, a point on which I shall elaborate below.

Implicit in my argument is the notion that all contemporary states are internally Lockean, even those that are not visibly democratic or even capitalist. A Lockean state rests on the proposition that the government is representative of the people rather than simply a sovereign unto itself. While practice is often quite distant from theory, there are few states whose constitutions do not include such principles and that do not hold periodic elections, however meaningless the latter might seem. Those governments seen as consistent violators of the human rights of citizens are under constant pressure to fulfill the terms of the Lockean social contract. To a growing degree, the practice of political conditionality makes the availability of international financial funds contingent upon fulfillment of those terms.

The Economic Bases of Human Rights

The conventional story tells us that citizenship and human rights are political entitlements, having emerged through a historical and somewhat teleological process of political development, and culminating in democratization and the modern citizen. Globalization, it is sometimes said, threatens these entitlements because of relentless competitive pressures that force governments to make policy choices without public ratification (Brysk and Shafir, this volume). Others, however, argue that, notwithstanding these pressures and a "democratic deficit" at the international level, states are finding it necessary and possible to grant forms of national membership and protect rights of noncitizens.

Yasemin Soysal is an advocate of this latter view, arguing for a "postnational" approach to understanding the limits of state sovereignty where rights are concerned. On the one hand, she asserts, national sovereignty has become "celebrated and codified in international conventions and treaties." On the other hand, the "notion of human rights, as a codification of abstract concepts of personhood, has become a pervasive element of world culture" (Soysal 1994: 7). States are counted upon to assert their sovereignty over borders and immigration, but, at the same time, they are also expected to observe certain global standards regarding treatment of those who cross those borders and enter the national space. Soysal explains this apparent contradiction by reference to "new institutionalist approaches in macrosociology [that] contend that world-level rules and definitions are integral to the constitution of national institutions and social entities, such as state policies and bureaucracies, national economies, education, welfare, gender, and the individual" (Soysal 1994: 41). And, she continues,

> Human rights are now a pervasive feature of global public culture. They are the object of much public debate and social action and organization, enveloping and engendering a wide range of issues. . . . As such, human rights principles amount to more than formal arrangements and laws. They constitute a binding discourse, according frameworks that render certain actions conceivable and meaningful. . . . [G]lobal discourse creates new actors and collective interests which, in turn, exert pressure on existing systems. Once codified and material-ized through conventions, legal instruments, and recursive deployment, this dis-course becomes a focal point for interest-group activities and public attention. It enables mobilization, opens up an array of legitimate claims, and amplifies action. (Soysal 1994: 43–44)

Based on her research in several European countries during the late 1980s, Soysal finds that migrants are slowly being incorporated into the body politic, albeit not as full political members. While the particulars among countries vary, depending on state structure, culture, and history, migrants are being granted a broad range of social and economic rights. These permit them to integrate, at least partially, into the political economies of their host countries, even though they do not assimilate as individuals or become "nationals" in the generally understood sense of the term. Soysal takes this to be an optimistic and promising trend, in that it permits the simultaneous maintenance of a class of "national" citizens while creating a parallel class of "postnational" citizens.

Yet, in characterizing the discourse of human rights as a social and political phenomenon—which does, of course, have visible distributive effects—Soysal manages to disregard the role of the human rights discourse in the neoliberal global political economy as well as the origins of human rights in liberalism and its political economy. More to the point, the human rights discourse is as much one of political economy as it is social or political.[9] Here, again, geneal-ogy is illuminating. If we return to the origins of human rights in natural law, we find that they were asserted as against those limits imposed on the emerg-ing European bourgeoisie by the divine laws of God and the divine rights of kings, as Brysk and Shafir note in their introduction to this volume. But it was only through the legitimation of such rights that the middle classes were able to protect their property from unjust seizure. Moreover, it was only through coalitions with the sovereign, against the landed nobility, that the bourgeoisie was able to obtain acknowledgment of these rights by sovereign and state. Ultimately, these first rights of property were expanded and extended to en-compass today's panoply of human rights, as I suggested earlier in this chapter.

This argument is not meant to suggest that concepts of human rights did not exist prior to the promulgation of the UN Universal Declaration of Human Rights in 1948 or, for that matter, the French Declaration of the Rights of Man and Citizen in 1789. Nor do I suggest that human rights are some kind of conspiracy by capital or a liberal imposition. Rather, my argument is that human rights—political, social, and economic—are associated with individuals living in a liberal market society and are necessary to a fully realized but largely imaginary form of that society. As I have written elsewhere (Lipschutz 2000), human rights are best understood as a form of individual sovereignty exercised within liberal systems and their markets, which frees the consumer citizen from the constraints imposed by states pursuing national advantage. One's right to purchase an item produced anywhere in the world trumps the state's interest in restricting such choice only to national products (Friedman 1962; Friedman and Friedman 1980).

Human rights have quite different meanings (if they have any meaning at all) outside of this liberal framework (see, for example, efforts to extract similar rights from the Quran), and this is one cause for conflicts between countries over their human rights records. By focusing on the individual at the expense of society, human rights privilege individual self-interest, a necessary element of market society. Individual freedom is conventionally clothed in those negative freedoms that offer liberation from any obligations to society, but is more often judged in terms of success within the market. The specific human rights discourse analyzed by Soysal has been pegged to the spread of laissez-faire liberalism to the four corners of the Earth over the past fifty years, a result of the post–Second World War economic regimes, institutions, and practices established by the United States (with an early assist from the United Kingdom). The goal behind the Bretton Woods project was to reproduce domestic American society (or, at least, its underlying structural conditions), as much as possible, the world over. Such a system would be wide open to American products, investment, and extraction. To a significant degree, the project was a success, laying the groundwork for the most recent round of globalization that began in earnest during the 1980s (Lipschutz 2000: ch. 2).

Some observers, such as Stephen Gill, have commented on the extent to which citizenship has come to be defined by the individual's relationship to the market rather than the political community. Gill points out that wealth is necessary for access to credit, and credit is a prerequisite for citizenship in contemporary liberal democracy. He writes that "the substantive conception of citizenship involves not only a political-legal conception, but also an economic idea. Full citizenship requires not only a claim of political rights and obligations, but access to and participation in a system of production and consumption" (Gill 1995: 22). This, he argues, acts to discipline and socialize consumers, beginning in adolescence. Failure to meet the terms of economic citizenship, through late payments or bankruptcy, means social marginalization. The threat of exclusion keeps consumers in line (Lipschutz 2000: ch. 7). The result, Gill says, is the replacement of "traditional forms of discipline associated with the family and the school" by market discipline (Gill 1995: 26; see also Drainville

1995). In this way, the workers of the world are bound into citizenship in the new global economy.

Under these conditions, property, and little else, does become the fundamental basis for citizenship, and many rich countries are more than happy to grant citizenship to immigrants who bring with them substantial amounts of capital. But economic citizenship of this type obviously leaves many out of the picture—millions in the United States; billions around the world. Even during the booming economy and long expansion of the 1990s, the wherewithal to become an economic citizen did not reach everyone. Moreover, bankruptcy laws pending in the U.S. Congress suggest that what the market grants it can also easily take away. In countries such as Indonesia and Thailand, many who aspired to join the global consumer class now find themselves shut out by a recession triggered by the 1997 economic crisis (Garson 2001).

Soysal's research was undertaken in the late 1980s and early 1990s, prior to the establishment of the single European market, the European Union, and the various agreements establishing more rigorous boundaries between the EU and the countries to the east and south. It is not so clear that national solutions to the treatment of migrants continue to be operative in the way she describes them. More to the point, Soysal's view of postnationalism is decidedly nonmaterialist, and fails to recognize, or anticipate, the continuing and growing tensions the mobility of labor, much of it illegal, has created in both industrialized and industrializing countries. These tensions arise from a fundamental contradiction between political and economic demands on states by the bourgeoisie, on the one hand, and capital, on the other.

Migrants seem to pose several challenges to the middle classes of Europe, North America, and other states that are mostly representative of a single or titular nationality. First, they appear to threaten the hegemony and power of the dominant nationality, making the latter feel insecure as cultural changes and commodification work their way through the society (Harris 2002). Second, because migrants are often unregistered, it is assumed that they pay no taxes and represent a net drain on state resources, which the dominant group believes it is financing (see, for example, Harris 2002: appendix I). Finally, the middle classes have no real sense of the employment structure of the economy and assume, as they are often told, that migrants take jobs at the expense of unemployed citizens (which seems not to be the case, even in countries with structural unemployment stuck around 10 percent) (Sassen 1999: ch. 7). The result of the combination of beliefs and insecurities are demands that "something be done" about immigration, both legal and illegal.

In response to such political pressures, governments engage in policies and practices that appear to be attempts to reduce immigration, in the effort to garner votes, without actually having a serious impact on labor flows (Harris 2002: 80). Such halfhearted efforts are mostly a favor to capital and its holders, who recognize their need for low-wage workers and the fact that middle-class citizens will not take such jobs, even in times of economic duress (Portes and Rumbaut 1996). One need only stand outside of Disneyland, or one of its clones, at closing time, watching daytime workers leave and nighttime workers arrive, to see this distinction at work. The difference is evident, and so is the demand for labor that structures that difference.

To accommodate immigrant/migrant labor, the state must provide some modicum of services, although, as Soysal shows us, the specific services offered depend on the specific state under investigation. But it is also interesting to note that political tensions affecting the middle classes do not wax and wane in direct relation to levels of economic activity. Periods of prosperity create as many, if not more, demands for controls on immigration as do periods of economic recession or stagnation. This occurs because it is during the former that the demand for labor is high, that domestic labor pools are unable to meet the demand, that migrants are more likely to move in search of employment in host countries, and that the cultural impacts of immigrants are likely to become most visible (Sassen 1999: ch. 7; Harris 2002: 98–104). These days, prosperity seems as likely as recession to engender anti-immigrant legislation.

Going Global: Is Cosmopolitan Citizenship the Answer?

The pervasive sense that the contradictions between transnational mobility and national citizenship generated by globalization cannot be resolved within the nation-state has led to a growing interest in "cosmopolitan citizenship." While the term *cosmopolitan* has a somewhat checkered past, it has now become shorthand for the enhanced international mobility and territorial disconnectedness of that growing number of people whose loyalties to the nation-state are no longer a given. There are a number of competing and contrasting conceptions of cosmopolitan citizenship, whose origins are to be found in the Stoics' notion of "cosmopolis," "based on the notion of the essential oneness of humanity as part of the universal natural order governed by natural law" (Hutchings 1999: 12). Although we no longer subscribe to either "natural orders" or "natural law," the sense of one humanity is stronger than ever.

Here, however, I wish to focus on two of these cosmopolitan notions: first, the idea of what is, essentially, an elaboration on a neo-Kantian, multilevel federalized citizenship, as proposed by David Held and his colleagues (1995b, 1996) and Andrew Linklater (1998, 1999), and, second, what some call "differentiated citizenship," which is based on memberships, with variable rights, in a range of differentiated political and social communities (see, for example, Young 1989; Kymlicka 1995). Obviously, I cannot do justice to either of these conceptions in this chapter and only summarize them here.

Federalized Citizenship

Immanuel Kant's conception of cosmopolitan citizenship is rooted, on the one hand, in the framework presented in Perpetual Peace, which is based on an international association of peaceful republican states. On the other hand, it is also rooted in individual membership in a transnational moral community based on the Categorical Imperative. In his writings, Kant did not suggest that cosmopolitan citizenship involved any kind of political membership in a transnational community, somehow based on individual participation in a global public sphere. As Andrew Linklater (1999: 41) puts it,

> The democratic moment in Kant's writing was confined to the principle that the citizens of separate states should imagine themselves as co-legislators in a universal communication community. . . . [A]ll human beings should act as if they are co-legislators in a universal kingdom of ends, although they will never take part in deliberations together. World citizens would remain members of bounded communities. . . . But the act of imagining themselves as participants in a universal society of co-legislators in which all human beings are respected as ends-in-themselves would place powerful moral and psychological constraints on the wrongful exercise of state power.[10]

Based on Linklater's description, it is evident that Kant's model lacks two components thought of as essential in our modern conceptions of citizenship. First, as noted above, there are no actual politics or political practices involved here: no deliberations, no voting, no public space. The cosmopolitan part of citizenship is a moral construction organized around some sense of commonality among human beings and requiring people to act as if they belonged to a global public space. This is akin to the contemporary notion of "consciousness raising": if we all came individually to believe proper thoughts, we would act on them and change the world.

Second, there is no obvious material element involved here and no institutions or organizations to provide rights or entitlements or to impose obligations on either states or individuals, as is the case within the nation-state. In other words, power is absent. If we take liberalism as the organizing ontology of this type of cosmopolitan citizenship (although Kant did not), there is no "payoff" to being a good global citizen, and therefore it is not in any individual's short-term self-interest to be cosmopolitan.

Held, Linklater, and others do not seem overly worried by the flaws in Kant's concept and recognize its shortcomings. It is for this reason that they express their particular concern about the impacts of the so-called democratic deficit on the potential for cosmopolitan citizenship. That is, the failure of the institutions of emerging transnational governance to legitimately represent the individual members of the states that belong to them eliminates power as a critical element. This deficit is especially evident in the relationship between the institutions of the European Union and its member states. The EU has a somewhat toothless parliament, whose MEPs are elected by citizens of member states, but the European Commission and Council are subject to no such electoral ratification. Article 8 of the Maastricht Treaty establishes a category of European citizens, but this has had little effect on the sovereignty of individual member states, and does little more than require a uniform color and seal on all passports.

Linklater (1999: 43) points out that each EU member accepts that the citizens of other signatory states may stand as candidates, and vote, in its local elections, and each recognizes similar rights regarding elections for the European Parliament; but there is nothing in the Maastricht Treaty that invites the citizens of different states to transcend their differences in a transnational citizenry that is empowered to elect the members of the European Commission.

To put the point another way, at the present time there is no trans-European public sphere in which the citizens of Europe can engage in political behavior and exercise some modicum of power, in the sense that is possible within the individual democracies comprising the union (I ignore, for the moment, the very real limits to democratic practice within the member states of the EU or, for that matter, all contemporary democracies). Because no one seems very keen to turn Brussels into even so weak a power center as is Washington, D.C.—and many believe the European Commission is on its way to becoming more powerful—the problem becomes one of empowering citizens while disempowering the European Commission and Council.

Federalized citizenship, or what Linklater (1999: 55) calls a "dialogic approach to world citizenship"[11] is, apparently, the answer. Again, to quote him (1999: 49),

> The point is not to reconstitute sovereign authority over a wider territorial domain but to promote multiple sites of political responsibility which represent sub-state and transnational allegiances as well as loyalties to nation-states. Citizens would then be able to exercise their political rights and express their different political loyalties within diverse public spheres.

In general terms, it is not altogether clear what might be included in these "diverse public spheres," although they could include states as they currently exist, subregions within which some identity might be constituted, and "solidarist structures" dedicated to the promotion of various social and environmental concerns (Linklater 1999: 55). In the European context, this begins to sound very much like the citizen's version of "subsidiarity"—that is, the arrangement under which functions and duties are performed, and rights and entitlements are granted, at that level of government that is most appropriate to the task at hand. There is little difficulty in having democratic garbage pickup, should anyone be interested in it.

What this version of cosmopolitan citizenship does not really address, however, are differentials of power, including the power of states to define and delimit those public spheres into which citizenship might be expanded. Indeed, there is a notable lack of attention to the material aspects of citizenship, and a seeming disregard not only of those social and economic entitlements that come along with "full" citizenship, but also the less visible structural inequalities and impediments that prevent many notional citizens from being able to participate fully in both the public and economic spheres. To put this another, less charitable way, there is the smell of idealism floating around federalized citizenship, an idealism that prioritizes and reifies liberal political rights above all others.

Differentiated Citizenship

Over the past decade, growing attention has been paid to the structural problem highlighted above, and a number of theorists have focused on the ways in which citizenship defined in political terms alone can reproduce and maintain discrimination against minority and culturally-distinctive groups within a society. Both Iris Marion Young (1989; see also 1990) and Will Kymlicka (1995) have addressed this concern, although their focus is almost entirely on citizenship within the nation-state. Young argues that, even with equitable political and civil rights, citizens experience differential consequent advantages linked to the relative social (and class) positions in which they find themselves because of their ethnicity, gender, class, and historical experiences. She proposes, therefore, that citizenship rights be granted variably among groups so as to protect minority rights and redress some of these disadvantages. This type of approach was, in fact, applied in Malaysia following communal riots in 1969, under a very broad structural affirmative action program (as opposed to the rather more individualistic form under attack in the United States), with a fair degree of distributive success (Lubeck 1992).

Kymlicka's proposals follow similar lines, and there is a growing literature debating the form, as well as the merits and problems with such an approach. Of particular concern to some critics is the possibility that differentiated citizenship will lead to further social fragmentation, as some social groups compete for advantage and others form to oppose them (as has been the case, to some degree, in California). Joe Painter (2000: 6) has pointed out that the possibility of gaining group advantage "may have the effect of consolidating groups rigidly around a somewhat static identity and may permanently lock in one specific set of groups to a formal position in the polity."

Ruth Lister (1998) has taken the idea of differentiated citizenship further, developing what she calls "differentiated universalism." She draws, in part, on Young's (1990: 105) criticism of universalism as impartiality (a criticism that applies, as well, to national citizenship), which Young defines as "the adoption of a general point of view that leaves behind particular affiliations, feelings, commitments and desires," and rejects. But, apparently, Young backs off toward a neo-Kantian conception of cosmopolitan citizenship in her emphasis on the "universality of moral commitment" to equal moral worth, participation, and inclusion of all persons (Lister 1998, citing Young 1990: 105). Lister's primary interest lies in articulating a differentiated universalism that can be applied to feminist conceptions and practices of citizenship. She identifies women as a transnational class or group oppressed by structural disempowerment in every society, but applies her proposals to citizenship within the national setting. At the end of the day, of course, public and private spheres remain largely contained within the nation-state and, even though those who struggle against oppression may be able to establish global solidarities with one another, the political action seems to remain on the ground, within the state.

Is Citizenship the Answer? What Was the Question?

In conventional terms, citizenship is currently conceptualized as a combination of entitlements and nationality (Lipschutz 2000). From the former arise political, civil, and social rights; from the latter, inclusion and exclusion. Generally speaking, however, it is the nationality-territory link, in a narrow sense, that grants access to most entitlements and generates the resentments that are visible in almost all of the world's societies in which there are large immigrant communities. So long as citizenship remains linked to territorial and cultural exclusivity ("national sovereignty"), the contradiction remains; if, however, the two could be decoupled, multiple "citizenships" (or memberships in political communities) might become possible. This raises, in turn, the question as to whether we might conceive of political communities that are neither territorial nor exclusive yet have the characteristics of "membership" that we have conventionally associated with citizenship.

In other words, is it possible to imagine political arrangements in which citizenship is feasible yet not dependent on territorial units, such as the nation-state?[12] An alternative political community might, for instance, be based not on space, but on flows; not on where people are, but on what links them together. That is, the identity between politics and people would not be rooted in a specific piece of reified "homeland" whose boundaries, fixed in the mind and on the ground, excluded all others. Instead, to slightly revise Michael J. Shapiro's language, this identity would be based on "a heterogenous set of . . . power centers integrated through structures of communication" (Shapiro 1997: 206), as well as knowledge and practices specific to each community. Kathy Ferguson (1996: 451–52) has suggested that

> [c]ollective identity based on control of territory sponsors a zero-sum calculation: either we belong here or they do. One can imagine collective identities that are deterritorialized, knit together in some other ways, perhaps from shared memories, daily practices, concrete needs, specific relationships to people, locations, and histories. Such productions would be more narrative than territorial; they might not be so exclusive because they are not so relentlessly spatial. Connection to a particular place could still be honored as one dimension of identity, but its intensities could be leavened by less competitive claims. Participation in such identities could be self-consciously partial, constructed, mobile; something one does and redoes every day, not a docile space one simply occupies and controls. Empathy across collective identities constructed as fluid and open could enrich, rather than endanger, one's sense of who one is.

These notions focus heavily on dialogic connections and communications, ignoring the material (welfare) side of citizenship. Unfortunately, political theorists are not very good at political economy, seeing it as epiphenomenal to politics, while political economists (in the Marxist, not liberal, sense of the term) are not much interested in political theory, regarding it as superstructural at worst, or highly contingent to the material base, at best. But citizenship as we commonly understand it is, as I argued earlier, a necessary element in the organization of the Lockean, liberal state, and liberal citizenship is only one form of possible membership in a range of possible political communities. The granting of citizenship as a property right in the self is both a cause and a consequence of the limited range of political participation allowed to the liberal citizen; as Painter (2000: 6) puts it, "Liberalism holds a limited and passive conception of citizenship which provides a minimum set of basic rights to allow each individual self-interestedly to pursue his or her private definitions of the good life. Active participation in the public sphere is discouraged, as this would imply an effort to promote a common conception of the good life, thereby reducing the liberty of individuals to pursue their own, perhaps different, conceptions."

Indeed, the very reification of "private" as a sphere distinct from the "public" serves to obscure the extent to which the public impinges on and intrudes into the private and the degree to which this division manages to depoliticize some very critical matters.[13] Relegating family, civil society, and social movements to the private sphere leads to the conclusion that they have nothing to do with either politics or power in the public sphere, even as the state routinely meddles in the private. Furthermore, the notion that the market is part of the private rather than the public sphere leads to the illusion that political freedom largely involves individuals' "freedom to choose," as Milton Friedman (1980) has put it. While these points are important in the national context, and have comprised the terrain over which the citizenship battles have taken place, they are even more important under conditions of globalization, when the realm of the market no longer fits very well with any public sphere and, indeed, seeks to colonize it.[14]

It is, of course, possible that we are asking the wrong questions. There are, I would propose, two areas of concern here: First, under conditions of globalization, what ought to comprise the public sphere and how ought individuals to be political within that public sphere? Second, what ought to comprise the ethical set of entitlements ("ethical" in the Hegelian sense) that is required to address both distributive and social inequities and, by extension, the questions of both citizenship and human rights? It is clear that the two matters are related, but how they might be addressed is not very evident. Young argues that "[a] model of a transformed society must begin from the material structures that are given to us at this time in history" (Young 1990: 234). In other words, we should examine "really existing social formations" without accepting them as either given or immutable, if we intend to answer the two questions I have posed here.

Reinstantiating the Political

As a number of writers have observed, globalization has had the somewhat unexpected effect of both marginalizing and constricting the public sphere of the nation-state, such as it is, and virtually eliminating people's access to whatever public sphere might exist in the international realm (Falk 1999). I concur, therefore, with Sheldon Wolin's (1996) argument that there is not much that is "political" in today's democracies; I am less sure of his contention that, under constitutional orders, the political must necessarily be both infrequent and ephemeral. I have argued elsewhere that the shift of political authority from the national to the international level, visible in institutions such as the WTO and the governmentalization of global governance, has been the result of a deliberate effort to "depoliticize" economic practices. I have also proposed that efforts to create a global public sphere are visible in the projects and campaigns of global civil society (Lipschutz 2001). It is clear, however, that these types of projects are liberal in inspiration, organization, and practice—not entirely surprising, given that global governance, such as it is, is largely based on the political system of the United States—and rely heavily on market mechanisms to accomplish goals of political distribution. To put this another way, global civil society is, for the most part, closer to liberal concepts and practices than to the liberationist ones. In any event, the creation of a separate international public sphere would simply serve to instantiate an institutionalized politics that would remain as remote from the individual as are the activities of most national parliaments. A cosmopolitan form of citizenship would be a thin and denatured version of national practices, and it seems unlikely that human rights would be observed or enforced any more strongly than they are today.

The struggle to achieve the political must begin with two objectives: first, ending the fiction of the separation between public and private as it exists in everyday life, on the ground; second, restoring constitutive politics in the political sphere. The first means resisting the penetration of market logic into all realms of human life, for political reasons; the second means creating public spheres in which the very uses and purposes of power can be subject to debate and decision. I am not suggesting here that everything, including the personal and sexual, be open to public scrutiny or politicized. Instead, I do argue that we come to recognize and contest the extent to which the "public," represented by an intrusive market, has already exposed so much that is personal. It is also important that we recognize that much deemed "private," including civil society and social movements, ought not to be excluded from the public sphere on the grounds that they have more to do with markets than politics. Only by reasserting the primacy of politics over markets can we begin to address the joint questions of citizenship and human rights.

One possible means of countering the continuing domestication of the political within and among market systems is through global networks of social movements, united by a shared epistemic vision, but differentiated on the basis of specific conditions, needs, and worldviews. Without glorifying or idealizing existing social movements—and recognizing that there are those that seek to severely limit the political realm by commanding obedience to a natural or immanent authority[15]—these are the sites that are, for the moment, the most political. That is, such movements come closest to the "spaces of appearance" that Arendt (1958) deemed necessary to reestablishing the separation between what is public and what ought to be truly private. Moreover, it is in those social movements most able to critically analyze the relationship of power and structure to their status—and I am thinking here of various women's and feminist movements, among others—that we also find greatest evidence of the political.

There is a second important aspect of this sense of the political, which has to do with strengthening our intellectual and epistemic sense of how we, as individuals, are situated locally in various kinds of relationships with others, many of which are of transnational extent. We experience and try to comprehend conditions, things, and events in which we are physically situated, but it is essential to remain aware and sensitive to the history, forces, and actions that have played roles in our individual and social lives (Scott 1992). For example, the conditions and experiences of women living in various societies and places are strongly dependent on both global and local history, processes, and actions, but the resulting circumstances are very contextual and contingent. Being political means, therefore, understanding how those factors have resulted in both difference and similarity and, more critically, how to exercise agency in those circumstances. These two elements are an essential part of (re)constructing a public sphere within which meaningful participation can take place and membership can be established.

I would argue that citizenship, conceived solely in terms of political and civil rights, does not, as such, enter into this equation. Although citizenship is understood in terms of a social contract between the state and particular individuals, it is a grant of title whose terms are largely up to the state. The kinds of political networks I have in mind here do not rest on the forms of authority exercised by the state, but are structured through mutual recognition and the diffusion, rather than the concentration, of power. Human and civil rights, which have come to be foundational to divided liberal systems ("divided" in the public-private sense) but whose sources remain rather mysterious, also have the character of entitlements by authority that can be given and taken away. To put this another way, there ought not to be debates about a "right" to basic needs such as food and shelter; these needs should be available without condition.

To repeat: First, it is necessary to recognize that the demarcation between the public and private spheres is a means whereby political action can be limited and disciplined. By limiting participation to institutionalized practices, such as voting in periodic elections, liberal citizenship is denatured of most of its political content, with membership represented by a thin set of rights and documents. Only by belonging—which goes beyond a membership card—to those movements that provide the tools to critically and constantly analyze and reflect on the political are we able, I believe, to fulfill the promise inherent in a richer notion of citizenship. Second, this awareness must encompass, as well, a recognition of how one has come to be located in a particular place, where place is understood not simply in spatial terms but also relational ones, and in which relations are not limited to those who live nearby but includes all those around the world who are also part of a particular episteme.

Distribution, Recognition, Justice

It is not enough, however, to articulate an intellectual conception of political participation and leave it at that; the "problem" of citizenship has, after all, a strongly material component brought about, as I have argued above, by the disjunction caused by globalization between the spatial reach of market power and the territorial limits of state authority.[16] Political membership and action must be grounded in the material realm in a way that enables others to construct and participate in their own movements and epistemes but, at the same time, establishes solidarity links among epistemes. I do not wish to engage here in some sort of policy-making exercise, describing how the material tools for these membership epistemes are to be provided, but it seems to me that considerations of both political recognition and distributive justice, as discussed by Nancy Fraser in her more recent work (1997, 1999), are of central concern. Once we begin to speak about distributive justice, however, we get caught, once again, in the debate over the relative merits of communitarianism and cosmpolitanism, and who is responsible to whom (see, for example, Jones 1999; Hutchings and Dannreuther 1999).

We need, consequently, to think in terms other than the nation-state, the welfare state, or their derivations. States are redistributive mechanisms, to be sure, however resources tend to flow within and among them in such a way as to empower some groups and disempower others. But there are various kinds of resources and other means of redistribution available. Inevitably, some movements and epistemes have greater access to these material resources than others, and the political use of such resources must include consideration of how those are distributed among movements and epistemes. This would require the creation of arrangements for the redistribution of material resources, a discussion of which I leave to another paper. My point here is that "citizenship" outside of a statist or federalized or neo-Kantian framework must enable people and groups not just to think politically but to be engaged and to act politically as well. And that will require a major rethinking about our contemporary understanding and practices of "politics."

Rather than engage in the intellectual contortions necessary to redefine or expand citizenship, it might be best to drop the entire idea and ask, instead, what ends we wish to accomplish? I have argued here that one concern has to do with the notion of meaningful political participation, while the second involves the means of achieving such participation and making it matter. Although the outlines of such a program remain cloudy and amorphous, to say the least, it rests on a conjuncture between social movements and political communities, linked together through epistemes, within which members can think and act politically, and outside of which communities and epistemes can do the same. Improbable? Perhaps. Impossible? No. In Justice and the Politics of Difference, Young tells us that

> [o]ne important purpose of critical normative theory [and speculation] is to offer an alternative vision of social relations which, in the words of Marcuse, "conceptualizes the stuff of which the experienced world consists . . . with a view to its possibilities, in the light of their actual limitation, suppression, and denial." Such a positive normative vision can inspire hope and imagination that motivate action for social change. It also provides some of the reflective distance necessary for the criticism of existing social circumstances. (Young 1990: 227, quoting Marcuse 1964: 7).

These seem like useful words to keep in mind.

Notes

1. I am not arguing that these are essentially contested concepts, although that is also the case.
2. A definition of *globalization* is warranted here. For the purposes of this chapter, I use the term *globalization* to denote both a material and an ideological/cognitive process. Globalization is material in the sense that it involves the movement of capital, technology, goods, and, to a limited degree, labor to areas with high returns on investment, without regard to the social or political impacts on either the communities and people to which it moves or to those left behind. Globalization is ideological in the sense that such movement is rationalized and naturalized in the name of efficiency, competition, and profit. And globalization is cognitive in the sense that it fosters social innovation and reorganization in existing institutions, composed of real, live people, without regard for the consequences. In all three respects, although globalization opens numerous political opportunities for social movements and other forms of political organization and action, a not uncommon result is disruption to existing forms of beliefs, values, behaviors, and social relations. A more detailed discussion can be found in Lipschutz 2000: ch. 2.
3. I take "membership" to be a legal status, while "belonging" is not. More anon.
4. I think here, for example, of related practices within the Ottoman Empire, which largely vanished after the First World War.
5. I suspect that even a democratic world state would not "solve" the citizenship question, inasmuch as it would be organized around extended and thin forms of representation, and could not offer the range of welfare services necessary to address the distribution problem.
6. "Social capital" is nothing more than the bonds of mutual obligation of social groups, a practice identified long ago by anthropologists, but generally relegated by economists to the realm of kinship and clan relations. Francis Fukuyama's *Trust* (1995) is a similar example of the wheel's reinvention.
7. It is interesting to note that, in many developing countries, "natives" have less proof of citizenship than legal migrants, who have had to be documented in order to live and work legally in the host country.
8. For instance, my maternal grandparents and their first-born daughter fled from the Russian Pale (now Poland) to Belgium prior to the First World War so that my grandfather

could escape the Russian draft. There, and in London, to which they fled in 1941, my grandparents remained stateless until they were able to acquire U.S. citizenship in the 1950s. My mother and her older sister, born in Belgium, were stateless until age sixteen, when they applied for and received Belgian citizenship. My oldest aunt was stateless until she became a British subject after the Second World War.

9. I use the term *political economy* here in its nineteenth-century sense, involving the interplay of power and money.

10. This idea has also reemerged in a slightly different form in proposals for a "Global Peoples Assembly," which would try to impose real constraints on the "wrongful exercise of state power" (see, e.g., Strauss 2002).

11. The "dialogic" notion is one drawn from the work of Jürgen Habermas and extended by others. It seems to involve the idea that extended, reasoned conversation will permit discussants to reach agreement on certain shared foundational assumptions about human value, human relations, and human behaviors. This sounds suspiciously similar to Linklater's discussion of Kant's notion of "co-legislators" (see above).

12. Some of what follows here is taken from Lipschutz 1999.

13. Arendt (1958) elided this problem by arguing that the "social," based on the extension of the household model to virtually all aspects of public and private life, had rendered the distinction moot. But Arendt's analysis, while rather convoluted and written from the perspective of the 1950s, remains one of the best fusions of political theory and political economy available today.

14. My take on this point can be found in Lipschutz 2001.

15. I have in mind here deep ecology movements. Quite evidently, the networks that planned and executed the September 11 attacks are not the type that I have idealized here.

16. Indeed, the question of where power is to be found in markets is a troubling one: it is, at once, everywhere and nowhere, exercised by individuals pursuing their own selfish interests, but reified by what Arendt (1958) called the "communistic fiction" of the invisible hand.

4

Latitudes of Citizenship

Membership, Meaning, and Multiculturalism

AIHWA ONG

The Debate on Multicultural Membership

For some time now, American citizenship has been a subject of intense debate. Scholars have moved beyond a tight focus on citizenship as a set of legal rights—either you have it or you don't—to an unavoidable consideration of *membership* that includes a variety of subjects, who include noncitizens. There are citizens (native and naturalized), and then there are green-card holders and legal refugees, who it is assumed will eventually apply for naturalization. Then there is a growing category of temporary visa holders—the skilled workers on H-IB visas, the overseas students, and the contract labor migrants. Finally, there are the illegal residents, those foreigners without papers who nevertheless live and work as part of society. Culture wars since the 1970s have broadened discussions beyond citizenship to membership of a variety of legal, partially legal and illegal residents. Great waves of migrations from Latin America and Asia, the circulations of business travelers and students, and the ever growing number of individuals with dual citizenship all add to a society of astonishing flux and diversity.

This chapter considers the symbolic and social *meanings* of American citizenship, and how it has been affected by forces of globalization, from increased immigration to transnational corporate connections. Recent debates show that the substance—the marrow, the soul, and the ethics—of American citizenship is in a prolonged crisis. As the idea of adherence to a single cultural nation wanes, there is a steady "desacralization" of state membership (Brubaker 1989: 4–5). Concomitantly, the demands for cultural acceptance, along with affirmative action mechanisms to increase demographic diversity in major institutions and areas of public life, has shifted discussions of *citizenship from a focus on political practice based on shared civic rights and responsibilities to an insistence on the protection of cultural difference* as new waves of immigrants have become more assertive about the hegemony of majority white culture.

For instance, in California, activist Chicano scholar-advocates such as Renato Rosaldo defined *cultural citizenship* as "the right to be different" (in terms of race, ethnicity, or native language) with respect to the norms of the dominant national community, without compromising one's right to belong, in the sense of participating in the nation-state's democratic processes. The enduring exclusions of the color line often deny full citizenship to Latinos and other "persons of color." From the point of view of subordinate communities, cultural citizenship offers the possibility of legitimizing demands made in the struggle to enfranchise themselves. These demands can range from legal, political, and economic issues to "matters of human dignity, well-being, and respect" (Rosaldo 1997: 27–38). Rosaldo and others point to the political and economic constraints underpinning claims to cultural citizenship. For instance, laws controlling the "normal" timing and use of public spaces conformed to middle-class norms, but undermined the civil rights of immigrant workers who could not avail themselves of public spaces in the same way because of work-schedule constraints and noise-level concerns. There is a sense, then, that dominant forms of normalization discriminate against the cultural difference of new immigrants, whose cultural expressions are at variance with middle-class sensibility and norms.

Furthermore, the struggles for a more open and multicultural America, against adherence to a single cultural nation—white Anglo-Saxon, (Judeo-) Christian, and heterosexual—have gained ascendancy, especially those movements for inclusions that stressed more the embodiment of middle-class values than fundamental values of egalitarianism and opportunity. Inspired as well by African-American Civil Rights struggles since the 1960s, gay proponents of what has been called "the politics of recognition" demanded public recognition of cultural diversity in connection with middle-class achievements. Building on the notion of contribution that earns worthy citizenship, early procedures of "outing" closeted gay individuals were intended to expose to society "worthy" persons who had suffered as a result of social discriminations, bias, and ignorance of their diverse and complex roles in society. The gay movement also puts stress on the more middle-class notions of self-realization and accomplishment as criteria for inclusion in the full benefits of citizenship.

The study of diasporas has also contributed to this view of immigrants as "people out of place" who continue to maintain their cultural difference in the host society (Gupta and Ferguson 1992: 6–23). Arjun Appadurai is well known for his argument that disjunctures in global spaces allow for a real politics of difference. He claims that diasporic communities—relocated in new differentiated and mobile spaces—now negotiate their positions in the setting of "postnational" orders (Appadurai 1996). There is this positive stress on difference—that is, on the study and valorization of culture and race "out of place," yet unassimilated and defiantly heterogeneous. In Canada, prominent liberal political theorists such as Will Kymlicka argue that liberalism must include the recognition of "*multicultural citizenship*," since the protection of the claims of ethnocultural groups must be protected in order to promote justice between groups, something that is a matter of both justice and self-interest in liberal democracies (Kymlicka 1995). Charles Taylor argues that equal rights are only realized when there is mutual respect for cultural difference, merely putting into practice the promise of Liberalism for nurturing of the modern, authentic self (Taylor 1994: 56–57).

While I agree with much of the demands of multiculturalism, my approach to the new America turns away from this use of cultural or ethnoracial difference as the framing device of inquiry (Ong 2003). There is an overwhelming assumption that the "cultures" of immigrants remain the same, and that somehow they are immutable to all kinds of policies, practices, and techniques that immigrants encounter when they come to America. Not only do anthropologists reject the view that cultures are static and seamless wholes, the assumption that claims that cultural differences are the key elements in recasting the substance of citizenship has obscured the *central importance of neoliberal forces* in shaping the content and conditions of American citizenship.

Latitudes of Citizenship: An Alternative View

I see America not simply as a heterogeneous cultural geography, but as a space problematized and transformed by intersecting domestic and global forces of neoliberal technology, governmentality, and ethics. The stress on multiculturalism does not tell us how American subjects are constituted in a variety of domains—biotechnology, bureaucratic forms, and liberal governance—in ways that that are not meaningfully described as simply an issue of ethnocultural difference, or attributed solely to the internal dynamics of race, class, and gender. America can be thought of as a new kind of problem space where the most significant changes deal with questions concerning how the human—as living creature, citizen subject, laboring being, calculative actor—is at stake. As an anthropologist, I am concerned about the different spaces of techniques—entrepeneurial, industrial, labor—about how the techniques are remaking the spatial, social, and moral borders of the nation. Contemporary logics of neoliberalism—on borderlessness, flexibility, deregulation, and so on—have had profound effects on the patterning of ethnoracial differences, and on material, social, and symbolic dimensions of citizenship.

Silicon Valley is the hub of supply chains that link multiple sites of production and government across the world. Assemblages of different elements—managers, techno-migrants, and low-paid migrant workers—are located in different geographies of production and of administration. The interrelations of assemblages, circulations, and multiplicities are increasingly shaped and dominated by the rationalities of neoliberal capitalism (Deleuze 1991: 3–7), so that the disembedding of rationalities from their local milieus—"deterritorialization" (Deleuze and Guattari 1994: 503–4)—problematizes our analytic model of government. People who are technically citizens or noncitizens of America may well exist in different latitudes of citizenship.

Globalization has intensified the connections between external and internal lines of differentiation, leading to a transvaluation of social capital and norms of labor, a patterning I call *latitudes of citizenship*. Specifically, the space-making technologies of economic liberalism have expanded external borders to include supranational spaces and noncitizens/transmigrant figures who create economic extensions of the American nation. Borders remain significant not so much for keeping sovereignty and citizenship tightly bounded in political space, but because they are demarking domains of value in this new economic territory. The capacity of entrepreneurial figures to cross, manipulate, and transform borders into lines of trade and production cut across national boundaries. Latitudes of citizenship thus refer to the transborder structuring of capital *and* of labor values—through the interconnected spaces of techniques—that has had repercussions for civil rights and social citizenship in America. In this case, the same "cultural group" plays different roles dictated by neoliberal logics of globalization.

I use latitude as an analytical concept to suggest the transversal processes that distribute disparate forms of citizenship in sites linked by the capital-accumulating logic that spans different spheres of worth across the world. Latitude suggests *transversal flows* that cut into the vertical entities of nation-states, and the *conjunctural* confluence of global forces in strategic points that are linked to global hubs like Silicon Valley. Because latitude points are transnational sites, they deviate from standard norms governing citizenship within nation-spaces. Thus latitudes of citizenship imply the freedom from narrow limits (of nation-states and legal regimes), the *scope and flexibility* to combine disparate forms of rights, privileges, and labor conditions. Such ensembles of unequally lateralized citizenship status are shaped by processes at once transborder and yet highly specific in constituting particular positions of subjection. Sweatshop labor and high-tech firms in the United States have accumulated a multiplicity of citizenship conditions and subjects.

Flexible Citizenship and Transborder Capital

The growth of the American nation has always depended on the activity and image of the pioneer, a figure celebrated as much for his sense of adventure in taming virgin or savage territories as for his capacity to generate wealth out of such territorial claims. California is a space where the American frontier once grounded to a stop, where the westerner saw an end to his dreams of self-realization. But throughout the twentieth century, the American economy has always exceeded the limits of the continent, drawing Asian immigrants for whom California is the Old World's New World, the West of the East, a place where the Pacific ends and a hypermodernity (skipping over the older modernities of Europe and the American eastern seaboard) begins. Or, at least, the immigrants were seeking through hard work and social mobility ways of sustaining and transforming those entanglements across the Pacific. While early-twentieth-century Asian immigrants became plantation workers, truck farmers, railroad workers, laundrymen, grocers, garment workers, houseboys, and restaurant operators, by the 1980s many new arrivals were already middle class, bearing financial, intellectual, and cultural capital that positioned them as actors who help extend the American frontier to far corners of Asia.

These new westerners deploy and reproduce the logics and asset specificities of neoliberalism that expand American economic territorialization in the Asia-Pacific. Much of the literature of globalization assumes a direct internationalization of production and finance, relying on a pure flow of capital, products, and people through networks, without any attention to how particular kinds of activities make such movements possible, and configure them in specific shapes and scales. Elsewhere, I have used the term *flexible citizenship* to refer to the assemblage of transnational practices for gaining access to different global sites—for business advantages, real estate deals, enrollment in top universities, or security for the family—as well as the versatile mobilization of business, legal, and social assets that facilities a high degree of mobility (Ong 1999).

I have identified the cultural logics that underpin such accumulation strategies of ethnic Chinese managers as they seek to deploy themselves, their family businesses, and their families in different sites of the Asia-Pacific. Such flexible citizenship strategies mesh with the neoliberal dynamic of interactions between capital, markets, and labor that have been spatialized in new ways. Neoliberal entrepreneurialism refers to versatility in adding value to commodities by shifting capital among multiple zones of exchange. New assemblages of the state and private actors have come into play in diverse arenas of market competition.

Since the 1980s, the growth of Silicon Valley industries has fueled a relentless demand for foreign economic and intellectual capital. Asian actors have come to play a crucial role because they possess not only economic and intellectual capital, but also the specific assets—practices and relationships—that shape firm-to-market relations across heterogeneous zones between Asia and America. David Stark has argued that this new entrepreneurial figure is an individual who possesses "asset ambiguity," or the kind of talents that can exploit the blurring of borders between countries, races, skills, and cultural signs (Stark 2001). The Asia-Pacific is a region where techniques for converting value across various spheres are very challenging, especially for mainstream Americans. Here overseas Chinese from different countries have region-specific assets that sustain relations of trust and manipulate the borders between cultures, languages, and nations. They can open doors to new places, translate instructions and values from low- to high-end labor markets, and build the institutional bridges for circulating information, capital, goods, and people.

For instance, Asian entrepreneurs are the creators and operators of many other kinds of transnational networks that have become central in the makeup of regional hubs such as Silicon Valley, Vancouver, and Los Angeles. In the high-tech field, Asian-American companies benefit from the cultural practices and rituals that forge links with Taiwanese venture capitalists, thus generating ethnic-specific strands in the industrial-capital circuit. Furthermore, Asian capital is frequently handled by accounting firms immigrant Chinese have set up in cities like Los Angeles that "baby-sit" newly arrived money through the regulatory channels of the American system (Yu Zhou and Yen-Fen Tseng 2001). A third example of trans-Pacific connections that circulate Taiwanese capital is in the aerospace industry. Because Taiwan is interested in developing its own aerospace industry, Taiwanese venture capitalists have bankrolled ethnic Chinese, formerly employed by Boeing and other aircraft companies, to set up workshops that manufacture avionics components for their previous employers. Intra-ethnic ideas and practices that can bridge transnational zones and be reproduced in new spaces constitute a hidden force in economic territorialization. In many cases, multinational companies in the region depend on Asian managers as much as Asian workers to translate across political, social, and cultural lines. Ethnic Chinese communities can be found all over the Asia-Pacific, and over time have developed templates for doing business in different places. We should not forget the centrality of bilingualism or multilingualism in these maneuvers and border crossings. Many ethnic Chinese activities are conducted entirely in Mandarin or Cantonese, or in local native languages such as Malay, Tagalog, or Vietnamese, with English as a language of technology and medium for communicating with mainstream Americans. Thus Asians come to personify the new entrepreneurial figures not simply for their intellectual or financial capital, but also for their capacity to keep in play multiple orders of worth in heterogeneous spheres of production, and for extending their strategy horizons into ever more remote Asian market landscapes.

An Asian circulating managerial class now shapes labor and immigrant policies in the national space because of their centrality to the growth of the computer industry that dominates northern California's economy. Santa Clara County, at the heart of Silicon Valley, has a total population that is half white, and a quarter each Asian and Hispanic (Breslau 2000: 52–53). In 1999, one quarter of the valley's businesses were run by Asian Americans, accounting for some $17 billion in gross revenue each year (Saxenian 1999). By the end of the century, almost a third of the chief executive officers in Silicon Valley were Asian-born (Sellers 2000: 134). Many of them are U.S.-educated and formerly employed by big corporations, and have become a crucial part of the supply chain in the informational industry. Immigrants, mainly from Taiwan and Hong Kong, operate small companies that constitute the manufacturing base of the local agglomeration of the globally oriented corporations. Indian entrepreneurs are also critical in forming trans-Pacific network economies that not only lead to mutual industrial upgrading, but also become supply chains for high-tech professionals recruited from Indian universities and cyber-cities who are needed by Silicon Valley firms (Ong forthcoming).

Flexible Citizenship and Transborder Labor

These transnational corporate networks have also brought into being high-tech spaces of labor under the control of an Asian expatriate managerial elite. The information economy is dependent upon a regime of production in which the outsourcing of most mass-production processes to sites in Southeast Asia has been synchronized with "a gradual but strategically important re-concentration of manufacturing activities in Silicon Valley," leading to the creation of unequal working conditions at both the global and local levels (Luthje 1998). This post-Fordist reorganization of global production has been called "systematic rationalization," a mode of labor management in highly flexible and segmented regional production networks that stabilize working conditions and wages below those established under union-represented, Fordist norms (Luthje 1998). Corporate giants such as Intel, Hewlett-Packard Co., and Sun Microsystems depend on contract manufacturers to assemble the elements and parts that make up "hot" products such as personal computers and cell phones faster and more conveniently than offshore manufacturing. Solectron Corp. of Milpitas, founded by two IBM engineers originally from Hong Kong, is the largest contract manufacturing business in Silicon Valley. The company has grown to become a manufacturing and design partner to their corporate customers. Manufacturing work is contracted out to smaller companies operated by Asian immigrants who, using local ethnic networks, employ largely nonunionized Southeast Asian female workers as "temporary workers" hired for ninety days at a time. These workers can be hired back at no improvement in wages or in contract security or grievance procedures. Indeed, the United States is the only liberal democratic country in which employers need not demonstrate cause to fire an employee (Colker 1998: 184). As contract manufacturers turn to smaller subcontractors and even to their own employees in order to meet stepped-up production schedules, nonautomated work is sent out through shopfloor workers to be assembled in their homes, work for which they are usually paid at piece rate.

The majority of pieceworkers are Southeast Asian women working at their kitchen table. It is estimated that, at any time, more than a third of the Southeast Asian immigrant population of 120,000 in northern California are hired to assemble printed wire boards (Hukill 1999: 16–22). Most are homeworkers who may enroll other stay-at-home relatives, and even children to assemble circuit boards and other components that involve using toxic solvents. Homeworkers made $4 to $5 an hour, or $40 to $50 per board, work that involves fusing components and wiring boards. The work is sometimes paid by the piece, such as a penny per transistor, and even with overtime workers barely earn the minimum wage. Piecework is not illegal, but it is subject to minimum wage and overtime laws. In many cases, workers were already employed by the same company at hourly wages, and then sent home and paid on a piecework basis for their home assembly work. In many subcontracting take-home arrangements, the labor practices violated laws governing piecework in the electronics and garment industries. A mid-1999 expose by reporters at *The San Jose Mercury News* triggered an investigation by the Department of Labor of the contract manufacturers who pay Vietnamese women piece-rate wages for work in the home (Ewell and Ha 1999b). In another case, Asian lawyers filed suit against Asian-owned companies for owing back wages and overtime compensation to a Cambodian worker who took work home and assembled components, earning a piece rate of $1 to $5 (Dang 1999). Almost a third of all workers in high-tech manufacturing are now employed on such ambiguous terms of contract and contingency.

What is striking is that local Asian network production systems deploy cultural authority, kinship, personal relations, and language to take advantage of employees working in substandard conditions. Two nonprofit organizations are focused on the plight of Southeast Asian workers in Santa Clara County; they have tried to organize unions among workers in electronics sweatshops and supermarket chains, but have faced obstacles because poor immigrants consider Asian employers (even of a different ethnicity) their patrons and protectors from the larger society. One lawyer said, "There's a lot of fear about complaining about employers. [The workers] are very desperate financially, and they're afraid that if they say anything they'll be retaliated against." The Santa Clara Center for Occupational Safety and Health (SCCOSH) use skits and radio dramas about the hazards of chemicals in the industries, and teach workers about their rights and laws against arbitrary dismissal. An organizer from the United Food and Commercial Workers' Union said, "In Chinese culture, employers have the same kind of authority as teachers and parents. If that's the case, you can't get workers to challenge them. And I think, partly, confrontation and conflict are not highly valued. I talked to one worker who said, 'We're in a new country. We don't want to start problems.'" (Hukill 1999). The use of personal relationships engender a sense of loyalty among immigrant employees who, because of language and skill deficiency, fear they have no work opportunities outside local ethnic networks. At the mercy of volatile market conditions, Southeast Asian workers shuttle in and out of the electronics, garment, and food industries, making hourly wages preparing cappuccino, and invisible to the cappuccino-sipping Internet employee high up the labor commodity chain. The greater capacity of transnational managers to move among different sites of production, and to shift rapidly among different streams of low-skilled workers here and abroad, has severely degraded work conditions in the United States. Ethnoracial affiliations, once the firm grounding for American mobilization and organization of communities of adversity, are now deployed in ways that control, isolate, and weaken workers, inflicting a symbolic violence that blurs the moral difference between loyalty and exploitation.

The restructuring occasioned by the high-tech boom is merely the most striking case of how the mix of globalism and nepotism in the national space has opened up opportunities for Asian actors to make money as expatriate entrepreneurs and techno-migrants at the top, and for low-wage migrant pieceworkers to struggle at the bottom. Each stratum has become distinctly gendered and ethnicized: there is, for instance, the male Chinese contract man-ufacturer, the male Indian engineer, and the Southeast Asian female piece-worker. This ethnic ranking is very much like the models observed in runaway electronics factories established in Southeast Asia more than a decade ago (Ong 1987). It is both eerily familiar and temporally disconcerting that the racially segmented industrial system spawned in Asian developing countries has returned to the United States and become a centerpiece of the high-tech economy. The integration of Asian immigrants into the top and bottom tiers of the transnational networks has come about as more and more people are employed, by footloose factories that can slither in and out of national spaces of production, to do piecework or homework rather than to work in secure jobs. As some have noted, American law in the age of hypercapitalism has always opted for undercutting labor rights in favor of flexibility and profitabil-ity (Colker 1998). In recent years, there has been backpedaling on union-protected workers' rights, and race-based rights, while the narrow space of civil rights that remains is focused on individual freedom, including the flexi-ble business practices that promise greatest profits. Indeed, the cases of worker abuse exposed by *The San Jose Mercury News* drew mainly angry letters to its website from long-resident Americans who argued that the main issues should not be the legality of uncompensated piecework assembly but rather the opportunities for "entrepreneurship, opportunity, advancement through hard work, individual choice" at the center of Silicon Valley values (quoted in Ewell and Ha 1999a). Flexible transnational production systems thus bring along a certain kind of moral capital as well, one that shapes working condi-tions on the ground.

Multiculturalism, Neoliberalism, and New Meanings for American Citizenship?

The question is thus posed: In what ways have the new circulations associated with hypercapitalism affected American citizenship? Do the new actors, Asian entrepreneurs and low-skilled workers, represent a break in the symbols of American citizenship? What are the implications of the new demographics of en-trepreneurship and widespread piece labor for the substance and meaning of citizenship? What kind of idealism remains in a moral project of citizenship in-creasingly governed by mobile, flexible, and supranational forms of capitalism?

From its inception, the American nation was imagined as a racial, class, and gender formation, one governed by an Anglo-Saxon hegemony that projected white race and class interests as universal for the entire nation (Horsman 1981; Archdeacon 1983). The concept of the American nation as specific, homogenous racial identity has been and continues to be the measure against which all potential citizens are situated as either within or marginal to the nation. Michael Omi and Howard Winant insist that race is a key "organizing principle" of social action, at the "macro level" of economics, politics, and ideological practices, and at the "micro level" of individual action (Omi and Winant 1986: 66–68). Historically, the intertwining of race and economic performance has shaped the ways different immigrant groups have attained status and dignity, within a national ideology that projects worthy citizens as inherently "white."

I have argued that the framing of immigrants in terms of a bipolar racial order has persisted, and that historically newcomers have been situated along the continuum from black to white (Ong 2003). It is obvious that these racial categories are fundamentally about degrees of undeserving and deserving citizenship. Such relative positioning in the national moral order is not state policy, but rather part of the political unconscious that variously informs official and unofficial perception and action. As Brackette Williams has pointed out, there is a black-white continuum of status and dignity, and the relative positioning of the (sub)ethnic group determines its moral claims to certain areas of privilege and advantage, and conditions fear or threats to these prerogatives from subordinated races (Williams 1995). Thus, these processes of relative positioning, group status competition, and race as group status envy mean that cultures become race-based traditions. Racial bipolarism has historically been part of a classificatory system for differentiating among successive waves of immigrants, who were assigned different racial stations along the path toward whiteness. Historical studies show that by the late nineteenth century, English, German, and to a lesser extent Scottish and Italian immigrants had forged patterns of financial and kinship networks within and beyond the United States. The consolidation of this white American elite with transnational connections has been celebrated in novels by Henry James and Edith Wharton. At the same time, as developed in the ideal-type construct of ethnic succession, there was the structure of expectations for how things ought to work out in a just, moral world of citizenship acquisition for less fortunate immigrant Poles, Italians, Germans, and Slavs, referred to by the derogatory terms PIGS (versus WASPs, the originary raced components). The succession model was about making racial identity that transcended the component nationalities of the immigrants to become an ideal generic white.

A legacy of white-black relations under slavery and Emancipation that "'naturalizes' the social order" was the use of "the Negro" as a "contrast conception" or "counter-race" of unfree labor (Copeland 1993: 152–79). The free working man came to embody republican citizenship, and any immigrant who failed to gain independent livelihood was in danger of sinking into wage slavery, the antithesis of the independent citizen. In the nineteenth century, this racial classificatory logic situated poor Irish immigrants on the East Coast and Chinese immigrants on the West Coast close to the black end of the continuum because their working conditions were similar to those of unfree black labor (Roediger 1991; Takaki 1990). Early Chinese immigrants were subjected to a process of "Negroization" and compared to black slaves as heathens who were a threat to republicanism. Chinese "coolies," like black slaves, were regarded as antagonistic to free labor. Chinese immigrants were cast as "a depraved class," "new barbarians" (comparable to the "Red Man"), money-grubbing, and a threat to white women, altogether having a cancerous effect on American civil society (Takaki 1990: 219–20). Thus, American orientalism that cast Asians outside the pale of white civilization operated within the bipolar racial forma-tion, assimilating "primitive" Asians to the "black" half of the model, on the side of unfree labor, and with no public status, clearly outside the nation. As for later non-Christian European immigrants such as the Jews, it was not until the mid-twentieth century that they ascended to white status through the euphemized process of ethnic succession (Sacks 1994: 78–102). The post–Second World War period also saw the slow whitening of Asian immigrants as their gradual attain-ment of middle-class norms earned them the label "model minority," as the contrasting category to the now black "underclass."

Currently, in the age of globalized capitalism, the process of honorary whiteness continues, and Asians for the first time have attained the status of ideal American citizens who have economic and intellectual capital, as well as the transnational networks and skills so critical to American expansion. As the new figures representing moral worthiness, Asian entrepreneurs strive not so much to be accepted as whites as to participate more fully in the national space through the combination of nepotism and globalism that is instrumental in producing wealth and power in the decentralized and dispersed systems of capitalism. Asked about being at the top of the ethnic hierarchy in Silicon Valley, a Berkeley-educated Taiwanese owner of an electronic company responded, "We carry our weight. Why shouldn't we be represented at the top?" He is considered a cyberhero, like Jerry Yang of Yahoo (Breslau 2000).

Thus the notion of citizenship tied to work and earnings gains a geometry value when humanity is more and more measured against mobile capital. George J. Borjas, a Harvard professor, has recommend more restrictive immi-gration policies against poor (Hispanic) immigrants, while laying out the welcome mat to the possessors of "human capital" (Borjas 2000). In a number of other advanced liberal democracies, immigration laws have been adjusted to ease the flows of favored professional and "investor-immigrants" (Jonas and Thomas 1999).[1] As I have argued elsewhere, the new citizen heroes are the Homo economicus of high tech and high finance, those versatile figures who possess many kinds of capital, redefine the norms of work routines, and transgress the borders of time and space (Ong 1999; Ong and Nonini 1997).

Regardless of whether they are foreign-born, alien residents, permanent residents, or citizens, high-tech managers and knowledge workers are now enrolled in a kind of transnational citizenship, one in which high education, capital accumulation, hypermobility, and flexibility are the passports to wealth production as well as the power to rule over others. The role of Asian entrepreneurs and knowledge workers in Silicon Valley, against the background of a looming Chinese economy, has done something to American thinking about Asians. Contrary to the rhetoric of Asian-American advocates, transnational skills, not intranational suffering, has become the moral capital of citizenship, and the racial coding of desirable citizens is increasingly Asian. However, while the variety of capital, and the kinds of actors who have come to represent the heights of American bourgeois citizenship, have changed, the process of honorary whiteness has, through the assimilation of such figures, become a force in global racial biopolarism.

Decentralized, dispersed, and flexible forms of capitalism have, however, ruptured the process of ethnic succession, which is more a sociological model than an empirical reality for many. Nevertheless, the structure of belief and expectation that minorities and immigrants could convert their sacrifices and suffering into identity claims, and contribute to the eventual benefit of the group as a whole, has been a very powerful force in giving a moral character to citizenship. In her essay *American Citizenship*, Judith N. Shklar argues that from the perspective of the historically excluded—racial minorities, women, and immigrants—the struggle for American citizenship has "been overwhelmingly a demand for inclusion in the polity, an effort to break down excluding barriers to recognition, rather than an aspiration to civic participation as a deeply involving activity" (Shklar 1991: 3). It is the intertwined process—the access to voting and income that is inseparable from attaining social standing worthy of respect and prestige—that has been central to the meaning and color of American citizenship. For minorities and poor immigrants, this promise took the form of ethnic succession whereby exclusions endured by earlier generations of migrant workers encouraged them to lay claim to a communal identity based in adversity and suffering. Such ethnoracial mobilization involved making a contribution to the well-being of later generations, and to that of society as a whole. Thus, the struggles of earlier generations of African-, Irish-, and Jewish American workers on behalf of their communities have resulted in laws intended to protect workers' health, wages, and social security, the forms of benefits that later contributed to the civil rights of all American workers. Besides fighting for the steady improvement of labor laws, communities of adversity have disrupted the structure of racism or gender bias in order to improve work conditions (Novak 1978; Milkman 1985). Historically, American slaves and immigrants have not merely broken down barriers to inclusion, they have struggled for the substantive expansion of the meaning of free labor and its link to the substance of citizenship.

This continuity—of intergenerational and ethnoracial class struggles that made the sufferings of past generations visible or available to be claimed by future generations—has been broken by the blurring of borders between nations, production sites, and industrial labor histories. The contemporary working poor do not have the material base to fight for and sustain older and better labor norms when their bosses enjoy greater flexibility to hire them as temporary, underpaid, replaceable workers. The reversal in the demographics of labor distribution, with a growing majority of people doing piecework and in-home work, has strengthened the power of corporations to erase or evade civil rights gains of the last century. The opportunities in older factory regimes for making substantial improvements in the quality of work conditions have decreased because of the movement of labor sites offshore. The floating factories, combined with the endless streams of migrant labor, provide a double means by which any constructive pressures brought by workers are undermined or simply evaded. Thus, forms of labor exploitation, coercion, and denigration that have disappeared from most work venues have reemerged, and the state apparatus is becoming even more experienced as a system of containment and restriction. For instance, police raids on sweatshops are a frequent pressure on illicit work conditions, producing a constant source of fear for undocumented workers. There is no longer the material capacity or the symbolic coinage to be produced out of advancing the well-being of others, whether of one's own ethnoracial group or of society as a whole.

The loss of potential that any substantive accomplishment will be achieved through communal efforts that can be typed as racial or ethnic means, therefore, that communal contributions to larger social norms for the overall well-being of all working peoples no longer constitute a structure of ethnic succession. Indeed, in many cases, migrants of the same nationality are the worst abusers of their countrymen. Peter Kwong has studied the extensive human smuggling networks linking Fuzhou to New York City's Chinatown. Debt peonage forces migrants to work under slaverylike conditions in the warren of Chinese garment, food, and service industries, places where American labor inspectors and unions have failed to penetrate (Kwong 2002). American unions have been severely weakened in their fight to sustain decent working conditions in all industries, but especially in those dominated by immigrants of color. For this reason, some Asian-American leaders have expressed the desire to reject the transnational linkages and claims increasingly shaped by global capitalism in favor of community-based politics (Hu-DeHart 1999). However, few of these activists have linked up with the Asian workers embedded in the webs of high-tech production and yet disembedded from the social protection of the state. The forms of labor reproduction are now changed in and through the structure of transnational capitalism, and are no longer directly responsive to long-term gains in labor norms and laws governing the well-being and dignity of free labor as the right of citizenship.

Furthermore, the ethical meaning of citizenship, of Emersonian self-reliance, is now reduced to an extreme form of market individualism, where all that is left is for individuals to try and fight off particular instances of personal discrimination and injustice in a globalized wilderness (Emerson 1985). Any claim to making a contribution to the good of society becomes empty, since workers are not putting in moral borders to protect the next generation, but have become totally replaceable in a new way by the constant influx of even poorer and more exploitable immigrants. So workers do not or cannot aim for higher moral laws governing working standards. The symbolics of suffering continue, but the evidence of it, and of accomplishments against it, are difficult, if not impossible, to fix and made available to be claimed by future generations of workers. Furthermore, the denigration of idealism in citizenship—the old moral worthiness of citizenship, that basic working conditions for the poor must be upheld, and that capitalists will pay back society through taxes—means that the entrepreneurial figures, whether local or foreign-born, do not feel the need to pay taxes, to protect the less fortunate, only to get rich by maximizing advantages of transnational mobility, links, and possibilities for evading taxes.

Flexible Production Erodes Labor Expectations and Rights

Michael Hardt and Antonio Negri maintain that "[t]hrough circulation, the multitude reappropriates space, and constitutes itself as an active subject" (Hardt and Negri 2000: 397). The concept of the multitude, as new revolutionary actors collecting in cities to forge battles against the globalizing empire of capitalism, is very appealing. The multitude, however, is but one trope in a much more complex picture of biopolitical control and labor permitted by floating industries sustained by streams of migrant workers. Hardt and Negri view the multitude as a subject drawn from the immaterial labor of analytical and symbolic tasks, and linked by the Internet. This political hero will lead the battle for cosmopolitan liberation, providing the "intellectual labor" and forging "the common language" against the global order of the empire (Hardt and Negri 2000: 293, 29, 57). This totalizing project of counter-empire shows great ignorance of the majority of the actual "mobile multitude" involved in high-tech and informational economies—the migrant, the nonwhite, the female refugee—who cannot be represented by a single or imposed language of political power. It is not merely the case of universalization "by telling a Eurocentric tale of everyone's histories" (Rofel 2001: 643); very few of our Internet multitude have ever noticed the multitude of invisible workers in America's cyber front yard.

I have identified a transborder stratificatory process in American citizenship I call latitudes of citizenship. These lines of stratification—associated with the lines of capital, value, and labor flows—are layering the possibilities and conditions of citizenship achievement, a structuring of life chances according to one's specific location in the new geographies of production. Market forces are assigning people different kinds of fate, lines of differentiation by skill and occupation that are continuous across national borders. By thus lateralizing and lowering labor value in production along with flow of network capital, neoliberal forms of capitalism are posing questions of what is at stake for Americans as citizens, in the global ethical way that transcends the most immediate differences of culture, race, and nation.

Being a worker in the American national space is no protection against a progressive degradation of labor and civil rights. The relentless manipulation and crossing of borders by capital and people enable the conversion of values across multiple economic zones, thus enriching individuals and companies in the American nation. But the floating of values has also undone the meaning of work in America, erasing the older established morality of labor dignity, while labor values float down to the lowest denominator of labor extraction and denigration. The neoliberal logic of exploiting the ambiguities of economic and social orders has meant erasing hard-won battles for labor rights, and tolerating historically inferior American working conditions for people judged to be socially, morally, and economically inferior—that is, minorities and the latest wave of immigrant workers. Globalized America now celebrates a new kind of entrepreneurial worthiness. Mobile Asians are honorary whites not merely because of their value-adding activities, but because of their space-defying agility in juggling different regimes of worth in an ever expanding American economy. Such flexible citizenship and leapfrogging of capital markets have ruptured the American structure of belief in the succession model, in the right of workers to make a living with dignity, and in the expectation that political representation will improve the working conditions of ordinary people in the nation. I am not proposing an end to immigration, nor do I think that it will be diminished, since intensifying circulations of people have become an irreducible force of globalization.

The old meaning of citizenship—based on unfree labor, and the succession model of social mobility—was first eroded with the deindustrialization of America (Bluestone and Harison 1982), and has now evaporated in the post-Fordist era when temporary, piecework, and sweatshop workers have proliferated in the shadow of a dominant service economy. Citizenship based on income, the dignity of work, and representation is now mainly achievable only in the service sector, among those workers—in office buildings, hotels, and other major institutions—who have secure jobs to fight for. In the past decades, one of the most vibrant labor achievements has been in the service sector, among office cleaners and lower ranks of white-collar workers. For instance, Justice for Janitors—from its beginnings in a struggle against a cleaning contractor in Los Angeles—has grown rapidly into the Service Employees International Union in sixteen American cities to secure for janitors living wages and to win health insurance and full-time work. The recent support of

Harvard University students and faculty for low-paid janitors brought the movement into the national spotlight. Their success only goes to show that there is a layering of possibilities for workers to fight for and defend the substance of free labor. More and more, service and skilled employees—in casino, commerce, finance, media and entertainment, telecommunications, business services, postal and allied services, and tourism, to name a few—are the ones for whom the American Dream is still attainable through labor organization. In the aftermath of the Enron scandal, as "the capitalist as hero" is being replaced by "the capitalist as villain" in public perception, there may be a backlash against declining work conditions. But for the low-wage, part-time workers in the shadow of high-tech manufacturing, as well as in the apparel and cannery industries, the structure of expectations building on earlier generations of workers' struggles is no longer sustainable.

Overseas, much hope has been placed in the proliferation of human rights regimes that can come with the stretching and deepening of connections across spaces, and the growing awareness of "overlapping communities of fate" (Bauer 2000). Like Hardt and Negri's multitude, NGOs are heralded as the new figures fighting to universalize human rights. NGOs that directly and indirectly put pressure on local governments to protect the rights of subordinated populations are extremely important, in some cases linking a variety of local struggles in a new form of transnational intervention. But the counter-empire model of global civil society is still an abstraction, and it does not engage questions about the specific forms of politics in a highly decentralized world dominated by global capitalism. In actuality, dispersed groups struggling for human rights in different latitudes of citizenship can operate only in a contingent and supplementary manner, and many come with their own mode of governmentality in shaping social needs. Tensions and distrust remain high in relations between NGOs, as local groups in the south fear domination or the appropriation of their agendas by well-funded NGOs of the north (Ong 1997: 107–35).

Transnational corporate networks present a formidable challenge to the advanced liberal state in safeguarding basic human rights in situ. This discontinuity in the cumulative gains of labor and civil laws has important implications for how we think about rights-based notions of citizenship, and appropriate strategies in democratic struggles in such scattered nexus of political disembeddedness. What kind of substitution can we suggest for new forms of civic responsibility and sociality, since the dispersed system of industrial-capitalist production has shattered structural conditions of class struggle? We are left with scattered laboring situations that should be considered in terms of human needs (not worker rights), and interventions by various parties are needed, as I suggested. Chantal Mouffe has asserted that a rights-based citizenship requires the liberal democratic state to have the commitment to defend our central political values and key institutions, to preserve the "unresolvable tension between the principles of equality and liberty" (Mouffe 1992: 11–13). Such rights, however, should no longer be thought of in discrete, individualized terms, but rather in terms of a shared moral economy with people whose lives help sustain our nation. Notions of rights can be translated into the concept of collective human needs and obligations, a rationality that informs governmental technologies that shape norms for a new kind of translocal human sociality. Liberal democratic states as the main guarantors of civil rights have—especially though not only through the welfare state—sought to divide up democracy as a social good. In the United States, labor laws and civil rights must be renewed and recast to sustain the moral substance of American citizenship against the transvaluation of indecent working conditions that come with the new geographies of production and trade. In the international context, human rights regimes cannot replace the crucial role of nation-states in enforcing basic rights of citizenship at home and abroad.

Furthermore, as Foucault has argued, fundamentally the politics of human life is a technological question, involving concrete questions about how production and wealth can be adjusted to the needs of the population. A politics of human needs would be rooted more firmly in a moral economy, a greater commitment to the exchanges of rights and obligations between states, corporations, and other major institutions on the one hand, and subjects (wherever they may be) who are structurally interconnected to these powerful actors on the other.[2] In other words, a state or corporate moral economy incorporates moral obligations to the substantive needs of employees and other affiliated subjects in a multitude of positions. For governments, citizenship resolutely based on a deterritorialized moral economy would be a contemporary response to the need to protect society against the ravages of globalization (Polyani 1944).

Human needs and fulfillment are a problem of government, requiring precise biotechnical calculations. The welfare state has been stripped rather than augmented in an era of globalization. Now, more than ever, human needs must be given priority in ways that go beyond the welfare state to ensure the substantive guarantee of the economy. A committed technology for creating substantive goals—the provision of housing, health, education, leisure, public services—would require, in practice, an entrepreneurial rationality that brings a calculative rationality to the management of substantive needs, using the application of business school concepts and skills to the creation of "public value" (Moore 1995). Stephen J. Collier has observed that there has been a gap between corporations' and states' recognition of the substantive goals in any economic system, and the logic that guarantees the system's existence: "the space of the magic of formal rationalization itself; it is the space of initiative, entrepreneurialism, audit, tough choices, in short, of the productive austerity of budgetary discipline" (Collier 2001: 57). Such efficiency, however, has to take into account the entire "strategic situation," patching together particularistic flows of resources for "better collective outcomes" rather than efficiency in the allocation of resources to different uses (Collier 2001: 53–54). In other words, laws, regulations, and biopolitical strategies are all necessary to secure specific bundles of human needs in order to sustain the moral project of citizenship and a particular ideal of democratic citizenry.

Again, whatever the achievements of NGOS in local or regional contexts, there is a need as well for governments and corporations, in mobilizing other kinds of resources and attending to other forms of substantive needs in various global sites. The creation and management of social goods should be extended to transnational sites of different kinds and scales, and the needs of different populations who are structurally connected to metropolitan nations and corporations. Attempts can be made to synchronize the dispersed geographies of production with a dispersed geography of administration. We can talk about different assemblages of human needs that have been created by the reorganization of global capitalism, and the imperatives for national regimes and corporations to more fully incorporate substantive ends in their global operations. Where advanced democracies and global corporations fully embrace the moral economy of human wants, we can have a more routine rationalization of substantive needs in transnational contexts. For the foreseeable future, we cannot do without effective government action in resolutely managing and protecting human needs and fulfillment in the face of proliferating networks of trade, industry, and travel. By working with some degree of coordination, governments, corporations, and multilateral agencies can secure assemblages of human needs and help foster the spread of civil norms for a common humanity.

Notes

1. For a recent critique, and an argument that north-south migrations are an index of the integration of the Western Hemisphere, see Jonas and Thomas 1999.
2. The working concept of moral economy I use here is inspired by Scott 1976.

III
Constructing Rights

5

Agency on a Global Scale

Rules, Rights, and the European Union

DAVID JACOBSON AND GALYA BENARIEH RUFFER

While our understandings of democracy have evolved within a particular conception of citizenship and nationhood, the emergence of new global structures, institutions, and modes of governance necessitate recognition that democracy, as traditionally understood, is not adequate to conceptualize current modes of political engagement. Note is often made of the global expansion of human rights, generally coupled with the assumption that this expansion is synonymous with the spread of democracy. However, we need to recognize that the expansion of rights, domestically and internationally, is associated with a partial but significant shift in the mode of political engagement, from democracy or republicanism to the principle of the individual as "agent." The "decline" of the nation-state, one could argue, is symptomatic of an even more dramatic but hidden revolution, the emergence of agency.

Indeed, issues of *agency* have supplemented and in significant part supplanted dedication to the *democratic* and *republican* process. Agency concerns the ability of the individual or the group to act as "initiatory" and a "self-reliant" actor and to be an active participant in determining one's life, including determination of social, political, cultural, ethnic, religious, and economic ends.[1] The foundational mechanism of agency is the dense web of legal rights and restraints that are mediated or adjudicated by judicial and quasi-judicial and administrative bodies of different kinds. In contrast to the past, no area of life today is beyond the potential reach of the law—its tentacles, for good and bad, reach into every sphere of life from families to corporations to nation-states. Individual access to the development of a dense web of legal rights and restraints has become the mechanism of individual "self-determination," not the civic sphere or the public square.

Judicial and administrative mechanisms, as opposed to the legislature, become central in this process. And, indeed, law as regulation has expanded massively in the last three to four decades (an expansion itself an upward loop in a century-long expansion), including international law. Such law is "expressed" through judicial, quasi-judicial, and administrative bodies. The European Union, in its judicial and administrative organization, is an especially notable example of this phenomenon.

Joseph Weiler has taken important steps in recasting the question of democracy in the debate regarding the European Union. According to Weiler, democratic deficit implies a given definition of democracy that needs to be explicitly stated. He points out that it would be incorrect to judge the operation of the EU by the same normative criteria that are applied to ordinary nation-states. Indeed, it is important to recognize that different aspects of the EU may best reflect entirely new modes of governance (Weiler 1999).[2] Similarly, to ground our current understandings of what we could call a "rule of rules" within traditional understandings of democracy, political engagement, and governance might prove counterproductive.

One can begin to unpack the logic of agency based in "rule of rules" by recognizing that certain political divisions are better categorized as disputes between claims for democracy or republicanism versus claims for agency rather than a dispute about the general content of the rights at stake. Simply put, the advent of "rule of rules" has been challenging executive and legislative power. Agency places a strain upon executive and legislative power in that individuals increasingly possess the capacity to assert their rights by accessing laws outside of the national structure and bringing them before the European Court of Justice (or, in the Council of Europe, before the European Court of Human Rights) or through new "cross-border" principles such as direct effect, subsidiarity, harmonization, and proportionality.

The threat agency poses to executive power became all too apparent as the United States and other governments throughout Europe turned quickly to extralegal measures, outside of the web of laws, in reaction to the terrorist attacks of September 11. The establishment of military tribunals, "closed" removal proceedings, and the interviews of five thousand foreign nationals is best characterized as a strike against agency. Specifically, there is the perception that it was the dynamic of agency that allowed the terrorist cell to legally appropriate the network of rights and laws to form such a devastating attack on not just the United States but democracy itself. The significance of the assertion of executive power is not the curtailment of rights of those subject to government suspicion but rather the stop it put on agency as a mechanism by taking security measures out of the realm of law altogether. In Germany, and other EU member states, entrenched rights such as the right of privacy were not so much questioned as bypassed by executive power. Thus, for example, Berlin's Humbolt University gave information on twenty-three Arab students to the German government. What we see is not a questioning of the right of privacy per se, but rather a questioning of the agency and a reassertion of executive power.

There are a number of steps to explicating this phenomenon of the changing modality of politics: the "universal individualism" implicit in agency; the international, regional, and national legal developments on which it is predicated; the changing contours of the institutional and organizational environment (including the state) associated with "agency"; and the institutional mechanisms that make it possible.

The Long Arm of the Law

One of the most remarkable developments of recent decades is the growing "density"of the legal milieu internationally, regionally, and nationally. Law is getting more dense not just in terms of the sheer number of laws through the proliferation of administrative rules, legal institutions, and arbitration mechanisms internationally, specifically in Europe, through the EU, the Council of Europe, and the Organization for Security and Cooperation in Europe, but also on a national level through the incorporation or tacit recognition of the international human rights instruments in national legal systems. The incorporation by the United Kingdom of the bulk of the European Convention of Human Rights into domestic law in the year 2000 is the most recent case. Internationally, we see the growing multiplication of multilateral international treaties. Although the sheer increase in legal webbing is significant in and of itself, more important about these developments are the qualitative shifts.

International human rights law has relocated the individual as the object of the law and, thereby, affected national citizenship status in the Euro-Atlantic arena and in some other countries both in its treaty density (that is, quantity of multilateral agreements and ratifications) and in case law (decisions in regional and national courts based on international human rights); the growing specialization of law (from intellectual property to the environment, for example); and the growth in importance of tribunals, arbitration mechanisms, regulatory mechanisms, and other legal entities that deliberate independently of states, and allow nonstate actors to arrive at agreements and arrangements independently of states, yet whose decisions carry the force of law in all states. The rising importance and salience of international private law—akin to the increasing importance of civil law in industrializing countries in the last century—are also of note. How has the proliferation of legal forms and mechanisms shifted or altered the nature and location of political engagement? It is through posing this question that the emergence of agency comes to the fore.

The growing number of cross-border actors of different kinds, including international nongovernmental organizations or corporations, also reinforce and grow out of this increasing density and specialization of law. Administrative and judicial rules grow in arbitrating the kaleidoscopic complexity of a social world with an almost geometric increase in the number of actors with disparate social, economic, and political concerns. This parallels the evolution of domestic law within nation-states since at least the nineteenth century, in which legal mechanisms of control became tighter and denser with growing economic and social differentiation, specialization, and complexity.

This growing legal density promotes, reinforces, and facilitates the phenomenon of agency. Indeed, agency itself presumes, by definition, universal and individual values and a concept of human rights. Agency is embedded in this dense legal web, and the institutions that arbitrate this legal framework—the judiciary and other administrative mechanisms—grow in significance. We see a growing density of law, including law that "enables" agency, in issues that "cross borders" legally or in practice, like migration, where the courts are in many cases drawn into transnational/international issues and agency in turn reinforces that legal framework.

Alongside the denser web of law, is a related phenomenon, namely escalating litigation, nationally and in the European regional institutions. Litigation activities are of interest because they reveal the extent of agency and how the law is facilitating that agency: litigation is about arguments over rights and prerogatives. Growing litigation reflects a growing legal and social readiness and "recognition" of rights that inhere in, or are presumed to inhere in, the individual as well as other entities. Increased litigation reflects growing agency.

The growing density needs little elaboration, especially in the European context. The scope, caseload, number of member countries, rise in nongovernmental organizations, and influence of the European Court of Human Rights has grown, as is widely known, substantially and to an extent undreamed of at its founding. The scope, caseload, and influence of the European Court of Justice (as well as the "legal presence" of the EU generally) have likewise grown significantly and need little elaboration. In terms of international law, we witness a similar picture: from the end of the First World War, there is a steady accumulation in the number of multilateral international legal treaties, and a dramatic increase after the Second World War. Evidencing an increasingly dense global legal environment, the number of "significant" multilateral treaties in force rose from 187 in 1950 to almost 800 by 1988 (Jacobson 1998–99).

But in a certain sense more striking is the evidence of litigation in its different forms that is evidence of "agency" at work. Even in a country with an impressive history of judicial review, we see a marked upturn in this regard in the United States (Jacobson 2001).[3] The increase in the caseload in the European Court of Human Rights and the European Court of Justice is widely noted, but there are other notable indicators: references under article 177 of the EEC treaty have increased as well. Article 177 allows and sometimes requires judges in national courts to request an authoritative interpretation of the laws within the ambit of community. In 1970 there were roughly forty references of this kind, and by 1990 there were almost two hundred. (U.K. judges refer more cases to the European Court of Justice under Article 177 than any other member state.) This is significant because it illustrates the growing role of the judiciary in a dual sense—it shows the extent that national judiciaries are acting, so to speak, "extraterritorially," and how the judicial arm of government is strengthened as a consequence. Migration is one of the topics that generates the most references (Stone 1997).[4] The proportion of litigation, at least in the United Kingdom, tends to be underreported in areas where European Union law has been most heavily invoked. Immigration, taxes, social security, and labor are areas in which quasi-judicial entities are dominant, such as immigration adjudicators, and their decisions are rarely reported (Chalmers 2000).

The growing web of judicial rights in all kinds of organizational contexts makes agency possible.[5] Agency of all kinds of individual actors generates adjudication of rights, interest, and the like. Thus agency reinforces the process of judicial rights that made it possible in the first place. The democratic process is not removed so much as contained. The density of the legal process not only exists on the public level—domestic or international—but has progressively filtered into private organizations and corporations, where individuals can "litigate" internally over, say, race discrimination. Thus the containment of the republican or democratic process is taking place not only in the political arena in the traditional sense, but in "everyday life," notably in the workplace. Patterns of litigation are growing across Europe (not just in the United States) especially regarding racial and sexual discrimination in the workplace. Sexual and racial lawsuits filed in employment tribunals in the United Kingdom rose 76 percent in the year ending June 2000 compared to five years previously (Kapner 2000).

Within the European Community, individual litigation is likely to be further encouraged by article 13 of the Amsterdam treaty. Article 13, originally adopted as part of the EC treaty in 1997 and revised through the Amsterdam treaty, includes stronger wording that seems to encourage or allow positive enforcement by the EC directly against the states. It was enacted in response to the recognition that although the Treaty on European Union (TEU) gave the European Community a specific competence to adopt general measures in the sphere of human rights, and to combat discrimination in particular, there was no positive mechanism through which the community could take effective measure against racism, xenophobia, and other forms of discrimination.

Such developments have implications for notions of multiculturalism and immigrant populations. The growth of "agency" enables different forms of cultural expression, and the courts facilitate this. Conversely, restraining "parliamentary sovereignty" restricts (but does not completely preclude) majoritarian and collective national expression.

The changed nature of political engagement reflected in the shifting balance between agency, empowered by legal rights and obligations, and more traditional "democratic" consent modes of "voice" or politics is illustrated in the following examples regarding sexual equality and discrimination. Political demands for greater protection for women in the workforce led to public service experimentation with various quota systems at the state level in Germany. There seemed to be political consensus throughout Germany that led to the enactment of sixteen separate statutes at the state level establishing various forms of quota systems. But through 177 references to the European Court of Justice, certain of these German provisions have famously been placed in doubt (Schiek 1998). The ECJ determined in *Kalanke* and *Marschall* that EC law, specifically the equal treatment principle embodied in articles 2(1) and 2(4) of the Equal Treatment Directive, distinguished between equality of opportunity and that of result and foreclosed any positive action going beyond that necessary to ensure individual equality of opportunity.[6] The new sex equality provision in the Amsterdam treaty, article 119(4), has strengthened the EC position regarding the underrepresentation of women in the workforce while setting the guidelines within which the ECJ will determine whether the measures comply with EU law. More recently, the EU has provided for stronger measures to eradicate sexual harassment that will place additional burdens on member state employers.

These and other legal provisions and directives at the EU level provide individuals with a forum through which sensitive issues worked out through political channels at the national level can be revisited and redefined in the ECJ. In an important respect, certain employment rights and protections are being severed from national citizenship. For example, in a string of cases the ECJ determined that sexual orientation is not a protected category under EC law. In forming its decision, the court ignored the general political trend in the member states toward providing protection for sexual orientation discrimination in employment and equal treatment for same-sex couples (Bell 1999).

In another work, Galya Benarieh Ruffer has attempted to characterize the nature of the set of organizationally based rights and protections as a "virtual citizenship" that is, in important respects, independent of national citizenship. Thus the rights and protections that accrue to an employee on, say, gender discrimination in a corporation, public or private, are not a function of formal citizenship status (though, of course, the presumption is that the employee is at least a legal resident) (Ruffer 2000). In this regard, the expansion of rights has diluted national citizenship, at least in its traditional republican sense.

The Nesting of Organizations and Agency

The critical question remains, however, regarding the institutional mechanisms of agency: this is an issue that has not been sufficiently addressed in the debate on globalism, nationalism, human rights, and, for that matter, immigration.

The civic and human rights that are embedded in, and institutionalize, agency are not expressed *primarily* at the international, regional, or even the national level. Rather, the dense legal webbing enables the "acting out," so to speak, of human rights (say, on gender issues) at the lower-order organizational level—such as, prominently, the workplace. What has happened in recent decades is that in order to generate change at "lower level" organizations, appeals have been made to the "higher-level" organizations to change institutional patterns at the original organization. We have a nesting effect;

people will go to a higher-nested organization to appeal judicially for recourse, but only as far as they have to go (for example, the province is preferred over the state; or the state over a regional organization). Once the change is generated, internal mechanisms are generated at the "local" organization that are less likely to necessitate appeals to higher-level organizations. The nesting works in reverse: higher-nested organizations—such as the European Court of Human Rights—will have wide-ranging effects. They effectively close off certain options for lower organizations. But once this has been integrated or "internalized" by states and private and public organizations, that human rights issue is less likely to be played out at the national or regional level.

This is, in a sense, another radically different form of the global-local nexus. Certain "rights," for example regarding gender discrimination, filter down to the point where they are so embedded that they are presumed, almost outside the discourse on human rights. "Global" norms are expressed most readily in "local" foci—local here being from workplaces and other organizations, to cities and counties, to provinces and the like. But this just points to the remarkable extent human rights has become, in the long term, the armature, the frame, the skeleton girding the social and political architecture of society. It is like the syntax of language; it is presumed, not thought about. The "present" discourse of human rights tends to shift, then, to new frontiers, with different parties trying to broaden its reach to new social categories such as, for example, female genital mutilation in asylum laws. And because new frontiers involve contested issues and thus frame the issue of "human rights" in the public consciousness, the embeddedness of the larger scaffold of human rights, the degree to which it has closed off options, is often overlooked. The institutional mechanisms here are primarily judicial and administrative.

This nesting process is also legally inscribed, as captured in the concept of subsidiary and layered legal authorities, and is characteristic of both the United States and the European Union (and, for that matter, the European Convention of Human Rights). However, it makes sociological sense as well: absent internal rules on areas like gender or racial discrimination, endogenous change within an organization is very difficult to effect. So the actor will move to a higher-level organization to generate change exogenously, but that actor is unlikely to go to a point beyond what is necessary. Judicial and administrative change is also dramatic (and rapid) because often—especially in the United States—the change will then affect a whole of class of individuals and organizations, such as in gender and race discrimination. Judicial and administrative decisions can and have had the effect of expanding agency extensively in this way. Once such rulings have filtered down and become institutionalized, "human rights" will be acted on endogenously to the organization.

The U.K. case is particular interesting in terms of the "nesting" of organizations and legal authorities. As we know, the British political system has been one in which the sovereign Parliament was at the pinnacle and the courts were secondary, with very limited powers of judicial review. The United Kingdom, though it has long recognized the jurisdiction of Strasbourg, in contrast to most other Council of Europe member states, only recently incorporated the bulk of the European Convention of Human Rights into domestic law. In this context, it is no surprise that the United Kingdom has received special scrutiny by Strasbourg and that British judges have made so many references to the European Court of Justice. The notion of the individual as agent was highly constrained in this circumstance, and thus had to appeal to exogenous legal authorities—notably the European Convention of Human Rights and the European Court of Justice—to effect change. The European Union and the European Court of Human Rights has in effect required a fundamental shift in the relationship between the individual and the state. Instead of a majoritarian institution in Parliament representing a republican collective will in which individual rights are derivative, a more liberal vision has been instituted by the European Convention of Human Rights and the European Court of Justice around which individual freedoms are promoted and where "as much space is preserved for autonomous behavior by private individuals as possible" (Chalmers 2000). It was due to the European Convention of Human Rights and the European Court of Justice that judicial review became a significant factor in the United Kingdom from the 1980s. Clearly, the Human Rights Act, which recently took effect in the United Kingdom, will reinforce this process.

The United Kingdom example also reveals how human rights become embedded, and no more so than in the immigration area. Both immigration and asylum legislation have been significantly affected by the Court of Human Rights. The immigration appeals system's very creation was rooted in significant part in the European Convention of Human Rights (see *Alam* [1967]). Through the *Abdulaziz* (1985) case, concerning articles 6 and 8 of the ECHR, sex discrimination was eliminated in U.K. laws. The Asylum and Immigration Appeals Act of 1993, facilitating appeal rights for asylum seekers, concerning article 13, was significantly prodded through by the N.K. (1987) case in Strasbourg. *Chalal* (1997), concerning article 3, most recently impacted the Special Immigration Appeals Commission Act of 1998. Home office policy guidelines have also had explicit reference to the European Convention of Human Rights (Story 1998). Human rights issues become embedded such that, for example, due to the *Abdulaziz* decision the concept of sex discrimination on immigration becomes inconceivable and not even an issue on the regional or national level. Other areas of rights now taken for granted, such as consumer rights, are no longer "debated" internationally and simply become part of the broader social fabric.

Part of what accounts for the variation in the turn to international instruments—comparing the United States to the United Kingdom, for example—is the extent to which the growing stress on "agency" can be accommodated internally. If, as described above, actors will (for legal and for

sociological reasons) move "up" the layers of legal and organizational authority only to the extent that they have to in order to effect change at lower levels
of organization, then insofar as change can be generated before resorting to international instruments or even national instruments that is what will happen.
In the context of the U.S. constitutional framework, the dense net of rights and
legal rules and the historical and ever growing role of the judiciary (especially
in recent decades) provide extensive possibilities to effect agency. But even in
the case of the United States, four points should be noted: the legal (as well
as social and political) discourse about *human* rights (not just civil rights) has
expanded dramatically in the last three decades[7]; even in the American context
there is growing reference to international human rights instruments in
that period, though it is not nearly as marked as in Europe; presumptions
about global human rights inform cases in the United States even without
explicit reference to international instruments (see, for example, *Nebraska v.
Al-Hussaini*); and postwar human rights instruments, especially the Universal
Declaration, was heavily informed by the U.S. Constitution, among other
sources, indicating a certain affinity.

But the shifting modality of politics to the politics of agency, with its
presumption of universal individualism and human rights, is revealed in the
remarkable convergence and growing isomorphism of law on agency—in the
example referred to here, in the area of migration—across the Euro-Atlantic
arena and in much of the democratic world: almost across the board, family
unification, economic, and humanitarian criteria are the touchstones of
migration policy (albeit with different definitions in each category cross-
nationally) (Newland and Papademetriou 1998–99). And as this law con-
verges, it trickles down to substate jurisdictions and organizations (and the
word *trickles* does not, perhaps, reveal the rapidity of this process). This novel
isomorphism reveals, on the one hand, growing legal density on a global level,
and, on the other, the "nesting" effect described above. We would suggest that
growing transnational activities, "judicialization," and agency as the modality
of politics are interrelated phenomena, and as such would have this effect of
generating isomorphism.

Issues such as "gender" and "race" are legally *closed off* as options for discrimination to remarkable extent across these countries. When we step back
and comprehend the extent to which human rights institutions and idiom
have closed off certain policy options to the point that they are simply assumed to be unremarkable, the impact of human rights begins to dawn on us.

The nesting process is legally and institutionally inscribed: legal sources,
terminology, and institutional structures have shifted in response to the changing modes of political engagement and demands of agency such that they allow
for the nesting process to flow quite naturally. For example, legal principles
have been created to provide mechanisms whereby the differing legal systems
and laws of member states in the European Union can successfully integrate

with emerging EU law. In order to coordinate the competing legal competency of the EU and national authorities, the TEU (Maastricht 1993) formalized "subsidiarity" and "proportionality" principles. In 1999 the Amsterdam Treaty added a protocol on the application of these principles.

The principle of subsidiarity derives from the first paragraph of article 5 EC and dictates that the EU can act only when they possess the legal power to do so, that the EU should act only when an objective can be better achieved at the supranational level, and that the means employed by the EU when they do act should be proportional to the desired objective. The Treaty on European Union further strengthened the notion of subsidiarity by making it a fundamental EU law limitation and stating in EEC treaty article 3b that EC action "shall not go beyond what is necessary to achieve the objectives of this Treaty." National powers, according to subsidiarity, remain the norm, with EU action the exception. On the other hand, the TEU enlarged the realm of EU competence to include the areas, traditionally within the exclusive authority of member states, of industrial policy, health, education, culture, and the particularly sensitive areas of immigration and social policy. But for the time being, "subsidiarity" and other such principles remain a one-way street. Whereas the Court of Justice is responsible for the interpretation of these principles and review of European institutional compliance in suits brought by member states, the European Council has taken the position that subsidiarity principles do not have direct effect in member states' legal systems and cannot be raised in litigation before member state courts. Thus, exactly how the principle of subsidiarity would work as a mechanism within the state judicial system is still largely an open question.

Although in practice subsidiarity remains ambiguous, it does appear to enhance the kind of nesting activity discussed in this chapter while at the same time contributing to the evolution of EU integration. For example, in the area of immigration, although the EU has moved in the direction of greater competence over the question of immigration by moving it to the first pillar and, more recently, forming a special committee to draft one policy for the EU, the fundamental determination of "nationality" still remains with the member states. Such divisions of legal competences provide the "cross-border" spaces within which nesting occurs.

The purpose of subsidiarity, from the perspective of a country such as Germany, which had urged its introduction, is to protect areas such as environmental policy, in which national governments might have taken great strides in formulating effective policies. The German fear was that "harmonization" might result in a lowering of national environmental standards. Thus, even harmonization has been interpreted as a regulatory floor, not a ceiling. Since it remains unclear which areas are within the E.U.'s exclusive competence, there is much room for maneuver. The effect of these principles, therefore, is that the ambiguity they introduce opens up a number of nests, so to speak, where litigation to enforce and affect environmental policy, for example, can occur.

In addition, these principles have been introduced in conjunction with what is, perhaps, a new form of "hybrid" national institution in order to enable greater fluidity between the national and EU levels. One of these hybrid institutions, the Committee of the Regions (COR) established by the Maastricht Treaty, has been given the task of ensuring that the principle of subsidiarity is respected. The COR fills in the gap of local and regional authorities' demand for representation within the EU. Through the COR, regions, towns, and local authorities can take part, in an advisory capacity, in the E.U. decision-making process. In part, it is a response to the question of "democratic deficit." Thus, it provides a mechanism through which EU citizens can defend their immediate interests in the community policy-making process. A primary function of the COR is to issue "draft opinions" after examining documents issued by the EU council, the commission, or the parliament to ensure that EU action has not already been handled on the national level. As an independent body, it will be interesting to see how this institution affects agency as it evolves and functions as a "cross-border" space.

Agency and "People Out of Place"

While the generally accepted principle of, for example, a state's right of immigration control is not at issue (and is not subject to frontal challenge), the secondary "web of laws," such as rules of nondiscrimination, empowers the individual as agent to affect how that immigration control is achieved. Thus political divisions get played out, in important part, between claims for democracy or republicanism and claims for agency. This creates interesting conjunctions on a policy level. Returning to the example of immigration control of asylum seekers and refugees: the legal instruments of rights, specifically human rights, do not prohibit immigration control, just that the form of regulation should be based on recognized universal, nondiscriminatory criteria as defined by international human rights instruments. In principle, the flow, restrictive or liberal, of migrants is independent of human rights issues per se. (An ongoing myth is that human rights law should necessarily increase cross-national flows; this is simply not the case.) One can argue that asylum laws can be legally interpreted in highly restrictive ways.

Thus we witness this interesting conjunction in border controls: in practical terms, because of internal pressures or because they feel that asylum laws, for example, are being unfairly exploited, states may become more restrictive, but the question remains whether those restrictions are within the criteria of international human rights standards as defined by the European Court of Human Rights, the European Court of Justice, and the like. Restrictive practices—based on nondiscriminatory criteria—reflect the intersection of these different forms of political practices.

We see these conflicting forces between the judiciary and the executive in relatively recent decisions; for example, the European Court of Human Rights condemned the French government for trying to keep asylum seekers in "international zones" that, though physically in France, were considered as not in France for the purposes of the European Convention of Human Rights, in effect placing people in indefinite detention (*Amuur* [1996]). The United Kingdom was similarly unsuccessful in persuading the court that a man who was not formally admitted to the country, but had been resident for five years, was not legally speaking within the country (*D* [1997]). One could add the decisions that upheld the right of an individual not to be returned to a country where they would face degrading treatment (*Chalal* [1996] or *Soering* [1989]).

Conversely, the member states' "common visa list," requiring visas in country of origin of countries that send, or may send, individuals seeking asylum, has the effect of barring individuals from reaching the European Union in the first place in order to request asylum. (It should be stressed that whether this action actually violates international human rights law—which sanctions the right to leave a country but not a right, as such, to enter a country—is certainly open to question.) Thus the struggle between the judicial arms, which have the effect (in this regard) of promoting agency, and the state, which seeks to promote republican national self-determination, is part of this process.[8] Part of the contention here, however, is that the increasing density of law, and law that promotes rights and prerogatives (and thus agency), is central to the growing role of the judiciary. It is the judiciary, at both national and regional levels, concerning both domestic and international law, that mediates and adjudicates this web of law. (It is interesting to note that the role of judiciary in the newly emerging democracies, such as South Africa, differs significantly from that of the judiciaries in older liberal democracies such as the United States and Germany. In the newer democracies there is not just the acceptance of, but the proactive vesting of power in the judiciary as a political body with a political function.)

In the continuing evolution of the EU, one can see an increasing shift of power toward formal commitment to human rights and mechanisms to enforce those rights within the member states. The Treaty of Amsterdam formalized measures to extend citizen rights and improve democratic accountability and participation in the institutions of the EU. In a significant departure from the past, the treaty called for enforcement of nondiscrimination within member states and opened the channels not just to address issues such as gender inequality, discrimination, public health, and consumer protection but to enforce these rights through the European Court of Justice. In yet another significant departure, coordination of immigration policy was transferred from the third pillar, where it was handled as part of justice and home affairs, to the first pillar.[9] Whereas legal provisions emanating from the third pillar are not part of community law, but rather norms regulated by public international law, legal instruments emanating from the first pillar become part of European Union law binding on each member state. Moreover, given that individuals have the legal capacity to invoke first pillar laws and bring them to bear against member states, the changes of the Amsterdam treaty may give the judiciary (on the regional level—here the European Court of Justice) more control over immigration policy, as well as the now formal commitment under Amsterdam of the EU to human rights.

Conclusion

As relations both regionally and globally become more multifaceted, and the legal frameworks that institutionalize such relations become more extensive, so are we likely to see the growing importance of judicial and administrative mechanisms to mediate these legally embedded relations. This will remain the case insofar as executive and legislative bodies are absent or relatively weak on the regional or even global level. The globalization (and regionalization) of law appears to have a certain affinity with judicial and administrative institutions. Thus, the clash we see between agency and democracy—as in the acute example of the executive orders following the September 11, 2001, terrorist attacks—will be reinforced through the current structure of human rights or EU law, global in import, and which promote the agency of the individual.

Notes

1. We draw this formulation of agency, in part from Block 2001.
2. Weiler has argued that "the originality of Europe has been in constructing a polity which to date has achieved a level of legal and material integration far exceeding that obtained by any historical confederation, and yet has managed to maintain the distinct political identity and essential sovereignty of its Member States and their nations in a manner which has defied the experience of all federations. . . . But the price of rejecting a federal state model and charting its own unique experience has been that there is no ready made democratic blueprint for Europe."
3. The increase in the salience of the judiciary and of the idiom of rights since roughly the 1970s and 1980s are illustrated in the following stark figures: the caseloads of the federal courts on all three levels—Supreme Court, Court of Appeals, and U.S. District Court— jumped in most cases dramatically between 1970 and 1995; in the Supreme Court there were 4,000 cases in 1970 and over 7,500 cases in 1995 and in the Circuit Court over 11,500 in 1970 to almost 50,000 in 1995. In the district courts the picture is a little more complex: "commenced" civil cases increased massively from 87,000 to 240,000 in that time period, but only a small and declining percentage of cases reached trial. The number of criminal cases increased from 1970 to 1995 more modestly—about 15 percent.
4. As the legal web expands, so we see growing legislative "mortality" (legislation that is undermined through judicial decisions). To our knowledge the evidence is mostly descriptive, but if the Canadian example is any indication, mortality rates of legislation rose significantly after the establishment of the Canadian human rights charter in 1982.
5. Consider the proliferation of NGOs as "pollinators," so to speak, of this process.
6. Id. at 152. The decisions in *Kalanake* (ECJ 17/10/1995—Case C 450/93, 1995 ECR I-3051) and *Marschall* (ECJ 11/10/1997—Case C 409/95 nyr) were both initiated by individual men seeking protection through EC law.
7. The growing reference to "human rights" in federal court cases is evident in the following figures: from 1945 to 1960 the term *human rights* appears in only 68 cases, and from 1961 to 1970 the figure is 159 cases. Then we witness a surge: from 1971 to 1980, 861 cases; from

1981 to 1990, 2,224 cases make reference to human rights, and from 1991 to 2000, in over 6,300 cases human rights are noted. Figures are derived from a legal database search.

8. One has to temper this statement, as states, in the democratic world, have increasingly desired to prove their credentials on human rights; for example, it is the executive arm that generates reports to the UN and other agencies like the OSCE showing their progress on fulfilling their human rights commitments on issues like racial discrimination.

9. The European Union is made up of three pillars. The first pillar represents the European Communities, the second pillar Common Foreign and Security Policy, and the third Co-operation in the Fields of Justice and Home Affairs.

6

Mandated Membership, Diluted Identity
Citizenship, Globalization, and International Law

PETER J. SPIRO

Citizenship practices have been thought the last bastion of national sovereignty. As international norms have aggressively invaded virtually every sinew of domestic governance, nationality law has remained largely immune to any acknowledged constraint from beyond. As a doctrinal matter, it has been allocated (in the characterization of a prominent international pronouncement on the question) to a "domain resérvé" in which states are free to rule according to their own preferences. But this regime is showing early signs of slippage, and is unlikely to persist into the future.

Nationality law was in fact once within the unfettered discretion of states. To the end of reducing related frictions among states, some nationality practices lost full recognition at the international level as a matter of choice of law, and many states entered into consensual, bilateral arrangements to prioritize competing state claims to individual nationals. These developments were oriented only by state interests, not those of individuals, and by the maintenance of international order. For domestic purposes, determinations of nationality were left wholly within state discretion. The international community took no cognizance of nationality as an individual right.

At least as a discursive matter, that changed in the wake of the Second World War. Statelessness, which had previously been framed by the order paradigm, was acknowledged to implicate individual rights. Even as the right to a nationality was articulated, however, it was not made actionable against any particular state. Some nationality practices were more concretely implicated by the human rights revolution. Widely subscribed international women's rights conventions have mandated gender equality in domestic measures relating to the acquisition and loss of citizenship, and human rights norms now limit state power with respect to the termination of nationality. Some of these constraints have emerged as clear norms of international law, enforceable directly against states.

Even as such, however, as far as they went these standards only peripherally affected state capacity to delimit membership. A state could not extend those human boundaries so far as to trespass on the sovereign rights of other states, and there was a vague understanding about reducing the number of individuals lacking the international protective attributes of nationality. Core qualifications for citizenship remained largely untouched by international standards. As citizenship increasingly comes to be framed as a right in itself, not a matter of state interest, international order, or an incident of other rights, an international law of citizenship is likely to emerge. As that framing becomes more pervasive, international discipline of state citizenship practices will become more exacting and universalist.

This new orientation is reflected in international approaches to dual citizenship and to naturalization and birth citizenship. Where the former was once considered obnoxious to international order, it is now perceived in part as a matter of individual autonomy and identity, and there are signs that, at least in some circumstances, the retention of more than one citizenship will be protected under international law. Naturalization and birth citizenship were once wholly outside the ambit of international law, and states were free to set conditions for the acquisition of citizenship. But that insulation may be eroding. As naturalization and birth citizenship regimes converge, there may be some baselines to which states will have to adhere. Unlike past constraints on citizenship practice, those baselines will constrain a state's core capacity to define its citizenry.

These developments are a logical extension of the human rights revolution and the triumph of liberalism as the metric of international norms. International law is in general assuming greater consequentiality as a determinant of state behavior. States are increasingly willing to press human rights agendas against other states, even in the absence of geopolitical gains; and nonstate actors, including international organizations, nongovernmental organizations, and interested publics, now garner power independent of states with which to advance compliance with international law. States, including powerful states, ignore hard international norms at their peril. Although norms relating to citizenship practices remain soft and undefined at the margins, their development in recent decades has been unidirectional. As the international law of nationality comes to focus more on issues of exclusion rather than of interstate stability, it should enhance the rights and status of individuals in their places of residence, especially as against the use of citizenship practices as a surrogate for other internationally proscribed types of discrimination (that is, where citizenship law is used as an instrument of subordination on the basis of race, religion, and other such characteristics). That trajectory is normatively consistent with a human rights frame.

But the ultimate implications of dictating access to membership may be less clearly rights- and status-enhancing. To the extent that national citizenship has in the past reflected internally constructed national identities, it has facilitated and consolidated community solidarity. That solidarity may be a premise to thick public governance at the national level. The exogenous imposition of membership standards could undermine the rough correspondence of citizenship and identity. That could in turn drive solidarities into other forms of collective association, not so constrained, and with them many of the functions of the modern welfare state.

This thesis is meant to be speculative and suggestive, but also cautionary. Some barriers to citizenship may be deployed as weapons of subordination within communities rather than as boundary lines around them; in those cases, international law's intervention should not threaten community self-definition. But insofar as international law compels the redrawing of the lines themselves, it could further undermine state power. Securing inclusive citizenship regimes, in other words, may reap only short-term gains, as authority moves to nonstate institutions. This observation is not offered to retard the insinuation of international law into the last bastion of citizenship practices; that insinuation seems inevitable. But it does point to an unintended consequence of such efforts that will require heightened vigilance of membership and governance standards in other institutions.

The Old World: Nationality Law as Sovereign Prerogative

From the advent of the state system, international law has largely conceived of membership decisions as falling to the discretion of states. That discretion was circumscribed at the margins during the late nineteenth and early twentieth centuries, driven by a public-order imperative to minimize interstate conflict arising from the intersection of domestic nationality regimes. The capacity to define the core conditions of membership remained unconfined through this period. Except where the interests of other states (narrowly drawn) were implicated, states retained the power to decide the conditions of citizenship.

Nationality law has three basic components: how nationality is acquired at birth, how it is acquired after birth (naturalization), and how it may be lost. In the early modern period, states enjoyed largely free rein over all three. This was possible in the absence of large-scale international mobility and of any concept of human rights protected by international law. The magnitude of "conflicts" with the nationality laws of other states was minimal in a world in which for the most part individuals lived and died where they were born. The feudal regime of jus soli persisted, under which nationality largely coincided with residence. Nationality was not an important quality in that context, and nationality law rarely gave rise to controversy in either domestic or international contexts.

American independence and migration from Europe brought nationality regimes to the fore as a point of contest in bilateral relations and as a threat to interstate order (Spiro 1997). Nationality controversies were framed at the international level as a problem of choice of law, not as a question of state power. It was assumed that states could formulate their nationality laws according to their unconstrained preferences, and that for internal purposes such preferences were supreme. At the same time, the intersection of nationality regimes could give rise to situations calling for a prioritization of state claims. Nationality thus required management at the international level, or at least such management was attempted. The public-order metric could result in nonrecognition of a country's nationality designation in some cases, but it did not delegitimize the designation as a matter of international law. These order-management problems dealt only with cases in which states had extended nationality to an individual, or maintained an individual as a national, not cases in which nationality was denied. Conflicts resulted from the extension or maintenance of nationality, not its refusal.

Dual nationality posed the most serious threat to interstate order, with states pressing competing claims on individuals or attempting to protect nationals from the claims of another state of nationality. States contested the capacity of individuals to expatriate, in the context of immigrants to the United States who naturalized there and sought to shed their birth nationality. Under the doctrine of perpetual allegiance ("once a subject, always a subject"), as of the beginning of the nineteenth century most European states rejected the possibility of expatriation (Schuck and Smith 1996). Conflicts resulted (the War of 1812 among them) when European states insisted on extracting military service obligations from those who had emigrated. Dual nationality proved a consistent irritant to America's bilateral relationships, when emigrants returned to their homelands for temporary visits to find themselves subject to conscription. European states continued to claim these individuals as nationals of their state of origin, refusing to recognize the legitimacy of naturalization elsewhere.

The order-management response to the expatriation controversy took the form primarily of bilateral agreements and other arrangements allowing for the transfer of nationality in most cases. The Bancroft treaties of the mid-nineteenth century with several German and Scandinavian states accomplished this by treaty, providing for the subsidence of original nationality for so long as an emigrant maintained residence in the United States (original nationality would revive for those who returned permanently to their homelands) (see Koslowski 2000: 76). In the wake of an intense controversy involving the trial of Irish Americans as British subjects, Great Britain recognized the capacity to expatriate by statute in 1870. But several nations, including Russia, Turkey, and (in certain cases) France, persisted in adhering to perpetual allegiance. That persistence was considered consistent with international norms. States could agree consensually to bind themselves otherwise by treaty, or unilaterally to recognize a capacity to expatriate. But international law dictated no rule on the question.

Dual nationality also generated conflict where one state asserted the interests of a national against another state that also claimed the individual as its own. Under traditional (pre–human rights) international law, a state could do as it pleased to its own nationals. When it came to the treatment of nationals of other states, however, a refined set of international law norms constrained state action. Those two premises faced contradiction in the form of dual nationals, with one state asserting unfettered discretion over its national against the intervention (under the moniker of "diplomatic protection") of the other state of nationality. Relatedly, with respect to international state-to-state claims made on behalf of nationals, defendant states would deny the right of another state to espouse the claim of a national who was also a national of the defendant state. International law resolved the resulting conflicts by establishing a prioritization of nationalities in such cases. For purposes of such interstate disputes, an individual was recognized as having a single "dominant and effective nationality." The state of dominant and effective nationality could assert claims against another state of nationality and against third states and (in some formulations, including the American) exercise diplomatic protection against the other state of nationality.[1] Thus nationality was subject to international law, but only for international order-management purposes. The "dominant and effective" test did not deny the capacity of a state to designate an individual as a national, so long as it did not infringe on the interests of other states. The test implicated the interests of states, not of individuals; both diplomatic protection and espousal of claims were exercised at the option of states, not the option of individuals whose interests underlay them. The aim was to resolve interstate conflict and maintain order, not to vindicate individual rights.

Of course, these public-order threats (some of which gave rise to serious diplomatic disputes) could have been avoided altogether through harmonized nationality rules. That objective presented a primary motivation for the Hague Codification Conference of 1930. Although the parties to the resulting convention could agree that "the ideal towards which the efforts of humanity should be directed in this domain is the abolition of all cases of statelessness and of double nationality," the convention imposed minimal constraints on the nationality practices of the parties. (Even so, only a handful of countries—most of them Commonwealth—ultimately acceded to the accord; and, unlike more recent, widely adopted multilateral conventions, it could not be taken as representing customary norms—that is, rules to which states would be assumed bound in the absence of specific objection thereto.) The pact evinced a weak norm in favor of recognizing a right to expatriation where a person held two nationalities "acquired without any voluntary act on his part" (most notably, by the intersection of jus soli and jus sanguinis models of birth citizenship rules), at the same time that it recognized the prerogative of states to impose conditions on such expatriation. While restricting the exercise of diplomatic protection against a state of alternate nationality, the convention recognized that "a person having nationalities may be regarded as its national by each of the States whose nationality he possesses." Indeed, as a background principle, the agreement (tellingly entitled the Hague Convention on Certain Questions Relating to the Conflict of Nationality Laws) provided in its first article that it was "for each state to determine under its own law who [were] its nationals."

Statelessness presented the other notable international concern implicating nationality practices. Like dual nationality, it was framed as a threat to international order and a matter of state interest, insofar as it created "friction between States" (Weis 1979: 162). Although a less constant irritant to interstate relations than dual nationality, statelessness did pose a threat to state interests, for example, where a state found large numbers of aliens in its midst denationalized by and thus not returnable to another country (Seekler-Hudson 1934: 251). Statelessness also challenged the order premises of international law by creating a class of individuals for whose conduct no state would stand responsible, presenting, in theory at least, a gap in the enforceability of international law.

But the obvious disadvantages of statelessness from the individual's perspective made the status difficult to situate completely in the order-management model, and in fact it is here that one finds the first emergence of a rights orientation for nationality questions. Interwar commentators lamented the consequences of statelessness for individuals. In a world before human rights, those without nationality were at the mercy of their hosts; "[a]s far as the law of nations is concerned, apart from morality, there is no restriction whatever to cause a State to abstain from maltreating to any extent such stateless individuals" (Oppenheim 1928: 521). Making some short steps to reducing the incidence of statelessness, the Hague convention provided that states should effect the loss of a woman's nationality by virtue of her marriage to a foreigner only where she acquired the nationality of her husband. Where children did not acquire the new nationality of naturalizing parents, the convention provided that they would retain their original nationality, and a protocol to the convention provided for the extension of nationality to the child born in the territory of a state to a mother possessing the nationality of that state and a father not possessing such nationality. These were patches, no doubt, in a convention not widely subscribed to, but they were interpretable as a nod to individual rights rather than to international order.

That rights conception was made explicit in the wake of the Second World War, with its obvious implications for statelessness. (It was in this context that Hannah Arendt delivered her dictum that all rights are national rights.) The 1948 Universal Declaration of Human Rights provided that "[e]veryone has a right to nationality," and that "[n]o one shall be arbitrarily deprived of his nationality nor denied the right to change his nationality." With this stroke, the discourse shifted away from an order-centered orientation, moving to recognize the individual's interest in nationality rules as a matter of international law, and entrenching the by-then near universal acceptance of both a right to voluntary expatriation and protection from arbitrary denationalization.

But the discursive shift did not result in broadly actionable international norms. The right to nationality, in particular, was not designated as the obligation of any particular state to satisfy. The declaration itself did not take the form of a binding legal instrument. When many of its protections were adopted in the 1966 International Covenant on Civil and Political Rights, the right to nationality, again without reference to any particular state, was scaled back to apply only to children. The 1961 Convention on the Reduction of Statelessness required contracting states to extend nationality to children born on their territory who would otherwise be stateless, as well as to children born to nationals outside the state's territory who would otherwise be stateless. The convention also precluded the deprivation of nationality on the grounds of race, ethnic, religious, or political orientation, and required that deprivation for other causes be made contingent on the acquisition of nationality in another state. The agreement left core nationality determinations to state discretion. Even so, it has attracted only twenty-five accessions, and cannot be identified as representing customary norms binding on nonparties.

Gender discrimination presents the single area in which midcentury international law imposed significant constraints on state nationality practices. Majority state practice had provided for a woman's nationality to follow that of her husband, both upon marriage to a foreigner (forfeiting her original nationality for that of her husband) and upon naturalization of the husband (in which case many states provided for automatic naturalization of the wife as well). In cases where loss, but not acquisition, of nationality upon marriage was automatic, statelessness resulted, and (as noted above) the 1930 Hague convention attempted to address this by making automatic loss contingent on automatic acquisition. Beyond the statelessness concern, however, the convention confronted the nationality of women as a matter of gender equality, by providing that a husband's naturalization should not result in the woman's change of nationality without her consent. This small step was furthered by full implementation of equality in the regional 1933 Montevideo Convention on Nationality and the amendment of the laws of major states to implement the principle. The 1957 Convention on the Nationality of Married Women eliminated automatic changes in a woman's nationality by cause of marriage or change in her husband's nationality. Relative to other nationality conventions, the 1957 accord was widely adopted, with seventy parties and twenty-seven additional signatory states. It has been superseded by the 1979 Convention on the Elimination of All Forms of Discrimination against Women, article 9 of which calls for equal rights between men and women to acquire, change, and retain their nationality, with specific preclusion of automatic changes in nationality triggered by the nationality of the husband. With over 170 parties, CEDAW has been nearly universally accepted, and can be posed to represent customary norms binding even on nonobjecting nonparty states. Gender antidiscrimination norms have thus resulted in a significant constraint on state nationality practice.

But that constraint should be seen as driven by women's rights, not by any human right to acquire nationality in particular circumstances. Indeed, to the extent that it is driven by an equality norm, it dictates no particular substantive rule for the acquisition or loss of nationality, only that women cannot be disadvantaged in the formulation of those rules. So long as men and women are subject to the same rules, both can be excluded. In this sense (other than to require that nations include women as well as men among their nationals, which has always held true, even when women were disadvantaged in other respects), international law rules regarding women and nationality do not directly impact national self-definition as executed in nationality practices.[2]

Indeed, that international law has not, at least not until recently, trammeled on such self-definition is evidenced by the treatment of nationality in the 1966 Convention on the Elimination of All Forms of Racial Discrimination. Even at the time of its negotiation, racial discrimination was emerging as an important norm of international human rights (the treaty has been accepted by 155 states). International law has highly circumscribed the use of racial classifications as a general matter (leaving aside affirmative action, the motivating purpose of which is to correct historical discrimination). And yet in its first article the convention brackets the use of race as a criteria for citizenship, providing that "[n]othing in this convention may be interpreted as affecting in any way the legal provisions of States Parties concerning nationality, citizenship, or naturalization, provided that such provisions do not discriminate against any particular nationality." The convention does govern citizenship distinctions made within an existing community, precluding, for instance, apartheid-type situations in which native-born residents are denied nationality on the basis of their race. But in its original conception, at least, it was not intended to constrain criteria for admission from outside the existing community. Until recently, international law would have had nothing to say about a citizenship regime that had the clear effect of excluding outsiders on the basis of race.

Thus in the traditional conception of international law, with the exception of gender equality, nationality practices have been left to the discretion of states. In the commentary, nationality law was considered a core component of the doctrine of sovereignty (Weis 1979: 65; Schwarzenburger 1967: 141; Weil 2001: 18).[3] Although sovereignty itself is a social construct of the international system, and never translated into complete freedom of action, the extent to which any particular authority was framed in a sovereignty discourse correlated to the level of state discretion. In the area of nationality law, that discretion has been broad.

The traditional approach to nationality law can be conceived as a matter of human geography confronted on the same terms as territorial geography. Both regimes are forms of boundary maintenance. International law refused to draw territorial lines in any particular way, relying instead on history and control. It did evince a strong priority on allocating all territory to one state and one state only, in much the same way that international law found an objective in ensuring that all individuals had one nationality, but only one nationality, working against the twin difficulties of statelessness and dual nationality. Sovereignty over space and sovereignty over people were both predicates to the maintenance of international order. Although the latter context implicated individual interests, those interests were only indirectly accounted for.

The Emerging International Law of Citizenship

The traditionally deferential approach of international law to nationality practices appears to be eroding. This erosion is suggested by recent developments concerning dual citizenship and the acquisition of citizenship. International law has until recently been unwilling to impose standards of conduct regarding either question. With respect to dual citizenship, reversing past disfavor, international law may come to recognize an individual right to maintain the status. With respect to the acquisition of citizenship, emerging norms suggest limitations on threshold requirements for long-term residents, and the trajectory could arrive at the required adoption of a jus soli basis for birth citizenship. Both developments suggest that the balance is tipping toward a rights, rather than an order, metric in how international law processes nationality questions. If so, international norms regarding nationality determinations are likely to harden in the medium to long term.

As described above, dual nationality was the bane of an order-based norms system, sparking the human equivalent of turf battles among states with competing claims to individuals. Although international law was ultimately incapable of resolving the problem at its roots (failing to establish a harmonization of nationality laws), a strong discursive disfavor attached to the status. So strong was this disfavor that dual nationality was cast as immoral (Bancroft 1849).[4] This opprobrium was uncontested (Kimminich 1996). Among the difficulties associated with the status, the infringement of individual rights figured not at all. That was, to be sure, in part because dual nationality may itself have constituted an infringement of rights; at least in the nineteenth-century context of the expatriation controversy, dual nationality often translated into multiple and conflicting obligations, including mandatory military service. But the prospect of burdensome obligations dissipated as states either abandoned conscription or made it contingent on residence (also the case with taxation). Dual nationality became a status that an individual might seek to maintain. Nationality has been central to individual identity. Insofar as an individual might want to identify with more than one nation, then, dual citizenship can be framed as a matter of individual autonomy—in other words, as a matter of rights. And yet into the late twentieth century it was never addressed as such, even in a suggestive manner.[5]

That may now be changing. Scholars are increasingly situating dual citizenship in a rights frame. The rights perspective has now been at least partially adopted at the regional level in Europe, in the form of the 1997 European Convention on Nationality. That convention's preamble "[r]ecognises that, in matters concerning nationality, account should be taken both of the legitimate interests of States and those of individuals." In contrast to its 1963 predecessor (and indeed all other multilateral accords on nationality), the 1997 agreement refrains from condemning multiple nationality as a problem, instead noting "the desirability of finding appropriate solutions to consequences of multiple nationality and in particular as regards the rights and duties of multiple nationals." In its operative provisions, most notably, the new convention requires states to permit multiple nationality in the case of children born with the status and in the case of persons acquiring nationality automatically by marriage.

It is possible to describe this protection as perfecting gender equality in matters of nationality, by way of recognizing what Karen Knop calls "relational nationality" (Knop 2001: 89). In this frame, the 1997 convention understands that mere neutrality will not accomplish gender equality. Insofar as family relationships may depend on shared nationality, recognition of dual nationality as a legitimate status is necessary to protect both those relationships and individual identity autonomy; without it, the individual (more often the woman) is forced to choose between the two. In this explanation one can characterize the 1997 convention as continuous to earlier international norms on nationality incidental to gender equality. It is also true that the 1997 convention is not protective of all cases of dual nationality, permitting states to terminate the nationality of an individual who voluntarily acquires another nationality. Finally, of course, the 1997 convention is a regional and not a global undertaking, and as such cannot by itself be taken to represent an international norm.

But one can nonetheless characterize the 1997 European convention as a watershed. It is the first multilateral undertaking that is protective of dual nationality in any context. Regardless of its source, that creates a foundation on which to build more expansive protections. The partial protection itself shifts the discourse, in the instrument itself, to one that accounts for the interests of individuals. Nor does gender equality provide the only account of the convention's terms. One can alternatively explain the line between protected and unprotected multiple nationality in identity terms, with a focus on the child's rights rather than the mother's. Who is to say that a child forced to choose between a mother's and a father's nationality would be more likely to opt for the latter? The provision also protects dual nationality of a child born to two parents of the same nationality in another state recognizing citizenship jus soli. In that case gender equality cannot supply the full rationale.

The regional circumscription of the 1997 agreement is at least in part overcome by its reflection of global trends. Recent state practice with respect to multiple nationality points to dramatically increased acceptance of the status. Few states persist in requiring those born with dual nationality to elect one at majority, at the same time as global mobility has resulted in an explosion of the number of such birth dual nationals. Although the law of many states (heavily represented among major Asian countries) provides for the termination of citizenship upon naturalization in another country, the numbers have declined to the point where it is the minority practice (where in the mid-twentieth century it was nearly universal), and pressure from immigrant diasporas appears inevitably to be diminishing the number of those states refusing to recognize multiple nationality.

Such important "sending" states as Mexico, the Dominican Republic, and Turkey have undertaken recent nationality law reforms to allow for the retention of nationality upon naturalization elsewhere; India, the Phillippines, and Korea appear poised to follow. These changes have been considered to be in the interest of the states involved (in terms of maintaining ties with emigrant populations that are an important source of foreign exchange and political influence) but also in the interest of the immigrants themselves, who have otherwise been faced not only with the choice of sentimental loyalties but also with the prospect of losing certain rights in their homelands upon the forfeiture of their original nationality (see, for example, Chander 2001).

This practice indicating acceptance of dual nationality has not achieved the sort of prevalence that would qualify it as establishing a customary norm of international law. (One of the primary sources of international law is found in the practice of nations, which if acknowledged as arising out of legal obligation can be binding on all states, even in the absence of treaty agreement or other formal assent.) But given the recent trajectory, it is not implausible that acceptance of multiple nationality could ripen into a customary norm and/or support conventional undertakings recognizing a right to maintain the status. In particular, as already reflected in the 1997 European accord, establishing a right to maintain birth dual nationality may not be so far over the horizon (and could be deployed, most notably, against Germany's recent adoption of an election requirement at majority for those born in Germany with dual citizenship). The model here could be the evolution of the right to expatriate (that is, to voluntarily renounce one's nationality), which was rooted in changed state practice subsequently buttressed by such instruments as the Universal Declaration.

International developments regarding naturalization may also stand at a crossroads. The 1997 convention is signal here as well, requiring that states party provide for "the possibility of naturalization of persons lawfully and habitually resident on its territory," and that any period of residence required as a condition for naturalization not exceed ten years. More so than with respect to dual nationality, this treaty requirement reflects a nearly universal practice among states, under which naturalization is possible, often subject to additional qualifications, after a residence period of ten years or less (in most states closer to five years).[6] It still may take a leap to characterize this practice as required by international law, in the absence of some evidence that states feel obligated to sustain such standards as a matter of law rather than simply of preference. Again, however, that evidence may be supplied by the incorporation of this naturalization parameter into other multilateral instruments. Most notably, again, the European convention requires parties to provide for the possibility of naturalization after a period of residence not to exceed ten years. Unlike the protection of birth dual nationality, this development cannot be explained as a perfection of gender equality. An international norm requiring the possibility of naturalization for habitual residents would represent a qualitatively new international standard.

The significance of the European convention on this score is buttressed by recent developments relating to citizenship regimes in Estonia, Latvia, and the Czech Republic. Estonia and Latvia adopted restrictive regimes in the wake of the end of the Soviet occupation that encumbered the acquisition of citizenship by large Russian ethnic communities, most of whom (or their forebears) had settled after the Soviet occupation. Both imposed difficult language and history requirements as a condition for naturalization. The first Latvian citizenship law made it especially difficult for longtime ethnic Russian residents to naturalize as Latvians, adopting a system of age brackets that postponed the eligibility of most adults.

International condemnation of these restrictive citizenship regimes was sustained and ultimately succeeded in securing the adoption of eased requirements. The Council of Europe and the Organization for Security and Cooperation in Europe actively opposed the Baltic citizenship practices (the OSCE launched a "mission" on the subject that is only now winding down). Although both organizations carefully recognized the breadth of state discretion over citizenship under international law, they challenged the legitimacy of a regime denying citizenship to a substantial component of the resident population. As a Council of Europe report concluded, "if substantial parts of the population of a country are denied the right to become citizens, and thereby are denied for instance the right to vote in parliamentary elections, this could affect the character of the democratic system in that country." In the face of the European pressure, both Estonia and Latvia have implemented laws and other administrative practices to facilitate the naturalization of Russian residents.

The citizenship law of the new Czech Republic generated similar pressures. Under the original 1993 Czech nationality legislation, those with designated Czech nationality under Czechoslovakian law and resident in Czech territory automatically acquired citizenship in the new state; those resident but not designated as Czech nationals were barred from citizenship if they had a criminal record. The condition barred thousands of Romany residents from citizenship, and attracted CoE and OSCE criticism. A CoE report concluded, "Admittedly, a State may decide who are its citizens but it is doubtful whether, in a case of State succession, under international law, citizens that have lived for decades on the territory, perhaps are even born there, can be excluded from citizenship just because they have a criminal record." The Czechs desisted in 1996, repealing the clean-record requirement with respect to residents as of the breakup of the federation.

These developments, again, can be drawn as evolutionary, rooted in existing international law constraints on nationality practice. They implicate, most notably, the norm against statelessness; a clear concern in the Baltic and Czech contexts was the prospect of large numbers of stateless individuals resulting from the practices under scrutiny. But it is also possible to characterize them as a departure from past premises. Diane Orentlicher argues that the international response to these measures evidences a shift to a "territorial/civic" model of citizenship enforced through international norms, in which the extension of citizenship to residents is considered necessary to the full realization of human rights (Orentlicher 1998: 296). This represents a departure from past approaches to statelessness in two respects. First, as an operative matter, the norm devolves an obligation onto a particular state; the right to nationality becomes a right to a particular nationality. Second, as a normative matter, the new conception recognizes the democratic self-governance values; the point now is to guarantee political participation in a person's place of residence. The right to some nationality, by contrast, reflects an international protection norm; that is, that individuals should have some state to turn to protect them against mistreatment by other states.

Recent developments respecting German nationality practice, though not framed in international law terms, present further evidence of the possible emergence of international norms respecting both multiple nationality and the acquisition of citizenship. Notwithstanding its emergence, along with many other European states, as a country of immigration, Germany had been a holdout in both denying the legitimacy of dual citizenship and, more exceptionally, in maintaining a strict jus sanguinis regime of birth citizenship. Under the nationality law as it stood before a 1999 overhaul, immigrants were eligible for naturalization only after fifteen years of residence, and were required to satisfy onerous cultural assimilation requirements. Naturalization was also contingent, in almost all cases, on proof of termination of original citizenship. Citizenship was not extended at birth even to those children whose noncitizen parents had been born in Germany.[7] The difficulty of naturalization and the lack of any jus soli citizenship gave rise to a significant population of second- and even third-generation residents who nonetheless lacked German citizenship, most of them of Turkish nationality. Germany was proving an outlier, at least within the European context, on nationality acquisition issues.

Consistent with international trends, the 1999 reforms relaxed the hurdles to German citizenship. The new law for the first time provided for jus soli birth citizenship of nonethnic Germans, for the children of persons born in or longtime residents of Germany. The measure reduced the residency requirement from fifteen years to eight, and reduced the cultural threshold to a demonstration of some facility in the German language. Although an initial proposal to accept dual nationality in most cases was shelved after conservative politicians successfully converted it into a domestic election issue, the amended regime nonetheless relaxes what were high hurdles to the maintenance of multiple nationality. German citizens may now retain their German nationality upon naturalization in another state so long as they can demonstrate continuing ties with Germany—for instance, the existence of family members there. Those naturalizing as German will still be required to terminate their original nationality, and those now enjoying birth citizenship by virtue of noncitizen parental residence in Germany will be required to elect between their German and alternate nationalities under what has been labeled the "option model." But even in these cases the new regime provides for liberal exceptions for the retention of multiple nationality, including where the other state of nationality would impose substantial economic penalties upon the loss of its citizenship. It has been suggested that the law could be interpreted to allow Turkish nationals to retain their citizenship upon naturalization as Germans, because Turkey imposes restrictions on the ownership of property by noncitizens. Thus, even in the short term Germany may in practice become accepting of multiple citizenship status.

The German case suggests the possibility of an international norm requiring the adoption of jus soli in certain cases (most notably, those involving second-generation residents[8]), even where statelessness is not a concern. Controversy surrounding the recent nationality reforms in Germany were not, to be sure, primarily framed in international law terms, although such major human rights groups as Human Rights Watch had condemned the previous regime as overly restrictive of citizenship access. Even if international law has not been determinative of the recent reforms there, liberalization of German nationality laws is consistent with a norm allowing access to naturalization after sustained presence, some allowance for jus soli birth citizenship, and increasing international toleration of dual citizenship.

This is not to overstate the significance of these developments respecting naturalization and the acquisition of citizenship. At this stage they qualify as no more than soft law, representing aspirational norms that are not yet amenable to direct enforcement against states. No doubt the emerging norms in this context would be contested before crystallization. But soft law norms often harden. The trend here is clear; as Patrick Weil notes, "All stable, democratic nation-states with immigrant populations have moved in the same legislative direction" (Weil 2001: 34). It is now possible to envision international law standards governing core nationality determinations.

Rights and Identity

The legalization of nationality has profound implications for definition of community and the strength of state-defined identity. In the short term, mandating access to citizenship on a territorial basis and acceptance of plural nationality will enhance the rights of those who would otherwise be excluded. In the longer term, however, such mandated inclusion may diminish state-based solidarities, as a legal definition of community replaces an organic one. At the core of globalization is an eclipse of space. In that context, a territorially defined community is unlikely to be a thick one. A high incidence of plural nationality will compound that dilution. As communal solidarity diminishes so will the state as its agent. In the end, the rights-reinforcing consequence of mandated inclusion may be counterbalanced by the declining importance of the state as a locus for the protection of rights and the distribution of resources. Such loci may institutionally migrate to forms of association beyond the scope of legalization.

Emerging constraints on nationality practices are more identity determinative than previous constraints, such as they existed. Indeed, earlier international norms in the area can be described as policing state discretion to define community to ensure that it did not overreach actual community lines. With respect to expatriation, for example, recognition of a right to transfer attachment from one state to another vindicated a change in community affiliation. In the absence of such a norm, states could persist in defining their communities in ways that did not reflect actual community boundaries. Likewise with respect to international norms on the nationality of women.

As the construction of marriage and family changed during the mid-twentieth century, measures providing for the automatic transfer of a woman's nationality upon marriage to a foreigner may not have accurately reflected the national identities or attachments of women.

The more recent prospective norms, by contrast, may impose constraints that are not correlated to identity or that blur identity boundaries. The emerging territorial citizenship norm could mandate membership for those who have no other tie to the citizenry than place of residence, which tie may be insubstantial and subordinate to other attachments. In the past, territorial presence has in most contexts presented a reliable surrogate for other, sometimes unmanageable tests of membership. Under an assimilationist model of immigration, especially in the United States, it was in fact the case that presence over time correlated well with actual membership. One could assume that a resident of five years would be, on average, committed to permanent residence,[9] and that the incidents of that presence would result in community membership. If this correspondence of prolonged territorial presence and nonformal membership persisted today, mandating access to citizenship for long-term residents would be identity reinforcing (or at least not identity diluting), at the same time that it would advance other rights norms.

But the predicate is becoming less stable in the face of globalization. Globalization enables communities both to persist over distance and to isolate in proximity. It has also been associated with increased migration flows, magnifying the significance of this persistence and isolation. Individuals can be present over long periods of time without developing community ties, or at least not ties to a state-defined community. Human existence has an inevitable spatial component, and so some community connections will arise from nontransient presence. But those ties can be restricted to the local level, and they may not come to represent an individual's primary identity, especially in the face of sustained networks with home-country communities eased by improved communications and mobility.

Governance, of course, is still largely undertaken on a territorial basis. That explains the continuing attraction of citizenship in some contexts. Mere equivalence of social rights will not always suffice in the absence of political ones. The postnational vision has not yet been realized (Joppke 1999: 187; Koslowski 2000: 92–93), or at least not universally so. Voice may not be amenable to substitution, and citizenship can still carry status and equality implications. Thus the virtue of the territorial/civic model.[10] The model also represents the dominant instantiation of liberal theory on the question. The persistent territorial presence of status-subordinated communities is anathema to liberal theorists. Liberals, Michael Walzer most notable among them, have long argued the normative basis for low or eliminated barriers to naturalization (see Walzer 1983: 52–61). Some would now go so far as to make citizenship automatic after a certain period of residence, even for those who would prefer noncitizen status (Rubio-Marin 2000).[11]

But the triumph of imposed territorial membership may collapse on itself. To the extent that territory no longer correlates with community, the agent of the communities so defined will lose authority. Individuals who do not share a sense of identity with other individuals may be unwilling to commit to decision-making structures that will decide the distribution of resources, whether in the form of rights or of material goods. Governance in the absence of community will be thin. An international law norm that requires that citizenship be afforded on the basis of presence will thus contribute to the diminishment of state power. The norm would be less consequential with the passage of time as authority migrates to other institutions. Mandated access to citizenship may not disprove the postnational proposition. On the contrary, by diluting the ultimate consequentiality of citizenship, international reinforcement of citizenship access rights may facilitate a postnational destination in which citizenship status emerges as a historical vestige.

A norm protective of plural citizenship could also undermine the strength of communities represented by the citizenship tie. On the one hand, plural citizenship reinforces the institution of the state to the extent it facilitates expressions of national identity that were precluded in the old order, in which multiple attachments were disfavored (Bosniak 2002). A person who has ties to more than one national community can formalize those ties through plural citizenship. On the other hand, protection of the status will inevitably be dilutive of the categorical importance of identity defined in citizenship terms.

The old regime of mutual exclusivity reinforced the primacy of national identities, the distinctions among national communities clearly drawn. Plural citizenship blurs those boundaries; identity boundaries become less clear and as a result less defining.

Plural citizenship also lowers the costs of citizenship acquired or maintained for nonaffective instrumental reasons by eliminating the need to abandon citizenship representing primary community attachment. The costs of adding or maintaining citizenships is relatively low; few obligations are now contingent on the status. Plural citizenship is thus identity dilutive, facilitating the acquisition or maintenance of citizenship for such purposes as passport acquisition, immigration benefits (including protection against deportation and exclusion), social benefits eligibility, and property rights, for which no actual attachment to the national community may be indicated. This tendency appears to be most pronounced with respect to acquired citizenship, where the capacity to retain one's original citizenship may translate into the naturalization of some whose affective tie to the state of immigration is thin; the second citizenship may be subordinated. This is not, as it is sometimes tarred, a question of divided loyalties, as loyalty to states becomes increasingly meaningless in a world in which resource competition is not among states. But plural citizenship does lower the threshold for national membership in a way that may render national membership less meaningful. The end result, again, is accommodating to a diminished intensity of communal bond, which in turn will diminish the state as a locus of authority, at least marginally.

These observations are offered as descriptive. They cannot support a retrenchment of former approaches to citizenship determinations, in which states could act without the constraint of international law. Change is to a large extent made inevitable by globalization, the main driver here. International law is reflective of the changed nature of national identity and the citizenship tie. It may accelerate and enforce the universalization of these developments but cannot reverse them.[12] The absence of a new international law of citizenship will not enable states to resurrect strong national communities through exclusionary citizenship practices. The suggestion here is intended more as a cautionary challenge to liberal nationalists, who place much faith in the capacity of the state to be the primary agent for the protection of rights, and who would thus conceive of mandated access to national citizenship as posing no consequential risk. There is a possible downside here. If the dilution of identity does in fact result in the diminishment of the state, functions heretofore assumed by the state may migrate to less accountable private forms of association in which membership may be subject to no exogenous norms or standards not subject to public enforcement. Perhaps those other forms of membership should now come under the sort of critical scrutiny now brought to bear on membership in the state.

Conclusion: The Deepening Swath of International Law

That international norms are becoming consequential to national self-definition evidences the changing nature and expanding scope of international law. In the old world, international rules relating to nationality were to the end of minimizing friction among states; although these rules may have constrained the projection of nationality, they were ultimately to the benefit of states, not individuals. That was consistent with the orienting principle of international law, the management of order among states. Individuals were no more than incidental beneficiaries of that principle, and their interests as such were of no account under international law. To the extent that states desisted from conduct destabilizing of international order, international law protected state autonomy in the name of sovereignty. And at the core of sovereignty was the unfettered discretion to set the terms of membership.

In this sense, emerging international norms respecting national membership show how far international law has come. Community self-definition is constitutive and foundational, in the sense that it is prior to any act of the community; what states do is determined by the individuals that comprise them. If citizenship practices are not immune to international legal constraint, then nothing is; nationality law is the fallen last bastion in the citadel of sovereignty. That is not to say that international law now delivers a comprehensive regulatory regime, and indeed states will retain important discretionary powers into the future. But no function of governance will be shielded from international law as a categorical matter, membership decisions included.

Notes

1. Most notably in the International Court of Justice decision in the *Nottebohm* case, which denied the capacity of Liechtenstein to bring a claim against Guatemala on behalf of an individual whose "dominant and effective" nationality was German. The "dominant and effective nationality" principle was also used to resolve the problem of duplicative military service obligations, so that dual nationals would be subject to conscription only in their state of habitual residence; but this was through voluntary treaty undertakings, and not imposed as a matter of international law.

2. Of course, they may reflect national self-definition with respect to questions of gender equality. They may also reflect how community lines are dictated at the family level (whether, most notably, spouses can maintain a transnational divide). But they do not implicate first-level community boundaries, as do, for instance, eligibility requirements relating to ethnicity, language, or residence.

3. See, e.g., Weis ("There cannot be any doubt that this right [to determine the incidents of acquisition and loss of nationality] is a concomitant of State sovereignty"); Schwarzenburger ("In principle, international law leaves each territorial sovereign to decide which of his inhabitants he wishes to grant nationality. Thus, primarily, the topic is governed by the rules underlying the principle of sovereignty"); and Weil ("the attribution of nationality is inherently part of a state's sovereignty").

4. As George Bancroft observed in 1849, states should "as soon tolerate a man with two wives as a man with two countries; as soon bear with polygamy as that state of double allegiance which common sense so repudiates that it has not even coined a word to express it" (Bancroft 1850).

5. Nissim Bar-Yaacov's major 1961 study of dual nationality, for instance, continued to attribute serious "psychological conflicts" to the status, making it "detrimental to . . . the well-being of the individuals concerned" (Bar-Yaacov 1961: 266).

6. See Weil 2001: 17, 22–23 (setting forth naturalization requirements of a variety of states, none of which includes residency requirements of longer than ten years).

7. On the German nationality law before the reforms of 1999, see generally Neuman 1998: 263–85.

8. See Weil 2001: 25–26, for a survey of state practices with respect to second-generation immigrants. Of twenty-five major democratic nations, only five (Austria, Greece, Israel, Luxembourg, and Russia) do not entitle second-generation residents to citizenship in at least some cases (the variable being the period of residency required of the first-generation immigrant parent).

9. To the extent that such a period of residence did not reflect a longer-term commitment to permanent residence in the country of immigration, practice through the mid-twentieth century, in the U.S. context at least, provided for the forfeiture of naturalized citizenship upon return as a resident to the immigrant's country of origin. See Spiro 1997. Such enforcement of adopted community attachment is no longer undertaken today. A naturalized citizen retains her citizenship even if she abandons all ties to her country of naturalization and revives those of her country of origin.

10. Virtue, not primacy. As the rights of noncitizen residents (and in some contexts noncitizen nonresidents) approach those of citizens, questions of formal membership become less consequential. Social and economic rights are nearly equivalent in most immigrant-receiving states. Even in the political realm, aliens are securing channels of participation. In the European context, alien voting in local elections is now well established. In the United States, although noncitizens are barred from the franchise (with minor exceptions), permanent resident aliens are permitted to make campaign contributions—a far more effective route to political influence than the ballot. Noncitizens also garner power through their membership in powerful domestic interest groups, such as unions. Insofar as rights are not contingent on citizenship status, membership becomes less important, and community identity is diluted. The rights-equivalence analysis thus presents a different route to the same endpoint.

11. The proposal is, however, in tension with basic liberal premises of autonomy insofar as it would impose identity. It may also be symptomatic of emerging postnational conditions in some states. Assuming that naturalization barriers are already low, the need to resort to automatic naturalization evidences diminished perceived benefits in acquiring citizenship status.

12. One could, however, frame a countervalue in terms of the international right to self-determination. The connection appears yet to have been articulated, perhaps because the emergence of the right to self-determination was historically integrated with the end of colonialism and the self-determination of subordinated groups. The states most vulnerable to international discipline respecting citizenship determinations hardly represent subordinated entities. And yet the logic of self-determination seems no less applicable to, say, Germans than it should be for, say, various indigenous peoples. International norms mandating access to citizenship in Germany obviously compromises Germany's capacity to define its people as they might collectively prefer, at least insofar as the German state remains the institutional agent of the "German" people.

IV
Globalizing the Citizenship Gap

7

Deflated Citizenship
Labor Rights in a Global Era

GAY W. SEIDMAN

The tensions among globalization, national states, and the protection of individuals are perhaps nowhere more evident than in struggles to protect workers in developing countries. For the past century, labor rights have been defined through workers' localized struggles, in conflicts that have almost invariably been resolved through state regulation at the workplace. True, labor rights are increasingly discussed in universalistic terms: at the tail end of the twentieth century, there was broad international agreement about a core set of labor rights—freedom of association, freedom from bonded and child labor, freedom from discrimination—but the actual protection of those rights has been through mechanisms linked to citizenship, with more limited scope. In recent decades, however, globalization seems to have undermined the ability of national states to protect those rights, and weakened organized labor; many unions, especially in developing countries, seek new strategies to deal with newly mobile capital, in ways that highlight potential tensions between a language of universal rights and citizenship claims within the nation-state.

Since the industrial revolution, political citizenship has proved an essential component of workers' gains. Although militant labor movements generally focus on employers, for the past century labor's organizing strategies have almost invariably also targeted the state. Repeatedly, labor has used members' political clout to push democratic states to create social security nets, but even authoritarian states have sometimes regulated working conditions (Przeworski 1985; Rueschemeyer, Stephens, and Stephens 1992). While unions certainly negotiate with business, most labor movements have long viewed the political arena as crucial: national states set ground rules for collective bargaining, and state intervention is a critical factor in workplace conflicts. Around the world, militant labor movements have used the language of citizenship, often citing T. H. Marshall, to argue that full inclusion requires that states set a floor under citizens' living and working conditions, and to demand that states regulate the workplace in ways that grant greater dignity to workers and their families (Seidman 1994; Koo 2000).

Since the early 1990s, however, the discourse linking citizenship to labor rights has been steadily delegitimized: the neoliberal strategies pursued throughout the developing world have altered the relationship between states, business, and labor, in ways that often undermine states' willingness to regulate business or intervene in the workplace—and, increasingly, may reduce unions' willingness to call on states to intervene. An increased emphasis on global competitiveness has transformed relationships at work, raising new questions about how unions can or should defend their members' interests.

Globalization poses new challenges for organized labor: confronting a neoliberal state in a highly competitive global environment requires new strategies, each of which carries its own dilemmas. In this chapter, I first look briefly at how global market integration has reduced the likelihood that states, especially in developing countries, can protect workers' rights. Then I examine two very different responses on the part of organized labor to the dilemmas posed by capital mobility. In response to increased volatility and competition, many unions have sought a "high road" growth strategy, trying to raise skill levels and productivity in the effort to help their members compete in a global labor market. Many unionists hope that offering workers training and education will help attract high-wage jobs, but I suggest that these strategies create new dilemmas for unions, since they may undermine the bases of collective action.

A completely different approach seeks to avoid these dilemmas by completely bypassing what Gershon Shafir (in this volume) calls the "thinned" national state: many unionists seek to strengthen international labor links, looking for transnational mechanisms that might regulate transnational capital. In the penultimate section of the chapter, I argue that while this strategy may avoid the dilemmas of the first approach, most available mechanisms for international labor solidarity are limited at best, and at worst could exacerbate existing international inequalities. In conclusion, I suggest that unless international mechanisms are thoroughly reconstructed, organized labor will, almost inevitably, return to strategies that emphasize strengthening workers' citizenship rights and strengthening local states rather than looking to global institutions for enforcement and protection.

A Changing Global Context

Generally, discussions of globalization emphasize technological and institutional changes that create new possibilities for production, allowing greater flexibility in geography, design, and work organization. Many of these discussions mention, at least in passing, the way these changes alter workplace labor processes, suggesting that new patterns of production may realign the relationships between workers, unions, management, and states. An increasingly open international economy—in which trade, production, and financial processes increasingly operate on a global level, and capital moves around the world at will—is said to undermine national control over economic processes, reducing states' abilities to manage the domestic economy and complicating labor movements' relationships with states.

These views are not simply academic: they are expressed daily around the world, as policy-makers and activists confront what appear to be dramatic and rapid changes in the organization of the international political economy. Throughout the 1990s, aging social democrats like Nelson Mandela, Fernando Henrique Cardoso, and Kim Dae Jung promised fundamental reform of authoritarian, inegalitarian developmentalism; but in the face of global pressures, in an era when state-centered developmentalist options have been discredited by the collapse of Eastern European–style socialism, their reforms have followed the neoliberal pattern, removing tariff barriers, privatizing state enterprises, encouraging exports. Once, militant labor movements expected that democratization would bring to power governments sympathetic to workers' concerns, and through the 1980s labor movements tried to build strong ties to democratic oppositions, articulating class-based demands for better wages, social services, and full citizenship. In the late 1990s, however, unionists' conversations took on a slightly confused tone: the militant union strategies that seemed appropriate as a challenge to authoritarian rule now seem to threaten economic growth.

Throughout the developing world, former unionists who are now cabinet members entreat former colleagues to moderate their demands in the face of globalization, and union leaders express concern that their own members' militance will frighten away the international capital on which their jobs depend. Workers seem to accept that globalization brings a new precariousness: attempts to engage in the kind of general strikes that marked militant unionism in the 1980s have repeatedly failed in the more complicated climate of the 1990s, as many workers seem reluctant to risk their jobs for a larger struggle. Where once labor federations framed members' demands in terms of "full citizenship," they are likely now to speak instead of the need to maintain productivity and employment in the face of ruthless international competition (see Koo 2001; Webster and Adler 2000).

This shift is of course consistent with what Bierstecker (1995) has called "the triumph of neoliberalism" in the last two decades. Generally, discussions of globalization treat labor more as a factor of production than in terms of living workers, individually or collectively, and view unions' demands as threatening the very basis of economic growth (see World Bank 1996). Although business leaders frequently overstate the likelihood of capital flight, and underestimate the ability of states to intervene in labor relations in a globalized era, there is a great deal of evidence that threats of capital flight and job loss have undermined European social democratic coalitions, and led governments to back away from labor-friendly efforts to regulate business (Kapstein 1999, Golden and Pontussen 1992). In the United States, Human Rights Watch concluded in 2000 that "workers' freedom of association is under sustained attack in the United States, and the government is often failing its responsibility under international human rights standards ... to protect workers' rights" (Human Rights Watch 2000).

In developing countries, where organized labor must be as concerned about creating new jobs as about preventing capital flight, and where infrastructure and social services are often woefully undeveloped, those global pressures loom even larger: business and political leaders alike warn that investors will avoid countries with high labor costs or high tax rates, going instead to places where workers are paid even less, and where states are even more willing to reduce tax rates or environmental standards. In fact, it was largely at the insistence of developing-country government representatives— who feared that efforts to police global labor standards could complicate low-wage countries' ability to attract investors and to export their products to advanced industrial economies—that the 1996 Singapore Declaration of the WTO ministerial meeting concluded, "We reject the use of labour standards for protectionist purposes, and agree that the comparative advantage of countries, particularly low-wage developing countries, must in no way be put into question" (WTO 1996).

What does globalization mean for labor in developing countries? The optimistic view focuses on job and skill creation: by spreading industrial growth around the world, globalization's new possibilities for far-flung industrial siting is expected to give historically undeveloped countries a new basis for integration into the world economy. From this perspective, an increasingly liberalized trade regime will push countries to more efficient, cheaper production processes; the combined effects of the GATT and of new production possibilities will stimulate countries to be more productive, seeking niches in which they may have a comparative advantage—and leading to greater economic growth around the globe. Countries that manage to attract new industrial investment may gain jobs for more skilled workers, with new opportunities for high-wage industrial employment and job creation (World Bank 1996).

In this view, globalization promises new factories, new jobs, and new skills to workers in far-flung parts of the world; new technologies offer new possibilities for economic growth and productivity, and workers should be grateful for the chance to participate. By working together with management to find new productive niches—new efficient production processes, new products, or new international markets—this perspective suggests that workers and unions can help find a "high-skill, high-wage" route to prosperity and development. Workers' skills will provide the basis for future negotiations with employers: skilled and efficient workforces, cooperating with management to raise productivity, will be able to demand higher wages, since employers will be more dependent on their workers' participation in production; gradually, the bene-fits will trickle out to the entire economy, and all boats will float in a rising tide (World Bank 1996).

More skeptical analysts, however, suggest that international competition narrows workers' options. First, economic restructuring—particularly the pressure on developing countries to open their markets and increase exports—has routinely involved massive layoffs in the large, often state-owned compa-nies that served as the basis of industrial expansion for most late industrializers, undermining the relatively privileged core of many developing-country labor movements (Candland and Sil 2001; Webster and Adler 2000). But even beyond the cold shock of restructuring entailed in the shift from import-substitution to export-oriented development strategies, many analysts suggest that globaliza-tion could lead to a "race to the bottom," as developing countries competing for new investments are forced to offer low wages and a stable cheap workforce in order to attract multinational capital (Greider 1997; Lipietz 1987; Ong, in this volume). Industrialized countries may be able to draw on historical assets to retain high-wage jobs—educated workforces, developed infrastructures and labor markets, and easy access to the world's wealthier consumers; but most analysts assume that developing countries—even those with relatively skilled workers—find low wages, low taxes, and limited regulation the easiest incentive to offer potential investors (Moody 1997).

Both of these perspectives probably hold some truth. New technologies have reorganized the physical location of industrial production, may involve new skill requirements for industrial production, and certainly permit new managerial strategies. New technologies have allowed the spread of industrial production to new sites, stimulated the production of nontraditional com-modities and products for export, and promoted increasing international competition. And some analysts suggest that these technological innovations increase the possibilities for migratory labor, as workers and their families travel to new work sites, remit wages, and send information about labor mar-kets back to their homes (Sassen 1998).

But this process of geographic expansion is far more uneven than a seamless vision of globalization often implies, and not all jobs are equally good ones. Regional differences in infrastructure and sectoral differences in the applicabil-ity of new technologies combine with managers' historical and racial preju-dices (Kaplinsky 1995; Posthuma 1995). Many parts of the world have been left completely out of the new wave of private investment, or have found that their new "niche" is limited to producing primary commodities—minerals or non-traditional crops for export to consumers in industrialized regions (Stallings 1995). Much foreign investment does not involve sophisticated new technol-ogy or require skilled workers: many export-processing zones simply bring old equipment to new, cheaper workers, especially in labor-intensive areas like apparel, export-oriented agriculture, the lower end of the electronics industry, or even pink-collar call centers and data processing (Bonacich and Appelbaum 2000; Cowie 1999; Freeman 2000; Kaplinsky 1993).

Even when sophisticated technologies are brought to developing-country locations, the change has not always strengthened the workers' position on the shopfloor. Workplaces may be organized to reduce the possibility that even skilled workers could disrupt production; technologies that seem linked to greater trust and cooperation in advanced industrial contexts—in what is often called "post-Fordism"—may look meaner, rather than leaner, when embedded in the more authoritarian and hierarchical workplaces that persist in postcolonial settings (Juarez and Babson 1998; Kaplinsky 1995; Shaiken 1995; MacKay 2001; Posthuma 1995).

Moreover, labor is often denied much support from its strongest potential ally in the neoliberal world, where states are severely constrained by the fear of capital flight. High tax rates could chase away investments, while higher wage bills undermine international competitiveness. Globalization may thus further erode state revenues in countries that already lack social services or infrastructures—a prospect that undermines the possibility that developing-country states will be able to educate workers to give them skills that might increase their bargaining power with employers, or create the social security net that historically strengthened labor's ability to organize in advanced industrial countries.

This tension is most clearly reflected, perhaps, in the proliferation of export-processing zones—sites in which states often agree not to enforce existing labor law, as part of a subsidy package offered to foreign investors. As a development fashion, these zones create new dilemmas, involving a complicated tradeoff between investment, job creation, and the enforcement (much less improvement) of existing labor law. Indeed, in the effort to attract new jobs to their countries, many developing-country governments have proved more likely to provide services to new export-processing zones than to their own citizens. Governments are more likely to publish brochures advertising the "nimble fingers" of their willing workers (Ong 1987; Lee 1998) than to insist that investors provide health and safety protections, more likely to call migrant workers who remit needed foreign exchange "national heroes" (Parreñas 2001) than to solve unemployment by funding public works or infrastructural development. From this perspective, globalization will inevitably intensify inequities, further weakening already poor nations, and making workers who are already unskilled and poor increasingly vulnerable to the demands of international capital.

Unions and Economic Restructuring

What do these constraints on development strategies mean for labor? As international financial analysts regularly remind developing-country policy-makers, workers who threaten labor militance to gain higher wages or better conditions could frighten away investment, losing union members' jobs. In this climate, labor unions from Australia to Zambia have found themselves cooperating in "social pacts," accepting constant or even reduced wages and benefits in order to sustain investment (Lambert 2000). Elected governments may have replaced authoritarian regimes, but economies have been hammered by the multiple processes that are often lumped together under the term *globalization*—reintegrated into the world economy under neoliberal economic policies. Again and again, democratically elected governments have found themselves unable to pursue any alternatives to private investment and the market as the sole engine of economic growth. In the era of neoliberalism, democracy has regularly coincided with privatization, restructuring, and the opening up of national economies— undermining (sometimes quite literally, as in the case of South Africa's mining unions) the main stronghold of organized labor.

Faced with the perceived threat that they are engaged in a global "race to the bottom," many union strategists have shifted their focus: instead of seeking to strengthen workers' claims on employers and the state through collective action and political strength, many unions have begun to look at improving members' skills, hoping to attract and retain investment by offering increased productivity and competitiveness. The "high road" vision generally demands cooperation between labor, management, and the state, all trying to attract and retain jobs at the higher-value-added, higher-paid ends of global commodity chains, generally by making workers more productive. At the enterprise level, unionists have often found themselves cooperating actively in employer-initiated efforts to restructure the workplace, to raise productivity, and to enhance efficiency. At national levels, union confederations seek strategies for creating new jobs, especially high-wage jobs, rather than engaging in combative negotiations with employers.

New technologies and new managerial strategies have provoked a new set of discussions among unionists. Especially from the enterprise perspective, a newly competitive environment has increased concerns about productivity and efficiency, reducing employer commitment to specific individual workers while raising employer interest in increasing workers' skills. From São Paulo to Seoul, firms are increasingly demanding high school or even university diplomas for shopfloor factory workers, and many analysts stress the value that firms place on keeping skilled, productive workers at work (Carillo 1998). Correspondingly, many workers may find that their careers are being reshaped by the demands of flexible production. Where workers and employers once aspired to relatively stable relationships, where a sizeable minority of workers could assume that they would spend their careers within a single enterprise, workers today may experience a more staggered career, as they move from job to job, selling their services on a short-term basis—sometimes not even as employees, but as independent contractors, a circumstance that further removes them from traditional industrial relations frameworks (ILO 1998a).

Labor market volatility is certainly exaggerated by the managerial strategies fashionable among transnational managers—strategies that may involve new technologies, but that also reorganize work to reduce managerial risk and vulnerability to state regulation. Casualization, outsourcing, piecework, and subcontracting, especially when combined with "just-in-time" techniques, undermine workers' sense of security in their jobs, redesigning the relationship between workers and employers. Often discussed as if they were primarily the result of changing technology, these managerial strategies reach further than technological innovation alone could predict: when a mine in South Africa subcontracts cleaning services to a company composed of the mine's former employees, there is almost no change in technology, but the relationship between the mine management and the cleaners has changed dramatically. Similarly, when an automobile company subcontracts different components of its autos to companies composed of former employees, sometimes even located within the same factory, the managerial strategy is less a reflection of new technologies than of a new emphasis on risk reduction and cost-cutting (Seidman 1997; Posthuma 1997).

These new managerial strategies erode long-term job security with a single employer, and they have been reinforced by legal changes throughout the developing world, as labor laws have been revised to increase labor market flexibility. Throughout Latin America, discussions of labor law reform focus on making hiring and the use of labor more flexible, a discussion no longer led by unions but by entrepreneurs (Marquez 1995; Frenkel and Royal 1997). In South Africa, black workers only gained protection from arbitrary dismissal or state regulation of workplace relations with democratization, in 1994; but under the impact of globalization employers now insist that these new labor rights introduce labor market rigidities that impede competitiveness. Even in a relatively high-employment context such as the United States, many analysts emphasize the increasingly flexible and unpredictable pattern of individuals' work patterns (Bluestone and Bluestone 1992); in developing-country contexts, where unemployment rates are often in high double digits, "flexible labor markets" create great insecurity for workers at all skill levels. The character of labor processes—still racialized, everywhere, but no longer rigidly so even in South Africa—is shifting, to incorporate a core of skilled, relatively privileged workers in a far more consensual factory regime, while leaving excluded and marginalized those workers who are less educated, often older. But even workers in that core are generally more uncertain about the future than they might once have been.

A volatile labor market, unemployment, and informalization threaten unions' ability to represent workers in collective bargaining arrangements. Even in Europe and the United States, where labor protections remain relatively strong, employers are increasingly concerned about ensuring that their workers can offer the skills and productivity they consider necessary for global competition, and become less willing to respect workers' seniority. Efforts to upgrade workers' skills, and to reward productivity rather than seniority, are increasingly commonplace in management strategies, and unions around the world have found themselves engaging in efforts to raise productivity in the workplace, cooperating with employers to increase industrial competitiveness.

But in countries still undergoing industrialization, these processes create real dilemmas for union strategists. In countries where formal sector workers could be said to represent a relatively privileged group, and where skill levels are generally quite low, the temptation to treat low wages as a comparative advantage in the international economy—to pursue what analysts sometimes refer to as the "low road" strategy of industrialization—are strong. To fight that temptation, developing-country unions seem increasingly prone to participate actively in efforts to increase training and skill levels. Accepting the language of competitiveness and human capital, many unions seek to raise members' skill levels, to attract foreign investment to mid-wage sectors as a strategy for sidestepping the "race to the bottom"—a shift involving a profound reorientation in labor strategies.

Rather than emphasizing citizenship and incorporation, organized unions increasingly aim to prepare individual workers for a competitive labor market. Instead of an older rhetoric of democratization and citizenship, union federations around the world have engaged in national policy discussions around employment, and in specific efforts to design and implement new training schemes for workers in the manufacturing sector. Working together with employers and the government, labor federations try to increase the skills that workers bring to the labor market, to ensure that workers' training meets employers' needs, and to strengthen the possibility of attracting well-paid jobs to their country.

In many developing countries, unionists and government officials, along with those industrialists who understand the changes wrought by a democratization and globalization, are beginning to move toward creating internal labor markets, factory-based training programs, and wage differentials based on productivity. In South Africa, the Congress of South African Trade Unions has been actively engaged in efforts to develop new training policies and certification programs across all sectors of the economy, as it seeks to ensure that black workers receive the skills and certification needed for jobs in a rapidly changing labor market. The thrust of union strategy has been to establish a new framework linking grading, training, skills development, and pay in the industry. These changes are linked to new forms of work organization, such as teamwork, which have in turn impacted on the broader skills development strategy of the country and led to a new Skills Development Act being passed in 1998 (see Hirschsohn, Godfrey, and Maree 2000). Similarly, in Brazil, the major union federations have been increasingly engaged in providing training to their members, and in helping members adjust to new patterns of employment and work. Even the Central Unica dos Trabalhadores, Brazil's most militant federation, has accepted a $20 million grant from the Brazilian government to create its own training program for metalworkers, hoping to both prepare union members for a newly volatile employment pattern and increase skills enough to attract future investment in the industry.

As they shift to an emphasis on training, unions struggle to balance two very different dynamics: on the one hand, labor continues to define itself through an emphasis on collective mobilization, while on the other, unionists are drawn into designing vocational training programs stressing common interests between employer and employee. This cooperation entails choices that can undermine worker collective action. Ironically, democratization outside the factory can create new divisions in working-class communities: when South African state policies no longer enforce racial segregation and hierarchy on the shopfloor, or when the Brazilian government no longer enforces a rigid wage squeeze, skilled and semiskilled workers may no longer see their interests as clearly linked to those of the unemployed, the poor, or their less-skilled neighbors. But new strategies aimed at raising worker productivity and worker-management cooperation are also divisive, creating new and difficult dilemmas (Buhlungu 2000; von Holdt 2000). Should unions enter into compacts with employers or even with democratically elected governments, representing the interests of employed workers while abandoning the concerns of the unemployed, when the unemployed are often themselves former union members who have lost their jobs in the course of economic restructuring? Should unionists restrain strikes over factory-based issues—wages, working conditions, new labor legislation—in order to attract more foreign investment, hoping to create new jobs and, hopefully, more sustainable economic growth?

The long-term implication of this approach remains unclear. Government officials seeking to create jobs and labor federations may view training programs as a way to raise skills and attract higher value-added industries to the region; but local employers trying to compete in international markets may be more concerned about lowered costs than about raising skill levels. Further, organized labor's efforts to raise skill levels risk reinforcing existing divisions in the labor force: older workers, often barely literate, are frequently ineligible for training programs, so that unions find themselves supporting programs that are closed to old stalwarts from the shopfloor. Lacking any alternative project or vision, unionists may find themselves narrowing their gaze to individual workers, preparing them to compete better for jobs in a savagely fierce labor market, rather than trying to build a broader, more coherent working-class identity.

Where the discourse of citizenship once provided the basis for an inclusive vision of unions' constituencies, the language of competitiveness and productivity is a narrow one, undermining labor's ability to develop collective demands, collective identity, or collective action. Over the past century, labor movements have frequently been faced with these kinds of dilemmas, which stem from the fact that while many unions represent a small core of employed, often relatively privileged workers they generally claim to speak in the name of the working class. Historically, unions have managed the tension by appealing to the state, to create a context in which labor rights are respected, to prevent employers from replacing militant workers with cheaper ones, to provide a social security net that benefits all citizens. In the context of global competition, however, when even governments in advanced industrial countries claim that they cannot control capital's movements, labor movements are more likely to find themselves in social pacts with democratically elected governments than in opposition to them, hoping to attract capital to create jobs for their members, and engaging in training programs to make their members more productive and competitive in global markets. The shift is an understandable one, but the strategy directs labor's gaze away from mobilizing collective identities, or articulating broad-based interests, to an individualized perspective that mirrors the logic of the market. In doing so, it risks further undermining the ability of the state to regulate capital, by complicating the possibility of building labor-friendly political coalitions in the future.

Seeking New Alliances?

For every unionist who has gotten involved in efforts to attract investment, raise productivity, and improve competitiveness, however, there are probably as many or more who favor a very different approach, one that seeks to create a different kind of globalization. Historically, labor's vision has long claimed to be transnational—even when most of labor's energy has been focused on national states. A discourse of international labor solidarity was already well established by the end of the nineteenth century, articulating a universalist appeal that was expected to transcend borders and underpin a new social order. Over the past twenty years, as ruthless globalization has intensified existing inequalities and created new ones, countless labor analysts have argued that so long as the voices of workers and their communities are ignored or silenced, globalization will continue to marginalize whole segments of the world's population. A transnational workers' movement, it is argued, could serve as the core of a democratic challenge to the current exclusionary pattern.

Labor's global history is not, of course, unproblematic. While organized labor often speaks the language of international solidarity, labor's actions have generally reflected a more narrowly defined nationalism: labor federations have been much more likely to protect workers' immediate interests rather than broader class goals. In the last century, European labor unions supported imperialist campaigns and colonial projects; in the United States, unions often led campaigns to restrict immigration or to impose segregation. After the Second World War, American unions purged themselves of internationalists, allying themselves with American foreign policy and supporting conservative unionists around the world. During the Cold War, although international labor organizations routinely called on workers of the world to unite, they remained closely linked to superpower foreign policies, and few union leaders superceded their national identities (Bergquist 1996; Silverman 2000).[1]

In the post–Cold War world, unions struggle to develop an internationalist vision. Militant unionists in recent struggles from South Korea to Nigeria have explicitly distinguished between workers: they frequently claim to represent citizens (especially male ones) while excluding migrants, women, and un-skilled workers. Even in South Africa, where progressive unionists are acutely aware of the dangers posed by exclusionary unionism, union officials face xenophobic pressures from members who see immigrants from the rest of Africa as competitors in an already flooded labor market. Though labor lead-ers try to redefine workers' interests to include broad issues like democracy, inclusion, or child care, nationalism remains an all too easy choice.

Labor's organizational dynamics certainly help perpetuate this pattern. Accustomed to working within a single national framework, within national laws and institutions that have few international parallels, union leaders often limit their appeals and their imagination to a local constituency. Moreover, union bureaucrats are generally stretched thin, focused on more immediate problems than those of building long-term links with workers around the globe, while sectoral "internationals" are rarely capable of mobilizing real sup-port, and have few resources to share.

Even with new technologies like e-mail and faxes, constructing meaningful international links takes time, money, translators, energy—resources that few unions have to spare, especially in poorer nations. Where international links between unions exist, they usually stem from the work of small groups of com-mitted activists—and even then, one can question the depth of these linkages. Creative attempts to find new bases for transnational union activism, such as organizing workers internationally by sector, by multinational employer, or by links along a commodity chain, have had little impact, especially considering the amount of attention those attempts have garnered (Alexander 1999; Wells 1999; Williams 2000; Wilson 2000; Zinn 2000).

How much international discussion has to take place before a majority of union members redefine their identities to privilege international worker soli-darity? Efforts to build transnational unionism run into persistent differences in workers' interests across national lines, stemming as much from differences in structural location as from simple organizational patterns. Aside from workers' perceptions that they are engaged in a global competition for new investment—since jobs that "move" from Los Angeles to Mexico could be seen as creating new jobs for Mexican workers—how far do the concerns of work-ers in Central America really coincide with those of workers in Milwaukee? At what point might they diverge, impeding a common project? Consider a basic aspect of the contemporary global economy: pressures from the WTO and the IMF have forced governments in developing countries to lower protective tariffs and slash subsidies, opening their markets to international competition and privatizing state-run companies. Workers are experiencing drastic insecurity, as economic restructuring creates new volatility in sectors once relatively privileged by state development strategies—a volatility often worsened by the elimination of hard-won legal protections for workers in the name of increasing labor market flexibility to attract investment. When the AFL-CIO presses the U.S. government to impose tariffs on foreign-made steel to protect the American steel industry—and thus to protect its members' jobs—those tariffs block sales of steel produced by non-American workers, in countries like Brazil and South Korea, and threaten those workers' jobs.

Given those real structural differences, transnational labor solidarity will always require some negotiation. Democratization of international trade bodies could create welcome possibilities for workers' voices, but we should remember that those voices may not speak in harmony: Will unions in industrialized countries be willing to support the restoration of protective barriers in developing countries, or to provide subsidies to developing countries' industries, if those tariff barriers restrict potential export markets? Conversely, how will workers in developing countries respond to persistent efforts by workers in industrialized regions to retain skilled, higher-paid jobs, particularly when those efforts are all too often phrased in terms that imply that less-educated third-world workers are less skilled, less productive, or less worthy?

Discussions of transnational unionism seem destined perpetually to reinvent themselves: countless volumes include the phrase "new labor internationalism" in their titles, as if this time, perhaps workers will find ways to supercede their differences. And there is, of course, a great deal of creative energy going into thinking about how unions might confront globalization. For the past ten years, for example, some of the strongest labor movements in the developing world have met regularly, seeking to develop a "southern" labor vision that could offer a unified alternative to current patterns of globalization (Buhlungu and Webster 2002).

But faced with the prospect of persistent global capital mobility, unionists around the world have begun to discuss creating new transnational mechanisms to protect labor rights, arguing that if national states in developing countries are too weak and too dependent to enforce rights, transnational mechanisms could help regulate working conditions and wages, putting a floor under the conditions of the most vulnerable workers around the world. But as I will suggest in the remainder of this section, many of these mechanisms are problematic: building on existing international hierarchies of power, they often seem likely to replicate or even worsen them, in ways that are often overlooked in discussions of transnational labor. The most commonly discussed mechanisms—including labor standards in trade treaties, corporate codes of conduct, and even the ILO's effort to develop core labor rights—tend to rely on mechanisms of international trade for enforcement, a pattern that may pose real problems for developing countries' workers.

Including labor standards in international trade treaties may be the favored mechanism of American unions, but the strategy is viewed with some distrust on distant shores. From the late 1960s, American human rights activists sought to tie American international aid to countries' human rights records, hoping to persuade repressive dictatorships to reduce human rights violations (Keck and Sikkink 1998). Following this example, American labor rights activists have argued that by including labor rights concerns in trade treaties, the United States could push its allies and trade partners to protect their workers in return for favored access to American markets (Harvey, n.d.); under the Clinton administration, some trade treaties included American insistence on labor law reform. Some sympathetic academics suggest that bilateral trade treaties—especially the promise of easy access to North American and European markets—can push countries like Cambodia to adopt labor legislation (Candland 2002). Others point to the inclusion of labor side agreements in the North American Free Trade Agreement, which have allowed Mexican, U.S., and Canadian unions to insist that each government enforce existing labor legislation (Compa 1996)—a mechanism that could certainly enhance worker protections in many countries, since labor laws on the books are often stronger than their execution in practice would suggest.

Nevertheless, many developing-country unionists remain skeptical. Trade treaties are by nature blunt weapons: economic trade sanctions could be imposed on a country like India because of poor working conditions or child labor in agriculture, for example, but the workers most immediately affected would be those in export-oriented industries, where organized labor might well be stronger. Even more important, trade-related social clauses give leverage only to the governments of countries with large markets—that is, to governments in advanced industrial countries. Given current American and European domination of world markets, the imbalance is striking: if the United States were to insist that Cambodia change some aspect of its labor regulation, Cambodia risks losing access to its most important market, while if Cambodia were to block U.S. imports over some issue, the United States would probably barely notice. How would poorer nations, with insignificant economic clout, enforce labor standards on anyone else? Or is this to be a one-way process, in which rich countries, whose workers are also global consumers, use their market clout to enforce standards upon the rest of the world?

Perhaps most important, many developing-country activists remain concerned that American and other powerful governments might manipulate labor-related trade treaty clauses for other political purposes—a pattern that has clearly been visible in the way human rights clauses have been invoked as tools in larger geopolitical conflicts. Many developing-country policy-makers worry that putting labor clauses in trade treaties would simply increase the already overwhelming power of advanced industrial countries over their neighbors. What would stop American presidents from invoking "social clauses" for the wrong reasons, to undermine trading partners' sovereignty rather than to protect workers? If the past history of American policy is any guide, labor clauses would as likely be used for American gain as to protect developing-country workers; as Pakistani labor researcher Karamat Ali argues, "Labor standards in trade agreements will always be susceptible to being used to pressure intransigent governments for political purposes" (Ali 1996: 271). Especially if trade-related labor clauses were used to pressure developing-country states—threatening employment and economic growth in developing countries by blocking access to markets—their use could effectively weaken, rather than strengthen, the voices of organized labor outside U.S. borders: if publicly revealing labor violations could place at risk a country's entire growth strategy, unions could easily find themselves caught between exposing labor violations and being blamed for unemployment linked to trade sanctions.

These concerns become recurrent themes in discussions of how to incorporate labor standards in multilateral trade organizations, especially in the workings of the World Trade Organization. Suggestions that labor unions and other groups in civil society might redesign trade bodies, creating mechanisms through which global trade institutions might be forced to respond to the claims of a mobilized global citizenry (Evans 2000; Howse 1999), reflect a very real concern for the problems workers face with globalization; but again, many developing country activists view these mechanisms with distrust. Even if hitherto closed panels were accessible, the uneven power wielded by different governments within trade bodies, and the uneven power of different countries to impose sanctions through trade, makes these mechanisms problematic. As a body, the WTO has resisted efforts to include labor standards in trade rules, insisting at its 1996 meeting in Singapore that although its members remain committed to the observance of internationally recognized core labor standards the ILO is the competent body to set and deal with these standards. Perhaps more significant, the WTO ministerial conference asserted, "We believe that economic growth and development fostered by increased trade and further trade liberalization contribute to the promotion of these standards. We reject the use of labour standards for protectionist purposes, and agree that the comparative advantage of countries, particularly low-wage developing countries, must in no way be put into question" (WTO 1996). But even if the WTO were to shift its position and agree to declare egregious labor violations to be "unfair trade subsidies," and even if it were to open its closed panels to voices from organized labor around the world, the threat that trade mechanisms would re-create existing international inequalities remains. So long as global trade rules rest on bilateral trade sanctions (currently the WTO's only enforcement mechanism involves individual countries decisions to block market access to offenders), they are vulnerable to political manipulation and would leave the protection of workers' rights more dependent on the global power of consumers in advanced industrial countries than responsive to the voices of the world's most vulnerable workers (Khor 1994).

The question remains open: Can global institutions create labor standards that would be universally applicable but still respect international variation, while simultaneously addressing and ameliorating existing international inequalities? The recent efforts of the International Labor Organization to strike such a balance are instructive, and, so far, disappointing. Founded in 1919, the ILO is one of the oldest institutions of global governance; though it lacks any direct sanctioning mechanism other than dialog with states found to permit systematic violation of workers' rights, it is also one of the few global institutions that has long institutionalized voices from civil society, with a tripartite structure that permits representation from unions, employers, and states. In the late 1990s, the ILO persuaded its member states to agree on a set of "core" labor rights: freedom of association and the right to bargain collectively; bans on forced labor and discriminatory labor practices; and efforts to eliminate child labor. At the same time, however, the ILO was compelled by pressure from developing-country representatives to accept that for many countries job creation, rather than job regulation, came first: within the very text of its 1998 declaration on core labor rights, the ILO affirmed that "the comparative advantage of any country should in no way be called in question by this Declaration and its follow-up" (ILO 1998a). Although most of the ILO's 175 member states had ratified at least some of the core ILO conventions by 2002, it remained unclear how, or even whether, the ILO could act in defense of these core rights if developing countries insisted that do to so would undercut their "comparative advantage" in international trade.

The ILO campaign to stop pervasive use of forced labor in Myanmar may be the exception that proves the rule. In 1998, an ILO commission found "abundant evidence" that the Myanmar authorities and the military had coerced large numbers of civilians to work in forestry, portage, construction, and even in private agriculture, for no pay and often under brutal conditions (ILO 1998b). In November 2000, the ILO called on member states to impose economic sanctions on Myanmar—the first time in its eighty-two-year history that the ILO took such action. By early 2002, largely because of economic sanctions imposed or threatened by governments including the United States and the European Union, the Myanmar government began to allow political opponents to appear in public, and allowed the ILO to open a special monitoring office in Yangon (Olson 2002). But should we understand Myanmar as the harbinger of increased ILO power to call attention to international labor violations, or as an international response to a larger campaign in which the United Nations, human rights and refugee organizations, and the ILO focused on broad human rights concerns, not labor violations alone? The initial impulse for ILO action regarding Myanmar came from human rights advocates, not from labor; but even if the ILO were the key actor, the question remains whether broad economic sanctions could ever be used to protect core labor rights in situations where violations are far less egregious, extreme, or widespread.

It is perhaps an indication of the long-term difficulties involved in global institutional design that many activists, including some working within the ILO, have turned instead to the private sphere, seeking to protect labor rights in developing countries through campaigns targeting individual transnational corporations rather than states. Through corporate codes of conduct and outside monitoring, this movement seeks to submit corporations who are inadequately attentive to workers' rights to the kind of international "shaming" processes that have effectively embarrassed governments guilty of human rights violations. The Internet and international communications, it is often argued, could allow instant access to corporate violations; some scholars suggest that consumers can effectively police the conditions under which goods are made, by refusing to purchase goods made under sweatshop conditions (Fung, O'Rourke, and Sabel 2001; Oliver Williams 2001).

This approach has been particularly visible in the apparel industry, especially in that part of the market dominated by well-known labels and aimed at college-age consumers. During the past twenty years, largely in response to changes in American tariffs on foreign-made clothing, brand-name apparel companies have shifted their production outside the U.S. Instead of owning their factories, they contract with smaller companies to produce clothes; the "label" companies provide design, quality control, advertising, and access to North American markets, while the contractors supply machines, hire workers, and compete with other small producers to meet the retailers' prices (Collins 2001; Gereffi 1994; Bonacich and Appelbaum 2000). Clothing companies are perhaps especially vulnerable to human rights–style campaigns: where marketing is entwined with brand labels, major companies are sensitive to the shame of association with global sweatshops, and—under pressure from American and European student and labor activists—some major companies have responded to activists' concerns. From about 1997, several large companies in North America began to discuss the possibility of working through outside monitors to improve working conditions in factories from El Salvador to Bangladesh, while nongovernmental groups in Europe and North America embarked on well-publicized campaigns around labor rights in the apparel industry. Many more companies were discussing building oversight of subcontractors' labor conditions into their global quality-control systems (Anner 2000; Schoenberger 2000; Ross 1997).

In 2002, even the ILO had apparently turned to global corporate managers as a last line of defense for workers in developing countries. In a program funded by the U.S. State Department, ILO personnel planned to work with managers in apparel factories in Sri Lanka and Central America, arguing that companies as well as workers could benefit if global managers tried to improve working conditions. The program was aimed at

> identifying management systems and practices that enable domestic and international enterprises to achieve their economic and commercial viability goals while at the same time meeting the increased social expectations of the market and society. Issues that will be looked at will include management of networks, commodity and value chains, and management systems and practices for achieving good corporate citizenship and business social responsibility. (ILO Management Development Programme, www.ilo.org)

But as a long-term mechanism for protecting workers' rights, this approach, too, has its limits. Corporate codes of conduct, shaming, and what some business ethicists call "total responsibility management" rest on the threat of consumer boycotts of sweatshop goods; but secondary boycotts have always proved complicated for organized labor. First, of course, it is hard to keep consumers informed, even when they have access to websites; but it is even harder to persuade individual consumers to act on information. Although proponents of corporate codes of conduct point to telephone surveys in which American consumers insist that they care about the conditions under which goods are produced (Fung, O'Rourke, and Sabel 2001), most studies of actual consumer behavior suggest that price, taste, and convenience, rather than social responsibility, probably drive most purchasing decisions (Frank 1999).

And while the "branded" end of the apparel industry may be vulnerable to shaming, most transnational companies, even in apparel, are less visible—and most consumers are more price-conscious—than recent successful campaigns against Nike, Gap, and other labels favored by college students would suggest. Although efforts to develop "social labeling" have had some success in drawing attention to working conditions in specific commodities (particularly coffee and more recently bananas), most products are less clearly identifiable than branded clothing. Most labor activists recognize that few consumers will check websites daily for updates, even for items with labels; even more difficult would be the effort to mobilize boycotts against goods included as components in a larger product. For example, the ball bearings produced at a specific factory in central Mexico may be used in a wide range of products, carrying different labels; relying on transnational boycotts would require that consumers pay careful attention to new information about labor violations, and that they remember to end the boycott when the problem is solved. During a 2002 campaign by the American apparel workers' union over labor conditions in a Gap subcontractor in Guatemala, UNITE president Bruce Raynor said, "Our goal, which I think we're achieving, is to tie in the consumer mind and the public mind, Gap and sweatshops"—an association, as the *Women's Wear Daily* reporter noted, that "can be a powerful and lasting one" (Malone 2002).

And, of course, developing-country activists point to problems that parallel those that plague efforts to incorporate labor rights in trade treaties:

transnational monitoring campaigns leave the power to enforce labor rights in the hands of global managers and consumers—largely located in advanced industrial countries—rather than empowering workers in the factories facing boycotts. Who will monitor the implementation of labor standards and codes, and will those monitors acknowledge all the local, contextual variations involved in defining labor-related concerns? Moreover, while it could be argued that transnational activism around labor in export-oriented sectors might improve standards throughout the economy through a demonstration effect, transnational campaigns carry the risk that they might inadvertently weaken efforts to organize workers to speak for themselves. The threat of consumer boycotts might get corporations' attention, but they may also undermine worker organization in developing countries, especially if workers believe that a transnational boycott might threaten the enterprise's survival—and thus their long-term job prospects.

Although labor rights are increasingly discussed in universal terms, there are no ideal transnational mechanisms for protecting them; specifically, there are no mechanisms able to increase workers' leverage in relation to transnational employers, or states' leverage in relation to multinational corporations. If globalization has complicated union efforts to mobilize workers for militant strategies, internationalist strategies may introduce another set of dilemmas. Like strategies aimed at attracting "high road" jobs, most proposed international mechanisms for protecting labor rights build on the logic of the global market, and thus they tend to build on, perhaps re-create, existing global inequalities, in ways that could further undermine the ability of developing countries to protect their citizens.

Conclusion

Globalization's tendency to "thin" the national state is perhaps nowhere more visible than in relation to labor rights: dependent on multinational capital to create new jobs, developing-country states are perhaps more likely to suspend labor legislation than to enforce it in their effort to attract investment, but even advanced industrialized countries have stepped back from protection of workers' rights. National-level unions have also experienced the pressures of globalization: neoliberalism has left workers' organizations around the world grasping for the "high road," hoping that by entering into corporate efforts to increase productivity they can protect their members' jobs against ruthless global competition.

And yet it may be too soon to abandon the nation-state. As Shafir (in this volume) points out, mechanisms for enforcing and protecting citizenship rights are fairly well developed; in the case of labor rights, at least, it is hard to see how global institutions will easily improve on the national state. Over decades, if not centuries, national states—often responding to politically mobilized workers, working through democratic processes—have created viable frameworks for industrial relations, to oversee health and safety conditions at work, and to prevent employers from polluting local communities. States can pay attention to local context and variation and can deal with labor violations in specific sectors or factories more easily than the global mechanisms would allow. Above all, perhaps, there are well-established mechanisms through which states can be prompted to attend to concerns of local workers—at least, when states are democratically organized, and when they are able to insist that employers pay attention to broader interests and longer-term issues beyond immediate corporate profits.

It seems oddly ironic, given the long history of labor's reliance on citizenship claims to further workers' interests, that most suggestions for how organized labor might meet the challenges of globalization essentially overlook the state completely. Approaches that promote a "high road" growth strategy turn labor's view inward, to cooperation with corporate managers in raising productivity, and to training individual workers to compete on a volatile labor market—but these risk further dividing labor's constituency, undermining labor's political strength at the national level. Approaches that look outward tend to replace state-based mechanisms with the power of global markets—but these tend to rely heavily on the willingness and ability of advanced-country consumers to respond to labor violations in far-flung corners of the world rather than strengthening workers' capacity to demand reasonable working conditions for themselves.

Perhaps labor advocates should consider mechanisms that might strengthen, rather than surpass, state mechanisms. Efforts to broaden labor's constituency—beyond already skilled workers, to include the informal, marginalized, less-skilled workers who have historically been excluded from unions and who are especially vulnerable to the centrifugal forces of globalization—could strengthen labor's voice within national political arenas and reduce the likelihood that organized labor will be seen as representing only a relatively privileged labor aristocracy. Instead of focusing on transnational trade and corporations, perhaps international pressure could be designed to reinforce rather than bypass labor-friendly political coalitions, strengthening the possibility of national supervision and regulation of workplaces. Perhaps it could be designed to give greater voice, rather than less, to workers speaking on their own behalf.

Citizenship claims have long been articulated in opposition to the logic of the market; by contrast, labor strategies that build on the logic of global competition risk undermining the very basis of labor mobilization and the protection of workers' rights and dignity. If labor rights are to be strengthened and protected in a global era, perhaps we need to find a different logic: instead of letting the global market pressures dictate labor strategies and transnational campaigns, perhaps global institutions should seek to regulate those markets in ways that would protect workers' rights rather than further undermine them.

Notes

I am grateful to Stephen Chiu, Nadya Araujo Guimaraes, Jeff Rothstein, and Eddie Webster, for discussions in which some of these ideas were first developed; and to the editors of this volume for thoughtful comments on an earlier draft.

1. This history proved to be of continued relevance as recently as 2002, when AFL-CIO allies in Venezuela briefly supported a business-friendly coup attempt against a democratically elected populist who had angered Washington.

8

Globalized Social Reproduction
Women Migrants and the Citizenship Gap

KRISTEN HILL MAHER

The global economy has produced a great many "people out of place" whose citizenship rights have been complicated by their migration. A growing proportion of those migrating internationally are women, particularly as part of what might be called "globalized social reproduction," the counterpart to globalized production (Truong 1996: 29). Earlier in this century, most social reproduction[1] needs in developed states such as child care, elderly care, cooking, laundry, and housecleaning were supplied by private households, especially by women who carried out these tasks as full-time, unpaid work. To some extent, the welfare state offered support, even while private households remained the primary locus for social reproductive activity. However, in the late twentieth century, women in developed states joined the formal economy in larger numbers, just as neoliberal economic policies began to dismantle the welfare state. Within this context, many middle- and upper-class families turned to the market—and to "importing" labor internationally—in order to meet their social reproduction needs. The resulting "trade in domestic workers" (Heyzer, à Nijeholt, and Weerakoon 1994) involves massive flows of female migrants from less developed states to more developed states and a new "international division of reproductive labor" (Parreñas 2001).

Women who migrate as part of the household service economy are subject to the same kinds of displacement from rights regimes that all relatively poor migrants face. Their home states are not empowered (and often not motivated) to protect their citizenship rights while they are abroad. And there are significant obstacles to their making rights claims in relationship to either the host state's citizenship regime or the international human rights regime. In addition to this general quandary of displacement, migrant women also find themselves positioned in strongly gendered ways in receiving states, such that it is particularly difficult for them to make claims to rights as legal individuals. For migrants such as these, the opportunities available through migration are counterbalanced by losses in rights and citizenship.

Ironically, the women whose own rights claims are compromised by migration enable and enhance the citizenship of those in receiving states in multiple ways. First, they enable the "social citizenship" [2] of those who hire them. As neoliberal and "trickle down" reforms in Western democracies have eroded state responsibility for providing social services, citizens' access to social rights increasingly depends upon services provided privately by migrant women. Second, the labor by migrant women facilitates the entry of more first-world women into the public sphere by liberating them from the most gendered and labor-intensive aspects of social reproduction. Women who gain independent public standing have access to a fuller form of citizenship than those isolated in the domestic sphere (Shklar 1991). Third, migrant women doing the difficult labor of social reproduction also build the standing of citizens more generally, whose citizenship comes to be defined in part as the right not to do "dirty work" (Maher 1999, 2002; Anderson 2000).

The citizenship gap in the global organization of social reproduction is therefore quite complex. It is a gap between migrants and citizens in terms of the political, civil, and social rights they can claim, as well as a gap in "standing" (Shklar 1991), public presence, or status. However, the citizenship gap is also transnational, a gap in the quality of reproductive care (and hence social citizenship) between sending and receiving states. When women migrate internationally for social reproductive jobs, they enhance the quality of care in receiving states at the same time as their own families and children suffer the loss of their attention. Children can be left without parental supervision, or may be attended by relatives or low-paid child-care help (Mattingly 2001; Hondagneu-Sotelo 1997). In any of these circumstances, the children of female migrants and those who care for them indirectly absorb some of the costs of first-world social reproduction. The transfer of female labor from less developed to more developed states initiates a transnational "chain of care" that exacerbates international inequalities.

Globalized social reproduction strategies thus have a whole series of unfortunate (and largely unintended) effects that enhance the citizenship rights of those who consume household services while undermining those of the migrant women who provide them. While this citizenship gap is troubling, it can be moderated through political action and policy change enacted in local, state, and international arenas. This chapter reviews recent patterns of women's migration, explains how the globalization of social reproduction creates a citizenship gap between migrant women and others in receiving states, and offers recommendations that would help mitigate the loss of citizenship and rights among migrant domestic workers. The analysis draws on my empirical work on domestic workers in southern California (Maher 1999, 2002), as well as on comparative literatures on women's migration, domestic work, and citizenship.

The Feminization of Migration

In the past twenty years, international migration flows have been significantly feminized, a trend that has captured the attention of both scholars and international organizations like the United Nations and the International Labor Organization.[3] In order to make sense of the increase in women's migration, it is necessary to consider both the conditions under which migrants are leaving home and the labor demand that draws them to particular receiving states.

One critical dimension of female migration has to do with conditions in sending states, such as the Philippines, Indonesia, Sri Lanka, India, Moldova, Mexico, Peru, and El Salvador. The governments in states that send female migrants abroad often actively promote the migration of their citizens, as migrant remittances serve as a key source of foreign currency. Migrant labor is an "export commodity" that can help balance their reliance upon foreign imports (Chin 1998; Pettman 1996; Parreñas 2001; Enloe 1989). In the Philippines, one of the biggest exporters of female labor internationally, migrant remittances are second only to electronics manufacturing as a source of foreign currency to help pay the country's foreign debt (Parreñas 2001: 52). The Philippine government has begun calling overseas migrants "national heroes" for fulfilling this role. President Vicente Fox of Mexico has also recently begun to call migrant workers "heroes," in contrast to the long-standing position in Mexico that migrants are national traitors who abandoned their home country for greener pastures. This shift in rhetoric appears to mark a new realization of how critical these migrants' remittances are to the Mexican economy. Even in states that are fairly new recipients of foreign domestic workers, such as Lebanon, the "maid trade" is active enough to produce an estimated $10 million per month in remittances (Jureidini 2002).

In addition to providing foreign currency, migration reduces the pressure of unemployment in contexts where there is substantial economic displacement. Economic liberalization policies in developing states tend to disrupt traditional economic structures. These disruptions and the inflation that accompanies it leave many families without the means to support themselves without sending at least one member to work elsewhere as a waged migrant worker (Sassen 1998; Small 1997). Increasingly, young women are the ones who leave home for work abroad.

Why women? A number of scholars suggest that patriarchy is "a hidden cause of migration for women" (Parreñas 2001: 69; see also Anderson 2000; Pettman 1996, 1999; Enloe 1989). Although women and men are both affected by economic displacement and the relatively weak position of third-world states in the global economy, sexual inequalities in sending states contribute to female migration flows. For instance, the segmentation of labor markets by sex limit women's occupational opportunities, and women tend to be paid less for comparable work. Patriarchal relations within families also influence migration, as women flee from highly scripted, subordinated female roles in their home communities (Small 1997) or from abusive marital relationships that they are not permitted to leave by divorce (Parreñas 2001: 66–69; Enloe 1989).

The most widely studied migrations are those that follow a south to north, or third- to first-world pattern. However, we are also seeing a great deal of migration between developing states, such as from countries like the Philippines, Peru, and Sri Lanka to countries like Hong Kong, Malaysia, Chile, Lebanon, and Bahrain (Heyzer *et al.* 1994; Constable 1997; Chin 1998; Maher and Staab 2003; Jureidini 2002; al-Najjar 2002).

The gap in economic development between sending and receiving states is an obvious part of why migration occurs and which flows develop. However, migration scholars (for example, Castles and Miller 1993; Sassen 1999) are quick to point out that international migrations are not simply random flows from poverty to wealth, like water flowing downhill into valleys. Some poor states send very few migrants, and migrants do not simply travel to the nearest advanced economy. Instead, migration flows tend to be limited in time and scope and to follow relatively predictable patterns. For instance, many migration patterns reflect what Saskia Sassen (1998) calls military, economic, or postcolonial "linkages," such as those between the Philippines and the United States, or between Peru and Spain. And, to some extent, they reflect the emigration policies of sending states, such that there is much greater female emigration from the Philippines and Mexico, which encourage migration in order to secure remittances, than there is from Bangladesh, which disallows female migration despite its potential economic benefits. Nana Oishi (2002) argues that female migration patterns also depend upon the extent to which it is considered culturally acceptable for a woman to leave her immediate family's household for work.

Women from less developed economies who had limited occupational options at home tend to have even fewer choices upon migration. Most common are "flexible" production work of some sort; sex work or other work in the entertainment industry; and domestic work or home care. Most female migrants from less developed states find themselves channeled into one of these three lines of work, even if they have training and experience in another field. In addition to these three kinds of work, we also see a growing number of women migrating for mail-order marriage, an old-fashioned practice that is—remarkably—on the rise, involving women with very similar demographics as those who end up in sex work or domestic work (Sinke 2001; Simons 1999). There has also been some growth in the number of women migrating for nursing or other health care work, although this pattern appears to be more common in the United States than it is in most other industrialized states. This chapter focuses specifically on domestic workers, given that their labor is central to the international organization of social reproduction.

In order to make sense of the increase in female migration, and especially migration for domestic work, we also need to consider the dynamics of the labor demand in receiving states. I have already mentioned that the demand for domestic workers has to do with the entry of more women into the formal economy and the neoliberal dismantling of the welfare state. But let me complicate this picture a bit more.

A number of scholars link the growing demand for foreign domestic workers to a cultural shift in receiving states, in which the norms of hygiene, leisure, and child rearing in middle-class life have become unsustainable without hiring household workers (Hondagneu-Sotelo 2001; Maher 2001). Houses are bigger, landscaping more complex, the cult of domesticity more demanding, and the standards for early childhood development more rigorous. Simply maintaining this lifestyle is a very labor-intensive process. Similarly, the very presence of servants helps maintain the class image, not only of the very wealthy, but also of the middle classes in many receiving states. Christine B. N. Chin's (1998) study in Malaysia notes that middle-class families have begun marking their class identities both domestically and internationally by hiring foreign domestic workers. The same is arguably true in southern California (Maher 1999; Maher & Staab 2003).

Another critical element in understanding the demand for foreign domestic workers is the organization of social reproduction and gender. Like in sending countries, the market for domestic workers in receiving states is structured by gendered inequalities, and especially by the relegation of social reproduction work to women. Once women entered the paid labor force, a veritable crisis in social reproduction threatened. Who would care for the children and the elderly? How will the daily tasks necessary to maintaining a family get done? Rather than challenging the gendered division of labor or making demands upon the government to take more responsibility for developing comprehensive child care and elderly care programs, the hiring of foreign domestic workers has tended to maintain the tradition of domestic labor as women's work—simply shifting the burden from one set of women to another. In the United States, migrant women not only staff businesses that provide house cleaning, child care, and elderly care, but they also are hired by individual families to provide in-house (including live-in) services. Live-in domestic service is a premodern social form that had almost completely disappeared by the mid-twentieth century, but has reappeared since the 1970s (Hondagneu-Sotelo 2001). The growth of live-in arrangements is also apparent internationally: one of the appeals of foreign domestic workers is that they are more likely than someone with a family nearby to accept live-in working conditions (Anderson 2000), which in all contexts tend to be plagued by physical and sexual abuse, a loss of independence and social networks, and very long and even unending workdays.

This solution to the crisis of social reproduction has appeal to the state, insofar as it is absolved from needing to increase social spending, and insofar as foreign workers make possible greater economic productivity by native-born workers. It appeals to intermediaries such as placement agencies, human smugglers, money wiring services, and others who make a profit from the increased migration of workers. It appeals to tired women who find themselves responsible for a "double shift" in their households. It appeals to men who wish to maintain the sexual division of labor. And this solution is widely affordable not only to the wealthiest classes but also to middle-class families. In some parts of the United States, even working-class families are beginning to hire in-home foreign domestic workers (Maher 1999). It is important to note that the affordability of migrant women's labor is structured not only by the wage gap between states, but also by the racialization and gendering of domestic labor, a topic discussed more fully in a later section.

The Social and Legal Position of Domestic Workers

Women who migrate internationally for domestic work tend to be socially and legally marginalized in ways that undermine their capacity to make rights claims. In part, their vulnerability stems from the fact and conditions of their migration. People who migrate from less developed states to more developed states often fall between the cracks of available rights regimes, and domestic workers are no exception. However, women who perform domestic service are also marginalized by virtue of the kind of work they do, which is gendered, racialized, and "private," such that state interventions or rights protections are complicated both practically and culturally. That is, migrant domestic workers experience the citizenship gap both because they have migrated internationally and because they are socially situated in a position from which rights claims are particularly difficult. I will discuss each of these sources of vulnerability below before turning to assess the potential for various means of mitigating the loss of rights and citizenship.

Vulnerabilities as Migrants

As people out of place, migrants tend to fall between citizenship regimes, not fully eligible for citizenship rights in sending states or in receiving states. Hypothetically, a migrant has multiple bases for rights claims. She can make claims to rights in relation to her home state as a citizen abroad (external citizenship), in relation to a receiving state as a noncitizen resident (alien or denizen rights), and in relation to international human rights regimes as a human being (universal personhood) (see Bauböck 1991; Soysal 1994). However, in practice, there are significant limitations to each of these venues for migrants' claims to rights, particularly for those from less developed states and for women migrants.

According to Rainer Bauböck (1991), the rights of external citizenship, or those aspects of a person's citizenship that she retains when she is not a resident of her home state, vary a great deal depending on the relative power and the policies of the sending country. Most commonly, external citizenship includes the right of return and the right to own or inherit property in the home state; less commonly, it may include the right to continue to participate politically while abroad. Those migrating from powerful countries with a strong diplomatic presence in receiving countries may also experience active intervention by their home state in protection of their rights. Migrating from the United States, for instance, entails relatively few risks of a loss of fundamental rights, given this country's strong presence abroad. In contrast, migration from less powerful and less developed states, particularly those that devalue or discourage migration, can be a very risky endeavor indeed. For instance, in Bahrain—where foreign workers comprised an estimated 64 percent of the workforce in 2000 and almost every household employs at least one domestic worker—major sending states such as Sri Lanka and Indonesia do not have any diplomatic presence at all. Other sending states such as India and Bangladesh do have embassies in Bahrain, but they are reluctant to have any relations with their nationals working in domestic service (al-Najjar 2002).[4] Similarly, in Lebanon, sending states without formal diplomatic presence, such as Madagascar, Ethiopia, and Vietnam, rely upon an "appointed honorary consul," who is an unpaid Lebanese national working on commission for services, and who serves to recruit labor more than to protect migrants (Jureidini 2002).[5]

Even those developing states that encourage migration and celebrate migrants as "national heroes" have not had a strong record of successfully protecting their citizens abroad. The Philippines has an active embassy in Lebanon, where tens of thousands of Filipina women work. The embassy serves important functions, such as providing legal assistance for migrants, providing mediation in labor disputes, and promoting a standard labor contract. However, they too are relatively powerless when it comes to enforcing labor contracts, as the Lebanese government has prosecuted very few employers who violate the contractual terms of employment, abuse workers, or withhold payment or passports. There are also more serious cases of migrants charged with murder, or who "commit suicide" under very suspicious conditions, and "no Lebanese have been charged or found guilty of such crimes against foreign domestic workers" (Jureidini 2002). These kinds of cases serve as bitter symbols for other migrant domestic workers about their vulnerability and their home states' lack of commitment to them. Indeed, states that rely strongly upon foreign aid and migrant remittances may be unwilling as well as unable to take a strong stance on migrants' behalf if doing so would mean jeopardizing economic gains.

Labor migrants also have limited options to claim rights in relationship to the states in which they are employed. In part, their rights claims depend upon the terms of their entry, whether they are authorized as permanent residents (also called "denizens" or "landed immigrants") or as aliens with temporary work permits, or whether they migrate without documentation. These three categories are accompanied by diminishing formal rights, from permanent residents, who can often claim most of the rights of citizenship, to undocumented migrants, who cannot make legal claim to any but the most basic of civil rights (Bauböck 1991). Among the latter, the migration process itself often entails rights abuses by smuggling or trafficking networks, by criminals who prey on vulnerable migrants, or even by corrupt state authorities.[6] Women migrants lacking financial or social capital are particularly vulnerable to trafficking or abuses in transit.

Scholars have identified two opposing patterns in relation to the rights of migrants in receiving states. On the one hand, there is some evidence that receiving states (particularly those in the EU) have been expanding the rights of all migrants, given the emergence of human rights norms in international law (Soysal 1994; Jacobson 1996). Yasemin Soysal argues that the human rights regime, in which rights are based on universal "personhood," is beginning to replace the nation-state regime that conceives of rights in more exclusive terms based on national membership. Within this international human rights regime, states have more accountability to protect the rights of both migrants and citizens, and migrants have some potential to make demands in relation to international treaties on human and migrant rights. Soysal offers evidence that human rights norms do, in fact, shape and constrain state policies regarding migrants in the EU. These international norms have had particular influence on the status of permanent residents or denizens, whose civil and social rights resemble those of citizens in some receiving states (Hollifield 1992).

On the other hand, there is also evidence of cultural and policy trends that move in the opposite direction. Many Western democracies have experienced a resurgence of nationalist sentiment and mobilization in the past decade, much of it targeting migrants. Right-wing parties with anti-immigration platforms have gained political strength in many European states, and neo-Nazi and other anti-migrant activities have continued despite elite discourse about human rights (Stolcke 1999; Bhabha 1999; Martin 1999). In the United States, the 1990s saw shifts in policy that served to reinforce the division between citizens and aliens, making both documented and undocumented migrants less eligible for social services and, in some cases, even for basic civil rights (Maher 2002). In the post–September 11 political atmosphere of homeland security enforcement in the United States, boundaries are being drawn even more strongly around citizenship in relation to many forms of foreign presence. These kinds of political and cultural trends toward reinforcing rights based on nation-state identity or membership make rights claims based on universal personhood less feasible.

One of the hot-button issues for anti-immigrant politics in Western receiving states is the provision of social services to noncitizens, given a popular perception that noncitizens place too much of a strain on public coffers. These kinds of concerns have tended to target female migrants in particular, given that women are seen as more likely than the traditional solo male to use social services and to have needs related to motherhood or children. In the United

States, where all children born on U.S. soil have citizenship, the concerns about female migrants' fertility and their families' potential claims on social services have been especially vocal in the past decade (Hondagneu-Sotelo 1995; Chavez 1997). Similarly, even while international treaties on migrant rights have emphasized family reunification as a fundamental right, popular sentiment has not always supported national policies promoting it. Hence, labor migration often breaks up families, making long-distance care and transnational motherhood necessary (Mattingly 2001; Hondagneu-Sotelo 1997).

Migration itself is an important right, and in some cases it permits economic mobility, independence, and even a means of escape for women who might otherwise be trapped in abusive situations. In this sense, some female migrants may be more empowered and have greater practical access to rights after migration than they would have had at home. However, migration also complicates citizenship for migrant women who have little protection from their home state while they are abroad and highly constrained possibilities for rights claims comparable to those of citizenship.

Vulnerabilities as Domestic Workers

Migrant domestic workers not only are displaced from their home institutions, but also occupy a position in receiving countries from which it is particularly difficult to claim legal rights or full personhood before the law. Because social reproduction work has traditionally been located in the household and performed by women, migrant domestic workers' position differs somewhat from that of laborers working in the formal economy. That is, their employers tend to think of them as filling the role of the "traditional woman" in the household, a position that is dependent, subordinated, feminized, sometimes racialized, and typically considered outside the bounds of civil society or the public sphere. Despite the great strides that have been achieved toward equality for women in most developed states, the traditional, subordinated feminine position has not been abandoned; rather, it is gradually being shifted from one group of women to another, from citizens to migrants. This position creates significant obstacles for migrant domestic workers to claim even those rights that are legally available and to secure some sort of protection from physical and sexual abuse as well as from violations of labor rights.

Part of the problem comes from the nature of the work itself, which is informal, unregulated, and imagined to be private rather than public. My use of the terms *private* and *public* follows that of feminist theorists (for example, Lister 1997; Pateman 1988) who observe that—along with industrialization and the emergence of liberal, capitalist society—a divide was constructed between the public sphere of politics and economics, and the private sphere of domestic life and social reproduction. The public sphere was imagined to be characterized by autonomous, self-interested behavior, as well as the implicit egalitarianism that accompanied liberal notions of democratic citizenship.

In contrast, the private sphere came to be imagined as a space characterized by sacrifice, devotion, dependence, and inequality. This divide was strongly gendered, as the qualities of the private sphere came to be understood as properly feminine characteristics and as women's dependent position as part of a household made them ineligible for full participation in public matters or independent existence as legal beings.

The public-private divide and the gendered division of labor in the household have long compromised women's legal claims and practical experiences of citizenship (Lister 1997). They also significantly shape the daily life and work conditions of domestic workers, who occupy the anomalous position of waged workers in the private sphere. The situation of migrant domestic workers resembles that of most female household workers historically. The relationship between workers and employers tends to be personalistic rather than contractual, such that domestic workers have trouble holding their employers accountable for fair working conditions and hours. Their job responsibilities (like those of the traditional housewife) tend to be ill-defined: they are commonly expected to provide service and support whenever a need arises in order to keep the household going. These open-ended, ever changing expectations lie "at the root of subserviance, the essence of which is not the performance of a concrete, defined task, but of being at the beck and call of another—of pleasing another without reciprocation" (Rubbo and Taussig 1978: 19). In addition, employers often do not conceive of the labor performed by domestic workers as "work" at all, in the same way that many woman's household labor tends to be discounted as activities that women do as a natural outgrowth of their femininity or domestic devotion. For instance, in a 1997 field study on domestic work in southern California, I observed many instances of employers who rejected potential domestic workers because they appeared to "just be in it for the money," as if even a complete stranger should be willing to labor long hours in service to their family simply because it is her feminine nature to nurture and serve others (Maher 1999). Most comparative studies of domestic work evince similar patterns in places as diverse as Hong Kong, Spain, Bolivia, and Canada (compare Constable 1997; Anderson 2000; Gill 1994; Bakan and Stasiulis 1994, 1995).

These circumstances all relate to the gendered, privatized nature of the position domestic workers occupy. A woman working in the private household is not thought to hold a "real job" subject to labor laws or minimum wage restrictions.[7] Like other women who have occupied the position of the "traditional woman" in the private household, domestic workers are often perceived not as individuals (with individual rights) but as subordinates subsumed under the head of the household's will and public personage. These circumstances constrain the rights claims of any worker who does paid household labor (Lister 1997).

Although all paid domestic work has in common the gendered construction of the job, there are *significant differences among domestic workers* in the daily conditions of their employment and their relative empowerment to make claims to labor rights. Based on a comparative, historical study in the United States, Evelyn Nakano Glenn (1992) argues that reproductive labor in this context has long been divided along racial as well as gender lines, and that within the "racial division of paid reproductive labor" the least pleasant, repetitive, or "dirty" jobs have been relegated to the women with the lowest social status or power. She notes that racial-ethnic women have largely borne the brunt of the dirty work since the 1920s, although the particular racial-ethnic group varied by region: African-American women in the South, Chicanas and Mexicanas in the Southwest, and Japanese and Chinese women in the Northwest and Hawaii (Glenn 1992: 8–10). In places where working-class white women also performed domestic work, they were generally hired for the most desirable jobs.

These historical patterns resemble the current hierarchy among women performing household labor in the United States, where there is a striking division in the status, pay, and professional image between white and racial-ethnic women. White women in high-end nanny or home care markets are generally able to represent themselves as professionals whose responsibilities are regulated by contracts.[8] In contrast, racial-ethnic women more often find themselves positioned as household servants. While citizenship, permanent residency, English language skills, good references, and independent transportation all translate into better-paying jobs among racial-ethnic women, their average salaries are lower than those of white women.[9] They are also more likely to work in jobs with ill-defined tasks and hours and with less room to exert control over the terms of their employment.

Live-in domestic service—the lowest status and lowest paid position in the hierarchy of household labor—is almost exclusively performed by migrant women from less developed states. The growing demand for live-in workers (particularly in the Northeast and Southwest) since the 1980s has been met in part by a growing industry of agencies that place immigrant women in private homes (Maher 2004). What we see operating in these patterns is not just a racial but also an international division of social reproductive labor (Parreñas 2001). The process of social reproduction is being effectively globalized.

The patterns evident in the United States bear a strong resemblance to those internationally, in which a growing market for migrant domestic workers rests on a division of labor shaped by race, nativity, and legal status as well as gender and class. For instance, Abigail B. Bakan and Daiva K. Stasiulis (1995) describe the ideologies and practices of agencies that recruit and place foreign live-in caregivers in Toronto, Canada. Most live-in caregivers in this context are Filipina, although there are also women from Europe, the United Kingdom, and the English Caribbean. These authors found that placement agencies actively projected racialized and gendered stereotypes about workers from different origins, and that these stereotypes helped maintain the "racial ranking within domestic employment hierarchies" (307). The representations of Filipinas exhibited a familiar double edge. On the one hand, some agencies represented Filipinas as "inherently suitable to perform domestic service" (313)—in contrast to Canadian women or men, for whom such work was assumed to be inappropriately demeaning. On the other hand, some agency heads and employers also believed that Filipinas were in some sense *too* debased (that is, not adequately "cultured" or professional) to effectively stimulate or care for children.

Bakan and Stasiulis also illustrate the ways that racialized stereotypes reflect workers' relative power. Caribbean caregivers were much more positively perceived (and praised as naturally suitable for domestic work) before they began to participate in visible organizing for domestic workers' rights in the early 1980s; afterwards, they were effectively blackballed by employers and placement agencies, who began to recruit Filipinas in much higher numbers, praising their passivity and respect for authority. As Filipinas have begun to organize to challenge exploitative conditions in recent years, these constructions have also shifted in a more negative direction (Bakan and Stasiulis 1995: 319–23; 1994: 23–24).

Ray Jureidini's (2002) study of migrant domestic workers in Lebanon also shows evidence of a racialized hierarchy, in which Filipinas, who carry higher prestige because they are perceived as educated and literate in English, are at the top. They make double the salary of Sri Lankan or African domestic workers,[10] and cost employers up to $2,000 in placement agency fees, in contrast to $1,000 for Sri Lankan or African workers. However, foreign domestic workers of all nationalities are subject to the same long hours, vulnerabilities to abuse by employers or agency personnel, and extremely restrictive daily conditions, in which they have virtually no mobility, leisure time, or independence. Additionally, the overall status of domestic work lowered as household positions began to be filled by non-Arab foreign women. Prior to about 1993, Lebanese families used to hire primarily young Arab women in their years before marriage, but once migrant domestic workers became more common, "such positions have come to be seen by Arab women as degrading and unacceptable. . . . This is not only because of the servile nature of the tasks, the conditions of work and relative low wages, but also because there is now a racial attachment to domestic employment" (Jureidini 2002: 2).

Studies in other international contexts repeat similar stories about the growing popularity of women workers from less developed areas for household labor, the racialization of domestic workers' position, and the workers' relative disempowerment (Constable 1997; Gill 1994; Chin 1998; Anderson 2000; al-Najjar 2002). Collectively, these studies suggest that the demand for migrant domestic workers is not solely the result of a need for social reproduction labor. It is also a desire for a certain *kind of person* who can fill a degraded, subordinated, dependent role within the household (Maher 1999; Maher &

Staab 2003; Anderson 2000). For reasons of economic inequalities, racial and gender constructions, state policies, and the displacement of migration itself, third-world women fit the bill.

The racialized and gendered constructions of migrant domestic workers' position have significant consequences for their daily working conditions and their capacities to make claims to rights. The potential for exploitation of domestic workers is in some part inherent to the job, which is commonly seen as beyond the scope of regulation by civil or international law. However, racism (and international class status) "deepens and provides additional legitimation for such exploitation" (Bakan and Stasiulis 1994: 24). When employers' expectations are to obtain a cheap, passive, natural subordinate to do the dirty work of social reproduction, the potential for workers to make claims to rights premised on universal equality seems quite limited.

The potential for migrant domestic workers to make rights claims is also limited by their commodification in a global market. When labor recruiters, brokers, and agencies represent migrant women as "merchandise" for sale (with different prices for different nationalities, like brand names), it is no wonder that employers tend to talk about "picking one [worker] up," as if they were purchasing a household appliance instead of hiring an employee (Maher 1999). Employers who "purchase" a domestic worker thereby tend to feel entitled to control her whole being rather than simply entering into a labor contract (Maher 2004; Anderson 2000). This feeling of entitlement or ownership underlies many of the specific kinds of abuses domestic workers tend to face, from employers who make claims on their bodies, to those who regulate what workers eat and wear, to those who make workers virtual captives in the house with no freedom of movement or social contacts even during nonworking hours.

Finally, racialized and gendered constructions of migrant domestic workers affect popular perceptions of the suitability of migrant workers as prospective citizens or full members of society. When the appeal of such workers is in part premised on assumptions that they are appropriately debased for demeaning work, there would need to be a significant shift in perception to have them later seen as civic equals. The relations of domestic service reflect existing social hierarchies, but they also shape and reinforce them (Colen 1990; Anderson 2000; Rubbo and Taussig 1978; Rollins 1985). The globalization of social reproduction reinscribes not only gender, race, and class divisions, but also the "social boundaries of citizenship" (Bakan and Stasiulis 1994). In this regard, globalized domestic service involves cultural and ideological reproduction as well as the maintenance and reproduction of the labor force.

Immigration policies often exacerbate rather than help these circumstances. For instance, some states (including the United States) have special guest worker visa programs for other sectors of the economy that rely heavily on migrant labor, but have no equivalent visa for domestic work, given that this labor is seen as private and personalistic. These states thereby virtually force women who migrate for these jobs to do so without documentation and to rely on trafficking networks for passage, circumstances that can leave women vulnerable not only to dangers and abuse in transit but also to sex trafficking (see Scanlan, forthcoming). Other states, like Canada, Spain, and Lebanon, do have special visas for live-in domestic workers, but they link the visa to continued employment or approval by employers, an arrangement that can resemble indentured servitude. In Lebanon, each live-in domestic worker is bound to her employer unless both the employer and the state authorities agree to release her.[11] The employer usually keeps her passport, rendering her both paperless and an illegal alien should she quit the job. These circumstances make live-in domestic workers effectively "unfree labour" (Jureidini 2002), given the coercive cooperation of state authorities and private employers. Either of these kinds of policies for domestic worker immigration—no visa access, or visas subject to employer control—undercuts the potential for rights protection. In a five-country study in Europe, Bridget Anderson (2000) found that the domestic workers most likely to suffer sexual, physical, or psychological abuses at the hands of their employers were those who were either undocumented or whose continued legal status tied them to a particular employer.

The Citizenship Gap in a Global Division of Social Reproductive Labor

Up to this point, I have argued that labor migrants experience lessened citizenship because they tend to fall between citizenship regimes. Women migrants performing social reproduction labor in the private sphere are particularly vulnerable to a loss of rights, given the ideologies of race, gender, and class that inform both daily practices in the household and state policies. These patterns alone illustrate a citizenship gap between migrants and citizens of receiving states. However, an ironic twist to this story is that migrant domestic workers also *enhance the citizenship of those in receiving states*, further widening the gap.

Most critically, foreign domestic workers enable the social citizenship of those who hire them. Neoliberal and "trickle down" reforms in Western democracies have eroded state responsibility for providing social rights in places with a strong tradition of social services, such as Canada, France, and Germany. Other states, like the United States, arguably never fully developed a concept of social citizenship (Fraser and Gordon 1998). In both kinds of states, many citizens' access to social rights now depends in part on services provided privately by migrant women, particularly the care they provide for children, the disabled, and the elderly. In effect, this transnational economy of social reproductive labor privatizes what otherwise would be state responsibilities toward citizens.

The labor by migrant women also enhances the citizenship of female employers, who become freer to take part politically and economically in the public sphere. Men's earning power has traditionally been subsidized by women's unpaid social reproduction work. When families hire migrant women to perform this social reproduction labor, both men *and* women have their earning power subsidized by the low-paid labor of migrants. In effect, hired domestic workers increase female employers' earning potential, while liberating them from the most gendered, "demeaning," and labor-intensive aspects of social reproduction work. Women who gain independent public standing have access to a fuller form of citizenship than those isolated in the domestic sphere (Shklar 1991).

This circumstance is not limited to migrant domestic workers, of course. The history of domestic work has long been a tale of privileged women gaining class status by hiring other women to do household labor. To some extent, women's entry into the public sphere in the past century has also relied on paid domestic labor: the early women's movement in the United States gained momentum in part because of "other" women doing domestic work in the homes of suffragettes. This issue has been a sticking point in the feminist movement, which has tried to build solidarity among women *as women*, when in fact different women have very different social positions, needs, and interests. With the turn toward social reproduction strategies that rely upon migrants, new divisions in the feminist movement emerge, making necessary "Third World feminisms" (Mohanty, Russo, and Torres 1991) grounded in the experiences and interests of women at the bottom of the international division of labor (Nash and Fernandez-Kelly 1983).[12]

Finally, migrant women doing the difficult labor of social reproduction also build the standing of citizens more generally. The counterpoint of constructions of third-world domestic workers as "appropriate" for demeaning household labor but unworthy of citizenship is that citizenship itself comes to be defined in part as the right not to do "dirty work" (Maher 1999; Anderson 2000). Geraldine Pratt's (1997) study of nanny agencies in Vancouver, Canada, includes apt illustrations of this understanding of citizenship. As one agent she interviewed expressed, "I don't think that there is a Canadian desire to be a nanny. As parents, we don't raise our children to be nannies." Another agent noted, "Society says that white ladies are not nannies. I mean can you imagine someone from Maple Street whose daughter goes to Kits [High School] as being a nanny? I don't think so. We don't bring up our people to do that" (162). These quotes illustrate an understanding of Canadian-ness and whiteness that are antithetical to the socially degraded status of jobs like nannying. "Our people," or real Canadians, should not do this kind of work. Canadian citizenship in this case is understood not only as a legal status, but also as a social standing (Shklar 1991) reflecting class, race, and national position in the international economic order.

In these ways, the globalization of social reproduction lessens migrants' citizenship at the same time as it enables and enhances the citizenship of those in receiving societies. The citizenship gap might therefore be conceived as the difference in citizenship rights and standing that these two groups can claim. However, from a broader perspective, we might also see elements of the citizenship gap operating between sending and receiving societies more generally. The globalization of social reproduction involves a complex chain by which social rights are effectively transferred from people in less developed states to those who employ migrants in more developed states.

Many of the women who migrate for social reproductive work are themselves mothers in their twenties and thirties[13] whose children remain behind in their home country, cared for by relatives or by paid child care workers. The "transnational families" (Small 1997; Hondagneu-Sotelo 1997) created by globalized social reproduction therefore pass responsibilities for caretaking down a female "chain" that is least compensated at the bottom. Consider a typical scenario for this chain of caretaking (Parreñas 2001; Hochschild 2000; Maher 1999). A professional woman in Los Angeles who earns a salary of $4,000 per month in the formal market hires a migrant woman from Guanajuato, Mexico for $800 per month to care for her children and elderly father and to perform some housekeeping. The migrant woman hires a woman living in Guanajuato to care for her own children remaining there, paying her $100 per month. This Mexican woman might then depend upon the unpaid labor of a female relative to care for her elderly parents.

While the details and geography of this chain may vary, it has a number of general effects. Most obviously, the wealth and care occurring at the top of the chain is subsidized by low-paid and unpaid female labor further down.[14] When social reproductive needs in the first world are met through global markets rather than through the welfare state, less developed countries end up providing an indirect subsidy through low-paid and unpaid labor, exacerbating already existing economic inequalities internationally. There may be less obvious consequences as well. In a study of the networks of caring labor in the global economy, Doreen Mattingly (2001) found that the female children of migrant domestic workers experienced a significantly different kind of childhood than those whose families hired a migrant nanny. While girls with a migrant nanny were able to invest time in their studies as well as lessons in music, drama, and dance, the female children of migrant domestic workers were expected to do household work and babysitting in their mothers' absence. Children further down the class-based chain may end up bearing some of the costs of others' opportunities and privilege.[15]

The migration of women for domestic work is not without its benefits for individual women, who thereby have the potential to gain both financial and social independence. Migration permits access to capital that may not be available in the home state, and it tends to be accompanied by empowerment for women in relation to their own families and expected gender roles. The remittances of domestic workers are at times essential to their families' care and well-being, and they can facilitate the mobility of children who are more able to invest in education. Women's migration for domestic work is not itself a problem; however, the system by which people in more developed states are importing migrant women for their social reproduction needs does have costs for the sending state, for migrants' families, and for the migrants themselves. The citizenship gap is an unfortunate byproduct of globalized social reproduction strategies.

Recommendations

What might be done about the citizenship gap in the case of migrant domestic workers? Clearly, ending migration is not an option, nor would it be desirable, given the benefits for workers and their families that are possible from spatial mobility and higher earnings. Instead, the following courses of action would help mitigate the worst of the effects of globalized social reproduction.

Eliminate the Position of the "Traditional Woman" within the Household. Rather than passing this subordinated role from one group of women to another, we ultimately need to make it obsolete. The problem is not that women are doing paid domestic work, but that the work is socially constructed as private, degraded, subordinated, and "natural" to women rather than being valued, contracted employment. One partial remedy would be for men to adopt their share of household and caring responsibilities, a long-term project of the women's movement. Another would be to have adequate state support for social reproduction needs, given the current reality of family structures that are increasingly nuclear rather than extended, and that often lack an adult available to work without pay on a full-time basis. Most critical will be the shift from thinking of domestic tasks as "dirty work that demeans those who do it" to a view of such work as a key pillar of both economic production and human development. This kind of cultural shift is unlikely to happen quickly or easily, but it must remain part of any agenda aimed at mitigating the inequalities of globalized social reproduction.

Bring Paid Domestic Work into the Realm of Contracted Employment Subject to Civil Labor Laws and State Regulation. Like the previous point, this plan of action requires a cultural shift—in this case, a willingness to expand the scope of the civil sphere to include paid household employment, rather than thinking of domestic work as a natural part of the private sphere beyond governmental intervention. This cultural shift seems entirely plausible in the short run, particularly in Western societies in which there is some precedent. For instance, the women's movement in the West has managed to transform domestic abuse and child abuse from private misdeeds—or even prerogatives—into crimes with civil consequences. There is no reason that there could not be a similar disruption of the public-private divide in the case of paid household labor. Labor laws in receiving states need to apply to household workers (as they often do not at present), and there should be a clear, accessible means for workers to seek restitution for breaches of contract or abuse, regardless of their legal status. This shift would certainly be easier to achieve if existing labor organizations more fully embraced domestic workers (and others performing "women's work") as people whose concerns belong on labor's political agenda. In the United States, labor organizations have begun to pay more attention to the service sector in addition to traditional manufacturing concerns, and have also recently embraced immigrants as compatriots with common interests rather than competitors for jobs. These changes bode well for the labor movement's potential to expand its base to household service as well.

Reform Immigration Policies that Leave Migrant Domestic Workers Vulnerable to Abuse by Traffickers, Labor Brokers, and Employers. States that import social reproduction labor need to implement or extend visa programs in such a way that women who migrate for domestic work do not need to do so without documentation. Work permits matter a great deal to migrants' potential to make rights claims in relation to host states.[16] They make the actual migration process less dangerous and make it harder for employers to use the threat of deportation coercively. However, these work permits must not be contingent upon continued employment with a single employer, and, certainly, employers must not have control over migrants' passports or other legal documents. In order to avoid near-indentured conditions of work, domestic workers need the freedom to choose and change employers. Finally, work permits should ideally include the option for eventual denizen status or citizenship, particularly if migrants are resident in a host state for a long time. Long-term labor migrants have some normative claim on membership in the host society (Carens 1989; Bauböck 1991) and should not be kept as a legally subordinate service caste, particularly in societies that call themselves democratic.

Encourage the Active Diplomatic Presence of States that Send Migrants in States that Receive them. While most sending states have very limited capacity to protect their nationals abroad, embassies can still serve important functions in relation to migrants. Most critically, they have the potential to enhance the external citizenship rights of migrant workers, such that the migration process does not entail leaving all citizenship rights at the border. They can potentially serve as safe houses for victims of trafficking or abuse. They can help promote a contractual basis for employment, mediate contract disputes, and provide legal assistance and information resources for those who need them. While not all embassies actually serve these functions, labor migrants would certainly benefit if they did.

Establish Bilateral or Multilateral Agreements between Sending and Receiving States. One precedent of such a plan is for bilateral agreements between states that each receive migrants from the other, granting the other state's migrants the equivalent of citizenship rights. Such agreements are most likely between states of roughly equal economic status that experience mutual migration, such as Sweden and Finland (Bauböck 1991). Most migration for social reproduction work does not fall into this category, marked as it is by economic (and often racial) inequality. However, bilateral agreements on the admission and rights of labor migrants may still be possible, particularly if both states acknowledge their interdependence—one dependent on imported labor, and the other on migrant remittances. Less likely but equally worthy as a goal would be bilateral agreements acknowledging the responsibility of receiving states for the costs that labor migration incurs in the sending society, particularly in relation to the care of children and the elderly in transnational families. In addition, multilateral agreements about the rights of migrants may be possible between states that respect and agree to the international human rights norms that underlie UN conventions and ILO treaties. Given its almost universal ratification, the Convention on the Elimination of All Forms of Discrimination against Women (CEDAW) might be an appropriate instrument if it were to include provisions to protect the rights of migrant women as workers rather than simply as victims of trafficking.[17]

Promote more Woman-Friendly Policies and Cultural Practices in Sending States. While there are ways to ameliorate migrant domestic workers' loss (or lack) of rights, the most effective solution would be to make it possible for these women to thrive in their countries of origin. Country- and culture-specific prescriptions should come from the women in each state themselves, as they are best equipped to identify what their interests and needs are. However, generally speaking, women in sending countries need the material conditions to facilitate their full citizenship, including access to education, capital, and social services. They need legal institutions that value them and function to protect their rights, such that migration as a means of escape is no longer necessary.

This chapter has focused on how the globalization of social reproduction makes certain migrants particularly vulnerable to a loss of rights and citizenship. However, at the same time, globalization has also entailed the emergence of human rights–oriented norms in a global civil society that offer some means to begin to address some of the above recommendations. For instance, international charters and conventions on human rights and the rights of migrants serve as important normative guidelines for state policy. While the effect of such conventions are limited to the extent to which states voluntarily comply, they can lead states to make gradual redirections in policy in order to maintain good relations and a positive image in the international arena. International conferences on women's needs such as the 1995 Fourth World Conference on Women in Beijing also have potential to introduce pro-woman legislation in both sending and receiving states, given high visibility and normative weight. Even more important, they bring together local activists on a global scale (Werbner and Yuval-Davis 1999: 24), generating conversations and networks of support that would not otherwise occur. Finally, the emerging global civil society includes complex networks of NGOs and voluntary associations that adopt feminist and human rights principles and work for the rights of women, migrants, and domestic workers. Some of the most effective organizations are regional or local. For instance, despite practical obstacles to organizing among domestic workers, such as social isolation, geographic dispersion, and a lack of resources, there have been instances of successful organization among domestic workers themselves. In Toronto, domestic workers have organized in a grassroots organization called INTERCEDE since the 1970s. Similarly, in Los Angeles, migrant domestic workers have organized under the rubric of the Coalition for Humane and Immigrant Rights (ChirLA) (Hondagneu-Sotelo 2001). Rather than adopting typical union tactics, these organizations serve the critical functions of creating communities in which domestic workers can discuss and distribute information about resources and rights. These kinds of local organizations, together with global conferences and lobbying at the nation-state level, can not only help protect migrant women's rights in the short term, but also lay groundwork for more substantial cultural and policy change.

Notes

1. Social reproduction might be defined as "the array of activities and relationships involved in maintaining people both on a daily basis and intergenerationally. Reproductive labor includes activities such as purchasing household goods, preparing and serving food, laundering and repairing clothing, maintaining furnishings and appliances, socializing children, providing care and emotional support for adults, and maintaining kin and community ties" (Glenn 1992: 1). This term can also refer to cultural or ideological reproduction, the socialization or "interpellation" (Althusser 1971) necessary to maintain a particular economic and social structure. In the following text, I focus particularly on the former definition.

2. "Social citizenship" draws on T. H. Marshall's concept of social rights, which refer to "economic welfare and security" in addition to education, or "the right to share to the full in the social heritage and to live the life of a civilized being according to the standards prevailing in society" (1998 [1949]: 94). See also Nancy Fraser and Linda Gordon (1998), who equate social citizenship more firmly with the right to a certain standard of economic welfare.

3. See Morokvasic 1994; Pettman 1996, 1999 for scholarly discussions of female migration. Also see the ILO report "Gender and Migration" (2001), which claims that "the proportion of women who are involved in global migration flows is increasing rapidly" and that in some countries women comprise as much as 70 to 80 percent of total migrants. The UN publication *The World's Women 2000* reports that women represent an estimated 56 million out of a total of 118 million migrants internationally.

4. Their reasons for noninvolvement vary. Bangladesh has curtailed official domestic worker migration, such that women who have been working in Bahrain since before the ban are now unauthorized, and others who migrate are doing so illegally. According to al-Najjar 2002, the Bangladeshi embassy in Bahrain does not consider these "illegal" workers its responsibility and leaves them instead to the Bahraini court. The Indian embassy, by contrast, does not have a clear policy toward domestic workers, does not want to have confrontations with local families, and does not have adequate staff to deal with worker-related problems. Bahraini employers also generally deny workers access to their embassies, such that it would not be a feasible resource even if the embassy were prepared to step in (al-Najjar 2002).

5. Sri Lanka, a major source of migrant labor in Lebanon, also relied on an appointed honorary consul, until 1998. The new Sri Lankan embassy takes a much more active stance on behalf of its nationals.

6. See, for instance the "Enrique's Journey" series in the *Los Angeles Times* (Nazario 2002) about the dangers Central American migrants face en route to the United States. Also see Wijers and Lap-Chew (1997), on the trafficking in women, and Dinan (2000), as a case study of the trafficking of Thai women into Japan.

7. In my California study, I found a number of instances in which even a worker's own family members—who were supported by her income—did not consider her labor as a domestic worker a "real job," but rather an extension of the kinds of responsibilities she had in relation to her own household. This kind of example illustrates the pervasiveness of the naturalization of women's household work and the difficulty of making rights claims as a domestic laborer.

8. The exception to this professional image would be among au pairs, who tend to be young white European women who are perceived as amateur caregivers who are undertaking this work in part for the cultural experience. Au pairs make considerably less money than other white caregivers, but their hours, tasks, and living conditions are federally regulated, and employers pay a substantial fee (roughly $5,000) for the initial placement through an agency. In this regard, their labor is also contractual and formal.

9. See Maher 2001; Hondagneu-Sotelo 2001; Wrigley 1995. In the greater Los Angeles area, typical salaries at the (white) high end of the nanny market in the late 1990s were upwards of $500 per week. In contrast, nonwhite women with legal documentation or citizenship earned $200 to $500 per week, and recent immigrants earned from $125 to $250 per week. In this final category, live-in workers with long, undefined hours sometimes found themselves earning less than $2 per hour.

10. Jureidini reports that Filipinas earn roughly $250 to $300 per month, while Sri Lankans and Africans typically earn $100 to $150 per month.

11. Lebanese employers are responsible for paying for workers' work and residency papers, their medical insurance, their return flight, and a hefty recruitment fee (Jureidini 2002). On the one hand, the availability of medical insurance appears a step up in living conditions from countries where workers have no access to medical services; on the other, these kinds of financial commitments appear to have contributed to employers' desire for control over workers, to keep from losing their investment.

12. Third-world feminisms are not a response solely to the international division of social reproductive labor, of course. Third-world women have historically found themselves on the wrong side of capital and colonialism, such that their interests have long diverged from those of white Western women.

13. The actual percentage of mothers among migrant women varies between migrant groups and between empirical studies, but this claim reflects general patterns found in the literature (e.g., Hondagneu-Sotelo 1997, 2001; Parreñas 2001; Maher and Staab 2003).

14. Of course, the earning capacity of men is also subsidized by female reproductive labor at every point in the chain. That is, the productivity and wealth possible in developed states rests indirectly on the social reproductive labor taking place in less developed states. The economic inequalities produced by this division of labor may be ameliorated somewhat through the remittances and trade migrants introduce into their home economies.

15. In addition, there are emotional costs to transnational family arrangements: parents and children who do not see each other for months or years at a time, and marital relationships strained by distance. See Parreñas 2001; Hochschild 2000; Hondagneu-Sotelo 1997.

16. Temporary work visas are no panacea, of course. Many scholars have pointed out the shortcomings of guestworker programs; about the U.S. case, see Martin and Teitelbaum 2001 and Calavita 1992.

17. As of 2002, CEDAW had been ratified by 170 countries, or almost 90 percent of UN members. Article 6 of CEDAW includes a commitment to "suppress all forms of traffic in women and exploitation of prostitution of women," but this provision is too narrow to address most of the kinds of abuses and losses of rights that migrant women experience. Text available at http://www.un.org/womenwatch/daw/cedaw/ (accessed Feb 25, 2003).

9
Children across Borders
Patrimony, Property, or Persons?

ALISON BRYSK

Despite the age of universal citizenship, there is one group of billions of people who do not have full citizenship in any society in the world. Children are a rapidly growing population with a history of special "private" status in states, burgeoning universal rights claims, and vastly increased mobility. Millions of these children are "out of place": doubly displaced from family and state in sweatshops, refugee camps, bordellos, and orphanages. Children across borders are often invisible, or treated as permanent exceptions to wider social processes. The movement of children across borders and state responses to their movement reveal important characteristics of the citizenship gap between international rights and global realities.

While previous chapters have focused on the competing global dynamics of production and institutionalization that shift the meaning and reach of citizenship, this chapter seeks to reemphasize the role of norms and identity. Children are an important test case, because children are a universal group whose primary social function is to reproduce identity. The patrimonial norms that govern children's lives permeate and undermine the historical tradition of citizenship in a way that shows its long-standing limitations. But at the same time, all forms of citizenship are increasingly challenged by global markets' norm of commodification and the human rights norm of universal personhood. Thus, children out of place are caught in a nexus of patchwork patrimonial citizenship, globalizing relations of production, and a nascent rights regime.

This chapter examines the special characteristics of children's migration, with an emphasis on transnational adoption, as a form of migration unique to children and a site where globalization, rights, and identities collide. After an overview of the argument, the next section discusses children's partial citizenship, while the following section describes the emerging international regime of children's rights. The chapter then considers the overall patterns of children's migration, followed by a more detailed analysis of transnational adoption.

Children—Perpetual "People Out of Place"

While childhood has traditionally been viewed by Western culture as a transient phase of incomplete adulthood for individuals, social science and international law increasingly treat childhood as a permanent marginalized social category with both universal and special rights—analagous to the disabled or the elderly. Like other dependent and politically disadvantaged social groups, children suffer special consequences from exposure to the social forces affecting their society (in this case, globalization). Since children lack full membership and participation rights, they have diminished access to resources—across generations, among nations, and even within families. This reflects a structural ambivalence between the requisites of modernity and the premodern condition of childhood. "If modernization may be interpreted also as a process of extending citizenship rights and responsibilities to an increasing part of the population, children are, however, still awaiting this process of extending citizenship rights" (Wintersberger 2000: 175–83). As Gershon Shafir's chapter in this volume suggests, citizenship has mediated the contradictions between the liberal modern expansion of markets and rights—but only for public individuals, not premodern and private subjects.

The status and condition of childhood represents an evolving relationship between premodern identities, modern citizenship, and postmodern mobility. As globalization pushes and pulls people across borders, it disrupts private and state modes of incorporation—family and citizenship. This essay argues that children's long-standing second-class citizenship becomes critical under conditions of globalization. Children cross borders as dependents, laborers, refugees, and adoptees. As a negative consequence of globalization, children's migration is generated by underdevelopment, political conflict, and a new division of reproductive labor in which shifting patterns of private life in the north are enabled by the south's "people out of place": from maids to prostitutes to orphans. On the other hand, migration and new human rights norms make children more visible. In response to children's newly visible common identity and common plight, international organizations and transnational civil society monitor and advocate their rights across states. Globalization also makes some states more receptive to international norms, especially concerning noncitizens. Extending the general analysis of globalization and human rights (Brysk 2002) to children's migration, globalization is simultaneously the greatest threat and the greatest opportunity for children's rights, and different forms of migration have systematically different sources and consequences for children.

Rather than a smooth evolution of the substitution of universal individual rights for second-class citizenship, children experience a series of contradictory, ongoing struggles between identity, commodification, and rights. Like domestic public policy on children and families, international treatment of children reflects a fundamental ambivalence between logics of patrimony, property, and personhood.[1] The logic of patrimony views children as the bearers of a group identity for the family, ethnie, or nation, which trumps their rights or needs as individuals. Patrimonial identities and practices serve as a general source of resistance to both commodification and rights, with a rationale of protection and naturalized private life. In addition, patrimony has predominant policy influence over intercountry adoption—the only form of migration that automatically transfers citizenship. Meanwhile, commodification displaces children into labor migration and trafficking, but there are unresolved tensions between children's economic value and their emerging liberal rights. In this sense, children as dependent humanitarian subjects are theoretically entitled to more rights than adult migrant workers, but their patrimonial invisibility within assumed family units reinforces the powerlessness of displaced second-class citizens. Finally, children displaced as refugees have gained rights more slowly than their adult counterparts, but have recently become the subject of new international norms and national practices. Even here, lingering patrimonial nationalist claims impede the expansion of rights for refugee children.

These struggles for rights cannot be fully resolved, as children remain perpetual "people out of place." While the halting and uneven growth of a children's rights regime does permit greater levels of intervention and agency across state and family boundaries, transnational rights can never fully encompass children—across borders or within them. The definition of rights for a class of individuals who are intrinsically dependent is problematic for the concept of rights, which is intimately tied to autonomy. Children's primary social role as bearers of identity also tests our notions of legal personhood, which is entwined with agency. As feminist theory suggests, cosmopolitan rights are based in a liberal order that cannot fully comprehend private identities. Neither existing forms of citizenship nor the emergence of a children's rights regime responds adequately to children's combined dependency and mobility, suggesting a deeper challenge for globalization—to preserve its own future.

Patrimonial Citizenship

The private status of children shows that despite Enlightenment claims regarding the public individual subject, political membership has long been defined via a public-private distinction and collective subject: the family. States construct citizenship around and through private family legal codes, family- and gender-based assignment of membership/nationality, and differential internal and international rights by family status.[2] Children's citizenship is peculiarly patrimonial; for all of the worldwide debate on the legal status and rights of fetuses, eggs, and even cell lines, once a child is born she becomes the unquestioned property of her parents and secondarily her state. The limiting features of children's citizenship are usually invisible under the assumed norm of stable nuclear families, peaceful functional welfare states, and limited or temporary migration—but contemporary conditions often violate these assumptions.

Children are provisional citizens who receive the civic dimension of nationality at birth, a tutelary and graduated package of social entitlements, and accede to political membership only at adulthood. As one study of citizenship in Germany concludes, membership is a multidimensional and sometimes contradictory concept:

> an international (or transnational) one grounded in universal human rights; a civil/political one that distinguishes between citizens and residents; a social one that provides collective insurance against individual risk; and an ethno-national one based on shared descent and cultural affinities. . . . In its administration of migrants, the FRG has further divided them by groups, for example, refugee/ expellee, guestworker, ethnic German, and asylum-seeker, and has allocated different menus of rights and entitlements accordingly. (Klusmeyer 2000: 2, 5)

Beyond these general layers of rights, states govern children's protection, illegal behavior, economic status, and guardianship through tutelary codes of family and juvenile law, which often lack the individual rights protection of conventional legal venues.

Citizenship modes of incorporation are generally based on either parentage (jus sanguinis), birthplace (jus soli), or residence (jus domicili). "The formal codification of nationality law is distinctly modern . . . as a result of increased inter-state migration" (Kashiwazaki 1998: 3). Different states base their citizenship regime on one of these criteria, so that children are not born equal in terms of membership status. But beyond this, when states are called upon to adjudicate a citizenship claim, children's claims usually devolve to jus sanguinis—even in states where an adult migrant would receive residence rights. For example, in 1996 Belgium refused to recognize the French nationality of three children traveling to meet their Algerian parents legally residing in France; the children were deported to Algeria (Bhabha 1998: 718).

Children's citizenship derives from that of their parents, which produces several shortfalls in universality. First, some states derive a child's nationality from the mother, others from the father, and some from both. Numerous international custody cases have arisen from the dissolution of marriages between U.S. mothers, generally presumed to pass citizenship to their children, and fathers from Arab countries, whose laws generally grant citizenship and control through the father. Conversely, "In Egypt, as in most of the Arab world, children born to women who marry foreigners . . . are not considered citizens at all" (Maefarquhar *New York Times* 2001). Furthermore, in the states utilizing a blood criterion, such as Germany, children born to foreign parents within that state may not have the right to citizenship despite birth and residence.

Even when nationality is not at issue, a child's rights and guardianship may depend on the marital status of its parents—"illegitimate" children may be wards of the state. For example, in Ireland until the 1970s, children of unwed mothers were routinely removed by state and delegated church authorities and placed for adoption without consent—resulting in thousands of international adoptions (Milotte 1997). On the receiving side, although U.S. law does not grant preference to "legitimate" children, INS classification of foreign children as "orphans" eligible for adoption by U.S. citizens does depend on the legitimacy laws of the sending state. In general, this means that acknowledged children must be released for adoption by both parents, while children born out of wedlock may be adopted with only the consent of the mother.

Finally, children may suffer a special risk of loss of nationality and even statelessness if their birth is unregistered, either within a state, in a refugee camp, or in a state that is collapsing or at war. A recent study by UNICEF shows that as many as 50 million babies born in 2000 were never registered, and explains the risks to these children of loss of nationality, vulnerability to exploitation and trafficking, and lack of access to citizenship functions such as formal employment, voting, legal migration, and marriage (Olson *New York Times* 2002; see also UNICEF 1998 for trends). Beyond physical and social impediments to the registration of children's identities, some states discourage registration by refugees and ethnic minorities—precisely to avoid granting citizenship. Russia and Bhutan have been cited by refugee organizations for laws that deny nationality to children of nonethnic nationals, excluding sizable migrant populations, while Myanmar has been criticized for its failure to register minority groups. Similarly, during the Central American wars of the 1980s, Honduras and Mexico refused to register births of Salvadoran and Guatemalan refugees in border camps, consigning tens of thousands of children to a complete citizenship vacuum (United Nations High Commission on Refugees 2000).

Alongside this patchwork, privatized mode of citizenship incorporation by states, a universal system of children's rights has begun to develop—to address both public-private and interstate gaps.

Children's Rights: The Globalization of Personhood

The shifting status and increasing rights of children have developed along with liberalism, while the consolidation of an international children's rights regime is both a component of and a response to globalization. Children's rights position children as universal and equal subjects of consistent international standards of freedom and entitlement. The comprehensive and widely endorsed UN Convention on the Rights of the Child (which entered into force in 1990) has been matched by the mobilization of international agencies (such as UNICEF), conferences, and campaigns. One of the key provisions of the UN convention gives an identity rationale for citizenship, as it states that each child has the *right* to a name and nationality. The Convention on the Rights of the Child specifies children's right *to* a family, while the Universal Declaration of Human Rights delineates the rights *of* families vis-à-vis their states. The International Covenant on Civil and Political Rights also has important provisions relevant to children, such as the right to protection, registration, and nationality. The movement of children across borders is specifically addressed in the Hague Convention on the Protection of Children and Cooperation in Respect of Inter-country Adoption, several ILO conventions that treat child labor, and the UN Convention on the Protection of Migrant Workers and Members of Their Families. ILO convention 182, which seeks to ban the "worst forms of child labor," has been rapidly ratified by more than one hundred countries. The 1990 Migrant Workers Convention reiterates the guarantees of Rights of the Child and the ICCPR, and adds that juvenile migrants accused of legal violations have the rights to separate custody from adults, family visits, and special state attention to family unity in the detention of any member. The United States, along with thirty-three other countries, has signed the Hague convention on intercountry adoption. All of the states in the United Nations, except the United States and Somalia, have signed the Convention on the Rights of the Child (U.S. objections are on patrimonial grounds). Regional human rights treaties, especially in Europe and the Americas, also address the rights of children and families. This international regime of norms and institutions has shifted the agenda on the treatment of children to a rights framework, and established international benchmark standards that most liberal states strive to achieve.

This institutional and normative framework has been matched by a growth in monitoring and advocacy groups for children's rights. Broader human rights organizations have founded special divisions and campaigns for children, such as Human Rights Watch—Children's Rights Division (founded in 1994) and Anti-Slavery International. An organization devoted wholly to children's rights is Defence for Children International; Free the Children is a campaign by children for children. An example of issue networks, in this case to address the issue of refugee children separated from their families, is the interagency working group formed by the UN High Commission on Refugees, UNICEF, the Red Cross, the International Rescue Committee, Save the Children, and World Vision. Sectors of the children's rights network address specific forms of migration: child labor, child prostitution, and transnational adoption. For example, both ECPAT and Captive Daughters focus on transnational child prostitution. Organizations such as the Rugmark Foundation campaign against exploitative child labor. Meanwhile, rights-based advocacy movements such as the International Union of Child Welfare review national social policies for conformance to international standards.

The treatment of children across borders may fall under several domains of international law, from immigration to labor standards to refugee norms to international private law. Different national legal systems classify migratory flows and cases under these distinct rubrics, and host states also differ in their level of adherence to international standards. Nevertheless, international law and norms of children's rights do seem to be increasingly influential, even as developed states are, overall, less receptive to migration. ILO member states have readily incorporated conventions on child labor abuse, child trafficking, and child prostitution, and EU institutions have initiated special programs in these areas. The U.S. Immigration and Naturalization Service has referred to the UN High Commission on Refugees' guidelines in reforming its procedures for the detention of unaccompanied minors. A U.S. immigration judge has ruled that deportation of a single immigrant parent must consider the "best interests of the child" (an American citizen who would be left behind)— explicitly citing the UN Convention on the Rights of the Child (Glaberson *New York Times* 2002).

In the identity-based area of intercountry adoption, international norms are stronger and more consistently incorporated by receiving states. Germany, Switzerland, Denmark, and the Netherlands have explicitly incorporated UN standards in their domestic legislation on intercountry adoption (Bagley, Young, and Scully 1993: 169). Sweden was forced to modify its adoption procedures by the European Court, in two cases brought in 1987 and 1989 under the European Human Rights Convention (Smith 1993). When Australia sought to draft international adoption legislation in 1978, it sent delegations to the major Asian source countries to discuss the provisions (Picton 1986); a subsequent set of standards incorporated the UN Convention on the Rights of the Child (Charlesworth 1993).

The movement of children across borders often threatens the fundamental rights clusters identified by the UN Convention on the Rights of the Child: survival, development, protection, provision, and participation (Wintersberger 2000). Given this framework of competing rubrics and evolving standards, what are the movements of children out of place—and how do states respond?

Displaced Workers, Misplaced Rights

As labor migration and refugee flows have increased worldwide, the participation of children within those flows has also intensified. Children are also a large proportion of "secondary migrants," who cross borders to join a parent or guardian who has previously migrated for labor or refuge. While secondary migrant children are not displaced from family, they may be displaced from home-state protection from family abuse or exploitation.

There are no comprehensive data on the economic migration of children, but some indicators suggest that millions of children cross borders each year as workers. Immigration raids on U.S. sweatshops and fields regularly result in the detainment of hundreds of children alongside adult workers. Children's transborder labor migration within developing regions is generally undocumented and often exploitative. In 1996, the ILO recorded 194,180 foreign child laborers in Thailand alone, most from Myanmar, Laos, and Cambodia—and many unaccompanied. In that country, there are estimated to be 5,000 foreign child prostitutes. An additional 49,000 child laborers have migrated from Nepal to India (www.ilo.org). Various forms of international child trafficking are common in poverty-stricken Bangladesh—boys as young as four are shipped to the Persian Gulf for hazardous work as camel jockeys, while girls are sold to India and Pakistan to work as prostitutes and maids (Sengupta *New York Times*, 2002).

States' policies on "family reunification" generally determine children's rights and membership possibilities in economic or secondary migration. The United States has fairly broad provisions for secondary migration in which children join resettled parents, but INS adoption guidelines explicitly exclude adopted children's biological families from immigration—so parents cannot join resettled children. And children's and family rights are easily forfeited: the INS has deported as many as ten thousand undocumented children of legal residents (Johansen 1993). In recent years, under public pressure, the INS has limited the conditions for "expedited removal" of juveniles and increased attempts to contact families. In Britain, the Immigration Act of 1988 removed the unqualified right to family unity, resulting in greater limits on secondary migration. Even in the Netherlands, a controversial ruling upheld by the European Court refused entry to the nine-year-old Moroccan son of a (widowed) permanent resident father with joint Dutch and Moroccan nationality (Bhabha 1998: 718).

Furthermore, children do not always migrate in family units as the law assumes. Older children may be unaccompanied migrant laborers, and children may be trafficked by strangers. Involuntary trafficking of children is estimated to affect 1.2 million children worldwide, with most girls forced into prostitution and boys exploited in commercial agriculture and crime (ILO 2002). Recent estimates indicate that about 11,500 foreign-born children are sexually exploited each year in the United States, generally unaccompanied or subsequently separated from their families (Hernandez *New York Times* 2001). With few and recent exceptions, commodification and border enforcement triumph over rights for these children.

In 1997–98, the INS reported 4,295 "custody occurrences" involving undocumented juveniles; 4,136 unaccompanied minors were detained for more than seventy-two hours by the INS in 2000 (Solomon 2002). INS detention of children under punitive conditions, in inappropriate facilities, and without access to legal counsel or interpreters evoked condemnation by Human Rights Watch, a 1985 class-action lawsuit (*Flores v. Reno*), and some reforms in 1998 (HRW 1998, Amon 2001). Thus, the INS established several special youth shelters for detained unaccompanied minors. But thousands of children are still detained for months or years—over one third are held in prisons, up to 80 percent of unaccompanied juveniles still lack legal representation, and their medical, educational, psychological, and language needs are often ignored. After exposure and advocacy by a coalition including Amnesty International, the ACLU, the American Bar Association, the Lawyers' Committee for Human Rights, Lutheran Immigration and Refugee Services, and the Women's Commission for Refugee Women and Children, legislation is now pending in both houses of Congress to establish an Office of Children's Services under the Department of Justice and remove jurisdiction for unaccompanied minors from the INS. In joint testimony before the Senate Subcommittee on Immigration, the U.S. Conference of Catholic Bishops and Lutheran Immigration and Refugee Service made an explicit appeal for universal rights transcending citizenship:

> The main theme of our testimony today is that unaccompanied alien children should be treated under the same standards and be afforded the same child welfare protections that are available to other children in the United States. Such standards were developed to protect children as vulnerable human beings; they should not discriminate based upon legal status or national origin, but they currently do. (Duncan 2002)

California Democratic senator Dianne Feinstein's Unaccompanied Alien Child Protection Act would also establish minimum standards for custody, institute a special immigrant juvenile visa, require family reunification or foster care where possible, and appoint child welfare professionals and legal representatives to represent unaccompanied minors (Duncan *New York Times* 2002; Unaccompanied Alien Child Protection Act, S.121—available at http://thomas.loc.gov).

Refugee Minors: Dependent Rights

In terms of refugees, the United Nations High Commission on Refugees estimates that 10 million of the world's 22.4 million refugees are minors. Children form such an important component of the refugee population that the UNHCR has a special set of guidelines, "Dealing with Unaccompanied Children Seeking Asylum," and recently established regional policy officers for children in half a dozen regions. In Europe, 13,600 unaccompanied minors applied for asylum in 1999 (UNHCR 2001). The United States in 1996 admitted 74,491 refugees, many of them children (there are no separate figures). In 1998, the INS also established special guidelines for asylum for children (HRW 1998). The largest single case of unaccompanied minor refugees in the United States, in 2000, involved 3,800 Sudanese war orphans who had walked to refugee camps in Kenya and were subsequently accepted for resettlement in the United States (Corbett 2001 *Economist* 2000: 5).

Juvenile asylum seekers go through a process similar to the one negotiated by adult refugees, but children often lack legal representation and sometimes translators. Once asylum claims are accepted, the U.S. Office of Refugee Resettlement provides financial support to unaccompanied minor refugees, and placement via the U.S. Catholic Conference and Lutheran Immigration and Refugee services (www.ins.usdoj.gov). But rejected petitioners can be deported.

Immigration policies for children persecuted by their states or families go further than the U.S. norm of screening and selective resettlement in many Organization for Economic Cooperation and Development countries. In Britain, Norway, Switzerland, Holland, and Canada, children cannot be returned to a home country without a suitability assessment of both country and caretaker conditions. This type of additional safeguard for juvenile asylum seekers is also a proposed feature of Feinstein's Unaccompanied Alien Child Protection Act (Duncan 2002).

The range and basis of U.S. migration policy for children is shown by three recent cases, which display disparate legal classification and rights outcomes. Economic migration by unaccompanied minors is generally denied, even when it challenges family ties and the rights of the minor. In June 2000, an eight-year old girl from Nigeria arrived alone in the United States and was detained by immigration authorities. It is believed that the child planned to join her mother, who had previously migrated illegally to the United States for economic reasons, but that the mother was unwilling to pick up the girl due to the prospect of deportation (this type of situation is apparently not infrequent, and the INS has been criticized for detaining undocumented children as "bait" to lure undocumented parents already resident in the United States). Since the INS has been unable to locate family in the sending country, the girl has remained in an INS foster care facility for over a year. Subsequently, a Nigerian claiming to be her father has come forward—but he is living illegally in London. She cannot be admitted to the United States or Britain, or released for adoption or even private foster care. While this case is unusually extended, INS children's shelters house hundreds of children for months at a time, indicating the scope of unaccompanied minors caught in similar immigration dilemmas (Schmitt *New York Times* 2001).

Meanwhile, in the infamous case of Elian Gonzalez, patrimony trumped rights and refugee status despite tremendous controversy and transnational lobbying. In 1999, this five-year-old Cuban boy was rescued from a raft approaching U.S. waters, where his mother had perished. While the boy's (noncustodial) father petitioned for his son's return to him in Cuba, Cuban-American exiled relatives of the mother demanded custody and pleaded for Elian to receive refugee status. After months of legal maneuvering, diplomatic tension, and exhaustive press coverage, a U.S. court finally ruled that the father's rights to his son and standard diplomatic practice determined the boy's return to Cuba. In a memo to Immigration Commissioner Doris Meissner, the Department of Justice noted that the key legal principle was who had standing to represent a minor's immigration claims. The finding concluded that Elian's father remained his legal representative under the Cuban Family Code, following U.S. practice of assigning jurisdiction to the legal system in which the family relationship arose (www.ins.usdoj.gov). An interesting feature of the case was the U.S. acceptance of the Cuban code's recognition of unwed paternity—and the United States did briefly consider and discard the child's individual fear of potential persecution. Yet even a child from an enemy state with an extremely vocal U.S. ethnic community advocating his cause was treated as the patrimony of his family, not an individual with political rights (Abraham 2001; Rabkin 2000).

Occasionally, humanitarian and rights considerations do triumph over both patrimony and property. On July 23, 2001, the U.S. attorney general granted "humanitarian parole" to a Thai boy who had been trafficked to the United States by smugglers, and was later discovered to be HIV-positive. The four-year-old had been rented by his Thai prostitute mother to a Thai trafficker who forced the boy to pose as his son to facilitate the entry of another Thai prostitute into the United States. In the year since the boy's apprehension, he was cared for by a Los Angeles Thai community organization, which has acted as his medical and legal advocate. Even though HIV status has been used to exclude adult migrants from the United States, in this case it was viewed by the courts as a condition mandating a right to treatment only available here. The legal claims of the biological family (although supported by the Thai government) have also been questioned by U.S. courts in terms of the "best interests of the child," because his mother rented the child, his father committed suicide, and the paternal grandparents seeking custody include a convicted heroin trafficker who served twelve years in a Thai prison. The boy will also be eligible for a new visa mandated by the 2000 Victims of Trafficking and Violence Protection Act, which grants rights-based asylum to many who have been coercively commodified. Meanwhile, the transnational Thai community group has placed the boy with a Los Angeles couple who wish to adopt him (Whitaker, "Ashcroft" 2001, *New York Times* 2001).

Transnational Adoption: The Globalization of Private Citizenship

Transnational adoption, while numerically small, has increased dramatically and reveals critical aspects of children's ambiguous citizenship. Debates on intercountry adoption dramatically highlight the competing policies of patrimony, property, and personhood that govern the movement of children. Thus, the First Lady of Soviet Georgia announced her state's restriction of transnational adoption during the post–Cold War economic crisis in the following terms of state identity over children's individual rights: "I am categorically against foreign adoption. Our nation's gene pool is being depleted. All the Georgian people are suffering hardships. Let our children suffer, too" (Simon and Altstein 2000: 109). In a more privatized assignment of patrimony, many Islamic countries forbid all adoption, because Islam states that children's identity and inheritance belong to their biological families and cannot be transferred to another family. Meanwhile, liberalism in receiving states shows a mix of property and personhood, balancing the "best interests of the child" with commodification. Within the same liberal state that admitted the Thai boy based on his universal right to medical care, one of the sponsors of U.S. legislation facilitating intercountry adoption referred to it as a "consumer protection" measure (for adoptive parents) (HR2909, Comments by Chairman Gilman, House Committee on International Relations, March 22, 2000).

Since the Second World War, there have been hundreds of thousands of intercountry adoptions—possibly as many as half a million (Simon and Alstein 2000: 8; Bagley et al. 1993: 135), and this migratory flow has increased with globalization. "The number of children adopted internationally has doubled since 1992" (Freundlich 1999). The United States currently admits fifteen- to twenty-thousand children per year via adoption, and the major European countries together take in a similar number. The size of the existing pool of children adopted across borders is indicated by a recent change in citizenship law that naturalized 75,000 children resident in the United States (Schmitt *New York Times* 2001). On the sending side, it is estimated that Korea exported almost 100,000 children from the 1950s through the 1980s (Altstein and Simon 1991). Since 1990, more than 25,000 children from Russia, Romania, Bulgaria, and former Soviet republics have been adopted by American families (Judge 1999).

Formal programs of intercountry adoption began after the Second World War, with the dual rationale of humanitarian rescue of war orphans and patrilineal resettlement in the father's state for children of returning soldiers. In the United States, the Displaced Persons Act of 1948 admitted ten thousand war orphans of specified nationalities (Bagley et al. 1993: 148). Since that time, large-scale intercountry adoption has usually resulted from some combination of recent war, socioeconomic imbalance between sending and receiving countries, and organizational linkages to facilitate the process (Altstein and Simon 1991)—the same factors that produce labor migration and refugees. Thus, postwar European orphans were quickly replaced by Korean children, who were a majority source through the 1980s. The 1970s saw an increase in Latin American adoptions along with political conflict in that region, while in the 1990s large-scale post-Soviet and Chinese adoptions increased. Currently, over half of U.S. "immigrant orphans" come from Asia—almost one third from China alone.

Despite the image associated with the term orphan, the majority of internationally adopted children have at least one living parent—usually the mother, who has generally abandoned or relinquished them under intense economic and social pressure. Around two thirds of foreign adoptees are female, and gender preferences in the sending country contribute heavily to adoptions from many countries, especially China, Korea, and India. This reiterates the patrimonial logic whereby females' identity is mutable and their citizenship correspondingly disposable. On the demand side, most U.S. and European prospective parents exhibit a preference for female children, often expressing a belief that girls are more adaptable to resettlement (Pahz 1988: 64).

At the same time, liberal states' changes in family patterns, globalization of markets, and communication links have increased the general demand for and feasibility of intercountry adoptions. Developed societies' changes in markets and mores have combined to produce an increased number of childless couples seeking adoption and a reduced pool of children available within those countries. As citizens of developed countries increasingly delay childbearing to an age of decreasing fertility, more couples are unable to become biological parents, increasing the demand for adoption. Meanwhile, the domestic supply of unwanted children is reduced by the increased availability of abortion and alternatively increased support for unmarried mothers. Thus, the focus of intercountry adoption has shifted somewhat "from parentless children to childless couples" (Altstein and Simon 1991). International regimes and state policies are thus pressed to also incorporate the rights and needs of adoptive parents.

Today, intercultural adoption comprises around 15 percent of U.S. adoptions, but one quarter to one third of adoptions in European countries such as Germany, Holland, and Sweden (Altstein and Simon 1991). Sweden has the highest proportion of intercountry adoption, which involved 30,000 adoptees from forty countries by 1990. Denmark, Norway, and Sweden have the highest proportions, currently 1,500 to 2,000 children per year in Sweden (Jantera-Jareborg 1990, 1994). People in the Netherlands have also adopted over 32,000 foreign children, and over half of Dutch adoptions are international (Hoksbergen and Bunjes 1986). "Foreign" adoptions in Germany include the abandoned German-born children of noncitizen guest workers (Baer 1986).

Objections to intercountry adoption range from the patrimonial to the universalist, and speak to the interests of each participant in the "adoption triangle": birth parents, adoptive parents, and children. First, some contend that displacement and adjustment ultimately harm the children. Since numerous studies seem to refute this charge at the individual level (Simon and Altstein 2000; Bagley et al. 1993), this argument shifts to a collective identity claim—or at best a psychologically latent child's right to racial identity. A related concern is whether adopted children from a racial group stigmatized in the host society, no matter how well cared for and secure in the adoptive family, will become second-class citizens as adults. Arguing against this identity-based blocking of transracial adoption in the United States, two social welfare professionals who have documented positive placement outcomes for the children contend that it violates children's "rights as citizens as called for in the 14th Amendment to the U.S. Constitution" (the rights to equal protection and equal opportunity for placement in a family) (Simon and Altstein 2000: 144–45, 150).[3]

A second set of arguments focuses on the sending states. Image-conscious states see the export of dependents as a mark of failure, and countries decry the loss of future productive citizens. A Thai social service official explains that "[h]anding Thai children over for adoption by foreigners is seen by policy-makers as a loss of dignity and a waste of human resources" (Dharmaruksa 1986: 128). It was also on this basis that Nigerian officials following the Biafran war refused to release an estimated ten thousand war orphans, insisting on resettling them within the nation (Bagley et al. 1993: 180).

At the same time, some children's rights advocates claim that intercountry adoption allows sending states to evade their social obligations to children by exporting the unwanted. Instead, they argue, the resources devoted to adoption should be invested in local development to serve the best interests of *all* of the society's children. For example, in Belarus adoptions rose 160 percent over a decade of economic crisis—but the proportion of children under three living in orphanages rose 170 percent (United Nations Children's Fund 2001). Critics reply that absent structural leverage and resources for improving children's welfare, in the short and medium term restricting adoptions simply condemns hundreds of thousands of children to abysmal conditions and even death in domestic institutions (Human Rights Watch/Asia 1996).

Finally, critics from all camps condemn the numerous cases of trafficking of children and coercion of birth parents (Bagley et al. 1993: 172–73). In its milder form, trafficking may refer simply to inadequately supervised and financially tainted adoptions—which are problematic and often exploitative of birth parents, but do not necessarily harm the child. A less recognized problem is that the growth of transnational adoption has also fueled the growth of an unsavory element of global civil society: adoption profiteers, including unethical overseas attorneys who exploit their access to state policy to coerce birth parents, extort adoptive parents, and endanger children through hasty or inappropriate adoptions (Pahz 1988: ch. 3). One response to this phenomenon simply seeks greater regulation and control of international adoption along with other global flows. For example, some sending countries and several states within the United States now prohibit private transnational adoption, in order to ensure government supervision. And U.S.-based adoption agencies have formed councils for self-regulation, such as the International Concerns Committee for Children (Pahz 1988: 17). But a stronger version asserts that the intercountry adoption process is inherently and irremediably exploitative as soon as children are assigned exchange value.

In addition, in rare but horrifying cases, children released for adoption have been illicitly trafficked for commercial or sexual exploitation. For example, a 2002 raid in Pakistan uncovered eleven infants held by a long-standing kidnapping ring that included three Pakistani nurses and three Maltese traffickers carrying passports and adoption papers to facilitate the children's sale in Malta (Bonner *New York Times* 2002).[4] Trafficking of children is universally repudiated, and stands on a par with other forms of international smuggling and slavery: it is explicitly condemned in article 35 of the UN Convention on the Rights of the Child, and a special resolution issued by the UN last year (see 54/263—Optional Protocols to the Convention on the Rights of the Child on the Involvement of Children in Armed Conflict and on the Sale of Children, Child Prostitution, and Child Pornography, esp. annex II).

In response to these issues, parallel to the children's rights regime, an overlapping international regime for intercountry adoption has developed, with universal, regional, and bilateral components. At the global level, general human rights treaties, the UN Convention on the Rights of the Child, and the Hague Convention on Protection of Children and Co-operation in Respect of Intercountry Adoption address the rights and safeguards of children and parents. The UN convention asserts the best interests of the child and respect for the child's opinion, but also specifies that children have the right to "be cared for by his or her own parents . . . as far as possible," and the right to protection from unjustified separation from parents (Lucker-Babel 1991). The Convention on the Rights of the Child clearly specifies that intercountry adoption should be a subsidiary option only when the child can not be cared for in the country of origin (article 21[b]). In such cases, the 1993 Hague convention mandates that signatories establish a responsible central authority within each state to monitor, adjudicate, and administer intercountry adoption. It does not definitively establish jurisdiction ("choice of law"), but in aspiration to universality admitted thirty nonmember states with full voting rights to the drafting convention—largely states of origin for adopted children. The key innovation of the convention is to raise the standard for transnational translation of consent: more limited parental consent in the country of origin for a "simple adoption" cannot be translated in the receiving country into a "full adoption" breaking all legal ties with the biological parent(s).[5] The Hague convention also specifies that the mother must consent to adoption *after* the birth, and encourages adoptive parents to personally transfer the child from the country of origin (Jantera-Jareborg 1994). Earlier and less comprehensive inter-American, European, and Nordic conventions on adoption facilitate legal recognition of adoptions among countries with close historic ties. This is all supplemented with bilateral agreements between countries with high flow levels (such as Sweden and the Philippines, Sweden and Ecuador, the Netherlands and the Philippines, and Norway and the Philippines), which generally reduce waiting periods, clarify jurisdiction, and sometimes guarantee repatriation if the adoption is disqualified.

Transnational adoption depends on and stimulates the formation of global civil society in several senses. Most directly, transnational adoption globalizes families—the most private and local social unit. Transnational adoption also often draws on previous patterns of travel, marriage, and migration across borders. And some adoptive families develop new relationships to the child's country of origin, including the growing tourist flow of "heritage tours" retracing the child's roots (Zhao *New York Times* 2002). At the organizational level, there are several types of distinctive transnational adoption NGOs. Historical humanitarian organizations, often based in relief efforts, promote the private liberal interests of children and families, prominently Holt International in the United States and Terre des Hommes in Europe. On the other hand, transnational professional groups of social workers (such as International Social Services) explicitly seek to regulate states, and are often delegated administrative responsibility and granted policy influence.

How do individual states deal with this anomalous form of migration of their most ambiguous citizens? Some sending states restrict, while others facilitate the export of "surplus" children; standards reflect the state's strength, history, and relationship with globalization.[6] A few countries, which comprise the major sources of adopted children, actively promote international adoption as a solution to domestic crises and inadequate domestic institutions. Most of the Asian countries do not require that the adoption take place in the sending state, in contrast to most of Latin America and eastern Europe.

In 1961, Korea passed the Extraordinary Adoption Law, which encourages international adoption, citing a low domestic social welfare budget due to the expenses of protracted military confrontation with North Korea. Despite some bilateral modifications during the 1970s, and an attempt to generally decrease adoptions along with development, Korean policy and intermediary organizations remain committed to intercountry adoption. Korea's adoption program sends internationally placed children books and cultural materials on their country of origin, and will subsequently help adopted adults to locate and visit their biological parents (Tahk 1986).

Similarly, China has generally welcomed international adoption as a source of relief for its overflowing orphanages. In that country, the economic pressures of poverty and globalization combine with a uniquely draconian population policy to produce a significant "surplus" of children without families. Accordingly, China set up a special intercountry adoption office in 1992 (Bagley et al. 1993: 190). While birth parents are not subject to direct coercion, their choice to relinquish a (usually female) child for adoption is severely circumscribed by globalizing economic pressures and their state's denial of reproductive rights, combined with patrimonial preferences for male lineage. Even in a nominally socialist state, children are commodified—China receives an average of $15,000 per adoption (Simon and Altstein 2000). Meanwhile, adoptive parents seek to secure their right to form a family. Thus, lesbian and gay couples effectively excluded from adoption in the United States have sought adoptions in China, which permits singles to adopt.[7]

For reasons similar to those of China, in the early 1990s Romania housed vast numbers of orphans who were initially released wholesale for adoption. But following adoption abuses, adjustment difficulties, and national embarrassment, Romania temporarily instituted a ban on international adoptions. Shortly thereafter, Romania created a state committee to redesign the adoption process—with a prominent U.S. consultant (Simon and Altstein 2000: 17). In Latin

America, due to internal political conflict Colombia has sent large numbers abroad relative to its level of development. But because of trafficking problems, during the mid-1980s Colombia banned private adoption and now requires that all adoptions be regulated through a government agency (Pahz 1988). Guatemala, one of the countries most negatively influenced by economic globalization, is currently the leading Latin American source for intercountry adoption.

It is also interesting to note that several countries that generate large numbers of abandoned children possess the requisite linkages but choose to drastically limit international adoption. Thailand sets a modest quota, permitting only a few hundred adoptions a year. After a series of scandals in the 1970s, Thailand reorganized its adoption process and transferred passport control to the Ministry of Foreign Affairs and Interior (Dharmaruksa 1986). It is suggested that one factor in this difference is the greater potential value of girls as continuing income earners in the Thai family, compared to in Thailand's more Confucian neighbors. With similar patrimonial rationale, Indonesia requires foreigners to live and work in Indonesia for three years to qualify as prospective parents (Indonesian National Council on Social Welfare 1986).

On the other side of the equation, receiving states differ in whether they treat international adoption as primarily an immigration or a private family matter. Do they grant automatic citizenship or require separate screening? Is the state's policy influenced by international standards? What is the role of private adoption and intermediary organizations? While the common law countries are generally liberal in their recognition of foreign adoptions, the continental tradition tends to require second adoption regardless of immigration requirements.

Since the United States is the destination for at least half of the world's international adoptions, U.S. policy is especially significant. U.S. policy is among the most restrictive and immigration oriented, but adoption is nevertheless the loosest area of U.S. immigration law. U.S. law requires that international adoptions meet three sets of standards: for the sending country, for the INS, and for the U.S. state in which the adoptive parents reside. Usually the INS requirements exceed those of the other parties, since the INS in these cases is mandated to investigate both the child's immigration eligibility and the adoptive parents' qualifications. As the INS reminds prospective parents, "adoption of a foreign-born child does not guarantee the child's eligibility to immigrate to the U.S." (US DOJ, M-249). Only U.S. citizens—not legal aliens—may file for a foreign adoption, which is technically known as a "petition to classify an orphan as an immediate relative." In addition to miscellaneous paperwork and fees, the parents must provide the INS with fingerprints for a background check, certification of marital status, proof that they have personally examined the child and satisfied the requirements of the sending country, and a "home study" documenting their domestic and psychological suitability for parenthood conducted by a licensed agency.[8] Regarding the child, they must show that the child is less than sixteen-years-old, free of specified communicable diseases, and meets the legal definition of an "orphan": a child whose parents are dead, have disappeared, or have relinquished the child in writing for emigration and adoption because "the sole parent cannot provide basic needs by local standards" (US DOJ, M-249).

However, popular pressure and sympathetic legislators (including several adoptive parents) have recently passed two key reforms that ease and coordinate the implementation of these requirements: the Inter-country Adoption Act of 2000 and the Child Citizenship Act of 2000. Under the Child Citizenship Act of 2000, adopted children now receive citizenship automatically rather than facing an additional set of applications and screening to naturalize the immigration visas formerly issued upon adoption. At the same time that U.S. policy has eased adoption flows and facilitated U.S. parents' rights, it has also strengthened the children's rights side of the liberal agenda through increased vigilance of suspected trafficking. Eight American couples were denied visas to bring home babies from Vietnam when their partner agency was investigated by the INS, despite pleas from a U.S. senator (Gootman *New York Times* 2002). Similarly, the U.S. embassy suspended all adoptions from Cambodia—which had been supplying almost one hundred children each month to American families—when it uncovered evidence of trafficking (Mydans *New York Times* 2001).

In general, the other major destinations treat adoption as a more private issue, consult more with international counterparts, and incorporate the child's rights and interests more systematically. In 1973, Sweden established a National Board for Inter-country Adoption, composed of political party representatives and experts, which certifies domestic and international counterpart adoption organizations (Andersson 1986). A 1979 adoption act restricted and regulated private international adoption in Sweden. Since 1988, the Swedish government has compensated adoptive parents for half the cost of international adoptions. However, Swedish courts have been presented with a series of cases in which adoption of adolescents and adults appeared to circumvent immigration regulations—these adoptions were generally rejected on that basis (Jantera-Jareborg 1990). Denmark requires dual adoption under Danish and sending-country law, but also permits the maintenance of dual nationality by the adopted child (Melchior 1986). In the Netherlands, a child-oriented foreign adoption policy privileges the child's interests over those of the (Dutch citizen) adoptive parents, encourages Dutch adoption agencies to work closely with sending-country counterparts, and expects adoptive parents to engage in "project help" activities for their children's country of origin (Hoksbergen 1991). Intercountry adoption stimulated the formulation of a national adoption policy in Australia, which had formerly relegated family law to state governments on the U.S. model (Charlesworth 1993).

Finally, patrimony exerts a greater influence on both sending and receiving countries with conflicted religious identities. On the host side, Israel's state monopoly on domestic adoption and lack of international regulation has shifted demand overseas, resulting in a high proportion of intercountry adoptions without a clear institutional structure to process it. Thus, children brought privately on foreign passports readily receive Israeli identity cards— but those cards carry a special notation, and there is the additional element that the children must be converted to Judaism to receive the full spectrum of membership in Israeli society (Jaffe 1991). India, a prominent source country, does not have any official adoption law, because Indian Muslims have blocked such legislation. Instead, Indian institutions operate under a substitute regime of "guardianship," which is functionally equivalent but widely variable in its application by local administrative units (Pandit 1993). India's guardianship laws apply only to Hindus, rendering Muslim children ineligible for the option of international adoption, and the status of members of smaller religious minorities is anomalous. In many sending countries, biological parents' sole specification regarding an adoptive placement is the religion in which the child will be raised.

Intercountry adoption is a growing form of globalizing connection that disrupts patrimonial citizenship and introduces a liberal logic of simultaneous rights-based cosmopolitanism and commodification of private relationships. Even within the universalist rights framework, membership in the form of citizenship/nationality is necessary to secure access to rights. And children's rights are balanced against the sometimes conflicting rights of birth parents and adoptive parents. Despite all of these conflicting interests, the children involved generally improve their material, psychological, and even political condition—but they are stripped without consent of membership in the country of their birth.

Conclusion

Children are one of the largest and most vulnerable groups of second-class citizens, across many types of social and political systems. One of the most promising features of the emergence of international human rights is the potential to extend legal personhood to such privatized, powerless, and socially anomalous groups. However, the children's rights regime is incompletely developed and unevenly internalized within domestic state structures, and thus proves inadequate to the demands of globalization.

Furthermore, the globalization of children's lives is largely unacknowledged and unregulated by either rights or citizenship. Children's status and membership are still largely subsumed under patrimony, which treats children as embodiments of the identity of their family, ethnicity, or state. Meanwhile, children's migration increasingly reflects commodification, which positions children as a uniquely vulnerable sector of the labor force. While liberal states strive to regulate the worst abuses of "displaced dependents," there is no comprehensive recognition of children's rights as individuals or potential independent membership. Even refugee children do not always receive the legal personhood to which they are entitled by international law, although the small subset of unaccompanied minors who are victims of trafficking or severe civil conflict are increasingly recognized by the liberal developed countries.

Transnational adoption, the smallest and most specialized flow of children across borders, is also the only area that systematically transfers membership and considers rights. Rooted in the patrimonial assignment of identity through family, transnational adoption now reflects the competing logics of globalization. Surplus children are produced by developing nations, while developed countries increasingly import all forms of reproduction. But in response to this commodification and transnationalization of the private realm, a strong sector of transnational civil society has developed to assert the rights of women, children, and migrants. Thus, evolving state policies and international agreements seek to realize an uneasy blend of collective cultural rights, individual "best interests of the child," and rights of the (birth and adoptive) family vis-à-vis the state. While states continue to exercise immigration vigilance over adoption flows, receiving states in this area are unusually responsive to private and transnational concerns, and do not systematically limit or generally disqualify intercountry adoptions. Furthermore, foreign adopted children imported into families of citizens ultimately receive full citizenship, in contrast to the many potential barriers faced by native-born children whose biological families are ethnically distinct, of mixed nationalities, unwed, or displaced.

The contradictions of children's citizenship show the need to rethink a number of assumptions concerning globalization and rights. First, people out of place are vulnerable not just outside of national borders, but outside of the social borders of their assigned family membership. Second, even the most cosmopolitan system of rights cannot yet protect people who are truly incapable of representing themselves. As in other cases of the citizenship gap, states are challenged to simultaneously extend greater membership to children currently excluded and to incorporate the full range of international rights of children and migrants within the citizenship package available to all. All of this means that children must move from a special privatized status to some form of civic personhood. The emerging global order must answer the claims of 2 billion children—to be treated as persons in policy and practice.

Notes

1. The United States shows an early liberal pattern, as patriarchal doctrines in family law were first challenged in the 1830s by the emergence of the doctrine of "best interests of the child" (Grossberg 1985).

2. A phenomenon that reveals the same logic of selective citizenship and migration rights based on an embedded domestic division of labor is the creation of special visas for foreign domestic workers to accompany diplomatic families to the United States. In the past ten years, over 35,000 such visas have been issued (Greenhouse *New York Times* 2001). Human

rights organizations link this second-class "private" citizenship with widespread exploitation and abuse (Human Rights Watch 2001).

3. There is a long-standing and controversial history of intercultural adoption following war or conquest. The sending culture framed these adoptions in patrimonial terms as an appropriation and loss of identity, while the dominant society depicted it in universalist liberal terms as both economically rational and in the "best interests of the child" to assimilate to the dominant culture. The history of adoption by dominant cultures has led to criticism of interracial adoptions by minority groups in the liberal states, which has sometimes extended to transnational intercultural adoptions. In the strongest case, the Indian Child Welfare Act of 1978 grants tribes "sovereignty" over children born on the reservation, and explicitly cites the rights of the tribe to preserve its identity through its children (Altstein and Simon 2000: 28). Similarly, at the international level most African states have taken the patrimonial position—perhaps recalling the appropriation of the slave trade—leading many African countries to ban international adoption despite large numbers of available children and a dearth of domestic placements and institutions.

4. The fear of loss of children may help to explain the persistent but unsubstantiated rumors in Latin America that adopted children have been secretly kidnapped for organ transplants (Pahz 1988: 16; Scheper-Hughes 1998). While illicit international traffic in organ transplants has developed, it overwhelmingly involves adults who could not medically benefit from children's organs. Although isolated cases of illicit local medical experimentation on street children have been documented in Latin America, to date there is no evidence of transnational trafficking of children to the United States for medical purposes.

5. Comparative and international law distinguishes between two forms of adoption. A "simple" adoption transfers guardianship to adoptive parents without severing the legal relationship to the biological family. By contrast, a "full" adoption completely transforms the child's legal identity to the natural child of the adoptive parents and extinguishes all claims to or from the birth parents.

6. General characteristics of the legal institution that differ among states are whether adoption requires a court order or a simple contract, whether it cuts off the relationship to the biological family ("full adoption"), whether adoption gives the child full equal status vis-à-vis the adoptive parents, and whether adoption is revocable. While most states are moving toward court-ordered, full, equal-status, irrevocable adoption, there are significant exceptions, such as Brazil's prohibition of full adoption to foreigners (Loon 1992: 138–39).

7. On the other hand, this particular phenomenon illustrates the potential for new forms of projection of collective identity at the expense of children's rights. In a relatively benign but still disturbing way, some lesbian adoptive parents preferentially seek female children from China's "surplus," as females are apparently harder to produce via artificial insemination (Rich 2000).

8. It is interesting to contemplate how many domestic biological parents could satisfy these criteria—and whether they should have to.

V
Reconstructing Citizenship

10

Citizenship and Globalism

Markets, Empire, and Terrorism

RICHARD FALK

The essential argument of this chapter is that the rise of transnational economic forces during the 1990s exerted a major influence on the understanding and practice of citizenship that marks itself off from the preceding period of statism, as well as the emergent subsequent period of global warfare directed at overcoming the challenges of megaterrorism traumatically posed on September 11, 2001. In the pre-1990s period the Westphalian model of world order based on a society of states prevailed to such an extent as to associate citizenship, as a meaningful dimension of political participation, quite totalistically with full membership in a particular sovereign state (Bull 1977; Jackson 2000). The state, with the reinforcing support of international law, deliberately subordinated the idea and practice of nationality to statehood, thereby attempting to coopt divergent nationalist loyalties of its inhabitants. This effort was not consistently successful. As a result, periodic attempts were made by dissatisfied minorities to reconfigure the boundaries of states or to establish zones of autonomy within existing boundaries. The rise of "nationalism" as the basis for community was itself a major dimension of the secularizing process that accompanied the rise of statism from the seventeenth century onward, and was complementary to the determined effort to exclude religious influence from the public sphere of governance. But it was always an ambiguous reality, conflating juridical ideas of membership and affiliation with a more spontaneous politics associated with identity and desire.

But there were all along important sources of popular resistance to this dominant statist trend arising from marginalized and dissatisfied ethnic identities and as a result of antisecular refusals to supersede religious solidarity or to accept a rigid separation of church from state. Captive "nations" remained trapped within state boundaries, giving rise to autonomy and secessionist movements designed to achieve a maximal overlap of personal and group solidarity, nations, and states in fully legitimate political units, what were sometimes privileged as "natural political communities." Also, especially during the colonial period, citizens of colonial powers were given varying degrees of extraterritorial exemption from and protection of their special status when physically present in various non-Western countries, an invidious departure from territorial law that inculcated relations of superiority and inferiority, leading the supposedly inferior over time to resist and revolt. Despite these qualifications, the core reality of citizenship in the modern era could be accurately related to the territorial domain of the sovereign state. To be sure, there were all along idiosyncratic and visionary claims of "global citizenship," particularly in the aftermath of the two twentieth-century world wars, but these were usually animated by antiwar fervor and associated with isolated yearnings of individuals for world government, world peace, and affirmations of human solidarity. These globalizing perspectives never acquired grassroots backing, remaining so marginal in their political relevance as to be treated as sentimental anomalies of an overwhelmingly statist reality, and of no conceptual or political importance. Exemplary individuals seemingly dedicating their lives and energies to humanity, such as Albert Schweitzer and Dag Hammarskjöld, were often identified as "citizens of the world" or "world citizens," giving a certain weight to this idealist image of an essentially unified human species (Little 2001: 3–38).

The secularization of politics was also generally descriptive of an evolving reality in the West, although from time to time the prevailing religious identity intruded on the affairs of state in ways that were contested by the mainstream tradition. This religious undercurrent that persisted in the face of ascendant secularism was in many respects a tension that could be contrasted with that of ethnic and nationalist resistance, as it tended to derive from those who were advantaged with the established order, and resented the self-restraints implied by the commitment to the body politic as a whole to keep the state free from religious taint. This bargain or implicit contract relating to citizenship meant that in exchange for subordinating particular identities and accepting the state as internally sovereign the society as a whole would benefit from law and order, from larger markets, and from protection against external enemies.

What the 1990s brought to the fore was the erosion of the modern prevalence of statism, the rise of regionalism and globalism as a restructuring of the reigning political imagination, and the prominence of such nonstate actors as global corporations and banks, as well as an array of transnational civic associations. At work was a cumulative process that was gradually giving shape to a post-Westphalian process most commonly labeled "globalization" (Falk 1999a, 2000a). Two principal tendencies began to reshape our understanding of citizenship in this period: first, a multilayered and flexible sense of secondary membership and participation in nonstate political and economic communities of varying scope; second, a vague but significant association of citizenship and loyalty with entities lacking territorial boundaries and not qualifying for membership in standard international institutions, most notably the United Nations.[1] An important part of this reconfiguring of identity and participation can be associated, especially in retrospect, with the declining prospect of *international* warfare following the collapse of the Soviet Union and the accompanying disappearance of socialism as a challenge to capitalism. The security functions of the state, so linked to its military capabilities to defend borders against intruders, were beginning to wither away, increasingly being seen as either unnecessary or useless. One result was to weaken the formal sort of nationalism juridically managed by the state, and the rise of a variety of ethnic and religious nationalisms that challenged from within the modern secular state, intensifying state-shattering claims of self-determination in many parts of the world. Of course, in the main, the state maintained its centrality in political life for most peoples in the world, including a military role seen as necessary for the security of territorial inhabitants.

And until the 1990s the state succeeded in defining the right of self-determination so that it could only be legally implemented in ways that did not result in the dismemberment of existing states. After the Cold War, the breakup of the Soviet Union, and, more so, the fragmentation of Yugoslavia into its constituent republics with the backing of much of the international community, introduced a measure of uncertainty as to the scope of the right of self-determination, thereby shifting some of the legal and moral ground from under the sovereign state (Falk 1997). Along these lines, as well, was the rise in the 1990s of the idea that international society had some responsibility for intervening to prevent severe abuses of human rights, and that under such conditions normal deference to territorial sovereignty would be suspended. The Kosovo war of 1999, operating under the dubious regional auspices of NATO, became the exceedingly controversial test case for so-called humanitarian intervention. In essence, the rise of human rights, the growth of external procedures for accountability and enforcement, further challenged the idea of territorial supremacy. This idea had been the crucial feature in the formulation of the sovereignty-oriented conception of citizenship that had dominated the doctrines and practices of citizenship during the modern era. This cumulative subversion of the foundations of statism also gave rise to a renewed interest in civilizational identities, reflected in the global resonance accorded Samuel Huntington's notorious thesis about "the clash of civilizations" (Huntington 1996). Beyond the hype, what was at stake was the realization that the state was being displaced from above by market forces and technological innovation, from below by a resurgence of traditional religious and cultural identities, and from without by a more aggressive approach to the implementation of international human rights standards. Even the computer played a role in this process, creating "virtual communities" exhibiting a contemptuous disregard for international boundaries and governmental institutions. Internet addicts began to refer themselves as "netizens," and professed their confidence in "self-organizing systems" and a libertarian ethos that had little need and a minimal desire for governmental institutions. These ideas, so prevalent in the dot.com world that was so ascendant in the 1990s, meshed perfectly with the neoliberal sentiments that were dominating global economic policy, and emphasized trust in the market to allocate resources in a far more socially beneficial manner than could be achieved by activist governments.

It was in this atmosphere of the 1990s that the state, struggling to retain its authority and legitimacy, generated more and more support for ambitious normative (law and morality) projects that did not call for increased spending on the discredited welfare sector. The state was seeking to recast itself, especially in light of criticisms of its top-heavy bureaucracy and heartless passivity in the face of market priorities, as a different kind of ethical actor, less preoccupied with the well-being of its own citizens and more concerned with its international role and reputation. Expanding political space existed for humanitarian diplomacy of various sorts that responded to the sufferings of vulnerable peoples, support was given for strengthening the human rights regime of the UN and in relation to foreign policy, past and current political leaders were being formally charged with crimes against humanity and severe abuses of their own citizens and were being held individually accountable, and suddenly historical grievances of long ago associated with the Holocaust, slavery, the dispossession of indigenous peoples, and other suppressed causes were gaining a hearing and were being assuaged by a variety of symbolic and substantive gestures of accommodation (Barkun 2000; Falk 2000b).

These moves were a consequence of unprecedented degrees of cooperation between moderate governments and a coalition of civil society actors, culminating in the treaty establishing the International Criminal Court that came into being in July 2002, giving a certain rudimentary institutional reality to the visionary idea that the rule of law did not stop at the borders of sovereign states. Such an evolution was difficult to assess in relation to citizenship, although it was clearly contributing to a sense that meaningful participation in political life, whether measured by rights, claims, entitlements, or responsibilities, was undergoing a profound set of changes that were building the foundations, at least, for the construction of an eventual global polity. These changes related particularly to the loosening of state-society bonds, and an increasingly plural sense of political community. It is this series of developments, promising yet preliminary and admittedly beset by uncertainties and contradictions, that has screeched to a halt, at least temporarily, as a result of September 11 and its aftermath.

What September 11 revealed, first of all, was the grim underside of globalization, including the moral and legal pretensions of this dominant strand of a post-Westphalian world order. By exposing the acute vulnerability of the most powerful and complex modern state to the extremist hostility of its Islamic opponents, a dynamic of action and reaction was unleashed with a wide range of divergent consequences the outcome of which remains to be determined at this point. In an important respect, the attacks reveal a continuity with the 1990s, exhibiting, in a shocking set of acts, the potency of nonterritorial, multistate networking and the functional necessity of global reach as the precondition for societal security (Castels 1996–98). Indeed, the al Qaeda network was also a post-Westphalian phenomenon in the primary sense that its struggle and Osama bin Laden's vision did not center on the seizure or reform of state power or a territorial base of operations, but seemed instead resolved to launch an intercivilizational war. The overarching stated political goal was to reconstitute the historic caliphate, abolished with the fall of the Ottoman Empire after the First World War, so that it could again over time unify the Islamic world, thereby overcoming the political and cultural fragmentation associated with the imposed Westphalian order, which was deeply criticized as a European invention and imposition incompatible with Islamic values of a single overarching human reality. The modernist ideas of nationalism, patriotism, and secular political life were all treated as decadent from the perspective of bin Laden, thereby explaining the sense of decline and the experience of humiliation in the Arab world of Islam. Al Qaeda's immediate goal was to resist Western, especially American, presence in the holy lands of Islam.

The American response was the mirror image in some respects, the exact opposite in others: in waging war against terrorism in general, the United States seemed to embark on a war without any clear lines of spatial or temporal demarcation, the battlefield could be anywhere, a global reach was claimed, and there was no prospect that an ending could be established with confidence (Ali 2002; Vidal 2002). Such a campaign was launched with an invitation issued to all foreign governments by the White House to participate in the antiterrorist coalition and a warning that a failure to do so would identify a government as part of the terrorist threat, and hence an enemy. This ultimatum was then extended to the American-led struggle against "rogue states" relabeled "the axis of evil." The relevant point is that the U.S. response was of a scope and intensity that ignored the sovereign rights of other states and refused to be bound by the contemporary restraints of international law governing recourse to force or the antiwar framework and procedures of the United Nations Charter. Given the exigencies of the situation in the immediate aftermath of the al Qaeda attacks, including the prospect of further attacks and the inability to be secure in a defensive mode against such suicidal extremism, there was a strong case for adapting the Westphalian template to the distinctive challenge of megaterrorism.[2]

Simultaneously, and with opposite effects, September 11 revived the security role and territoriality of the sovereign state in a dramatic form, at least for the United States, the current hegemon. And with that revival came one of statist American patriotism and nationalism in a variant more intense than anything previously experienced in this country. For this most powerful of states, citizenship suddenly reverted to waving the American flag, entrusting the government with dangerously expanded police powers and implicit authority to undertake warfare anywhere on the planet in secret and without the meaningful participation of the U.S. Congress. These dramatic developments had the effect of suddenly reversing the precepts of economic globalization by endowing the state with an activist and predominant *global* regulatory role that abruptly subordinated market considerations. Of course, it was not a Westphalian society of states that was being reconstituted in this setting, but an inchoate American informal empire that created a spectrum of responses elsewhere, ranging from willing subjugation to worried defiance.[3] What seems evident is that the patterns of citizenship in such a world beset by disruptive and confusing tensions are in the process of undergoing fundamental change, which will lead to a dynamic of growing differentiation for the next several decades. The regionalization of political community around normative ideas in Europe contrasts with the reinscription of imperial nationalism as the basis of political community and identity in the United States (Kagan 2002). Trends in other regions exhibit other features combining statist ideas with those of a less territorially specific character. There is also an important Asian anti-interventionist trend that emphasizes the inalienability of sovereign rights in a postcolonial setting.

This leads overall to two questions that underlie the discussion that follows: How does the switch from economic to military empire building by the United States bear on these diverse citizenship trends? What types of resistance to such a prospect are likely to take hold around the world, with what impacts on traditional and postmodern forms of citizenship?

Tensions of the Times

John Walker Lindh, the so-called American Taliban, exemplifies the deeper tensions of identity and obligation in a globalizing world. To the extent that the world is borderless, an altered sense of citizenship would be coming into being in such a manner as to take account of the complex multiple layering that individuals experience with increasing intensity. But to the extent that the security imperatives following September 11 achieve priority, the flattening of identity and obligation results from the imposition of nationalist criteria. Lindh is caught in the middle of this fire storm, apparently following his religious conscience where it would lead without regard to conventional boundaries, including nationalist affiliations, yet made criminally accountable by the application of territorially based criminal law, and in the spirit of vindicative patriotism. The fact that Lindh eventually pleaded guilty to some of the charges brought against him so as to avoid the likelihood of receiving a life sentence at trial does not change the realization that he found himself trapped between conflicting conceptions of primary identity and membership that are illustrative of a far more general cosmodrama pitting territorial affiliations against those of a nonterritorial or transterritorial character.

From another perspective, Osama bin Laden's worldview involves an uncompromising rejection of a world order based on sovereign states, and a demonic capability to pose a formidable threat to the life and liberty of his statist enemies. Bin Laden believes that Mohammed intended a unified Islamic *umma*, that the fragmentation of this community in the form of distinct sovereign states is itself a Western invention and intervention that by its very nature produces corruption and decadence. This negativity is decisively revealed by allowing the non-Islamic West to gain footholds close to the most sacred of Islamic sites on the Arabian Peninsula. It was the deployment of American troops in Saudi Arabia near Mecca and Medina in the setting of the Gulf War in the early 1990s that evidently represented the breaking point for bin Laden. So conceived, such an Islamicized individual has far-reaching duties to Islam, but not to the state of residence or citizenship. This rejection of a nationalist approach to membership in a community, and indirectly to citizenship, also represents a flattening of identity and obligation, but in the direction of religious and civilizational identity, and away from territorially based identity.

Such generalizations seem to pertain with particular force to the circumstances and ambitions of the United States, the target of the September 11 attacks, and the epicenter of globalization, and in an opposite manner to the followers of its hidden adversary. There is an irony manifest here that would be comic if its impact did not seem so tragic: the state most associated with dominating the policy agenda of globalization retreats to an apparent posture of ultranationalism, while its ultratraditionalist enemy carries into the lifeworld one vision of a clash of civilizations. Much of the rest of the world is caught in the middle, a zone of increasing danger and concern, and seeming impotence.

But there are further complicating factors. Even before September 11, the Bush administration was doing its best to move away from internationalizing effects of globalization. It was extremely busy repudiating multilateral treaties that were important pillars of international cooperation, making the antiglobalization point that it did not need or want the binding ties of multilateralism. Particularly significant, it was going ahead with the militarization of space (defensively and offensively) in defiance of the views of its closest allies. In the aftermath of September 11 these attitudes have persisted, even intensified. The overall situation has become confused by the seemingly inconsistent American demand that others cooperate in the global war against terrorism, and indirectly by the Enron scandal that makes a mockery of neoliberal claims that corporate globalization is best guided by the self-regulating forces of market capitalism. There is increasing reason to believe that the undisclosed priority of the Bush presidency is to establish the first truly global empire in history, and that it is to be governed from Washington (Lemann 2002). Arguably, prior to Bush there existed a strong imperial element in the American global role associated with presiding over a capital-driven dynamic of globalization (Hardt and Negri 2000). This imperial alternative to a deterritorialized economic globalization raised two linked concerns relating to the future of citizenship, globally conceived: How does the switch from economic to military empire building by the United States bear on global citizenship trends? What types of resistance to such a prospect are likely to take hold around the world, with what impact on traditional forms of citizenship?

On the one side, there is the revival of American nationalism associated with the anger and sense of continuing vulnerability associated with September 11 (Falk 2002). On the other side, there is the latent concern elsewhere about neutralizing some of the unilateralist and empire-building tendencies of this new American world crusade directed at terrorist networks. It is important to take account of the degree to which this "new war" pits the most globalized state against a nonterritorial network allegedly "present" in more than sixty states, including quite likely United States itself. In this latter sense there is a convergence of globalizations, the global empire versus the global network.[4] The American turn toward unilateralism and empire may thus be paradoxically interpreted as the state fighting for its life, the last stand of modernity so to speak, with the state fighting to save its soul (that is, the struggle to retain the primary allegiance of its citizenry). If this line of analysis has any purchase on reality, then the disposition of the Lindh case is of major symbolic importance, a collective reaffirmation of nationalist patriotism achieved by ritual sacrifice of a secular apostate, as performed by a compliant criminal justice system that is itself led by a born-again patriot.

There is one further preliminary observation relating to the modalities of resistance as bearing on the nature of citizenship. The most disturbing metaphor is that of the most severe cycle of violence unleashed against the Palestinians during Sharon's tenure as leader of Israel. Along this axis of speculation, if America persists on its present course, it will be confronted by the equivalent of "suicide bombers" around the world, resisting as the alternative to surrender and subjugation. The more hopeful alternative is the strengthening of regional tendencies as defensive shields, bypassing the state as the custodian of security, and building up a post-Westphalian hierarchy of overlapping political identities. An intermediate prospect is a regression from globalization to a new phase of "old geopolitics," the American imperial quest generating defensive alliances that seek to reestablish some sort of balance of power, which in the nuclear age would imply the deterrence of the United States. The peculiar feature of the period since 1990 is that the United States is essentially undeterred even with respect to nuclear weaponry, a condition that has not existed since the closing days of the Second World War, when atomic bombs were used in a context where no threat of retaliation existed (what I have elsewhere termed "the Hiroshima temptation"; Falk and Krieger 2002).

What this new global setting suggests is a highly dialectical dynamic bearing on citizenship. The leader of globalization insisting on chauvinistic patriotism, while much of the rest of the world is struggling either with the ordeals of statelessness (consider the entrapped nations: Kurds, Tibetans, Chechens, indigenous peoples, and many, many others), seeking to find regional or civilizational alternatives to statism, or relying on defensive statism to uphold its political and cultural autonomy in the face of economic globalization and empire build-ing. Global citizenship is for the moment, at least, eclipsed by these dramatic developments spiraling out from September 11, but also representing trends that preexisted the attacks.

Constructing Global Citizenship: The Unfinished Normative Revolution of the 1990s

With the ending of the Cold War and the collapse of the Soviet Union, several international developments ensued, and others that had been previously back-grounded by war/peace preoccupations, suddenly emerged into the sunlight of global consciousness. The most prominent of these adjustments was the shift in policy priorities of leading governments from security concerns to the chal-lenges posed by the world economy. The controversial labeling of this dynamic as "globalization" gave rise to a new phase of public debate, which pitted the dominant ideas of neoliberalism (globalization from above) against the perspectives of a range of critics (globalization from below; Falk 1999b). It was against this background that a renewed interest in citizenship emerged, especially to take account of the diminishing adequacy of relying on a purely Westphalian account of political identity in the face of the growing role of nonstate actors and the diminishing capacity of the territorial state to safe-guard and promote human well-being, as well as to provide political identity.

Such a reconfiguring of citizenship had several distinct features reflecting new patterns of thought, action, values, and sentiment that were achieving prominence. "Global citizenship" could be conceived as either the sum of these parts, or as those post-Westphalian identities that were global in scope or that rested on an ethical or anthropological premise of human solidarity.

If the first approach to global citizenship is adopted, then two strands of re-configuration need to be taken into consideration: the regional conferral of European citizenship as performed by the Maastricht Treaty establishing the European Union, and the more informal patterns of regional identification that achieve a certain kind of de facto "citizenship" for sub-Saharan Africa, for Asia, for the Arab world, and for Latin America. Closely related to this emerg-ing regional citizenship, itself diverse in effect, are overlapping patterns of reli-gious and civilization identity that both reinforce regionalism and extend it geographically and conceptually. The formation by Osama bin Laden of an Arab Brigade to join the Afghan resistance against the Soviet intervention dur-ing the 1980s is emblematic, linking this religious/civilization sense of engage-ment to the sort of security crisis that has been generated by September 11.

The second approach is what is more conventionally understood by the rubric of "global citizenship." It has several distinct orientations that need to be separately analyzed to assess their wider implications. There is the "one world" postulates of world federalists who seek to achieve by steps, or through a leap in political consciousness, a centralized form of world order capped by "world government." Such attitudes derive essentially from the belief that war is intolerable, and that the global path to peace resembles the state path—that is, through constitutionalism and governmental authority backed by police capabilities. Such views have no political base, derive from a detached Enlightenment consciousness that privileges the rational mind, formulated almost exclusively in the West, and are viewed with suspicion in non-Western countries as disguised empire building. A second dimension of global citizenship is associated with the operatives of the world economy who view the world as essentially a borderless market (Ohmae 1999). The role of states is to serve this market, to take their instructions from financial markets and to accord deference to any consensus that derives from the World Economic Forum (Davos). There is a cultural rootlessness that accompanies such "global citizenship," expressed by the empty homogeneity of international hotels, popular culture, consumerism, franchise capitalism, airports, life style, and the universalizing of the English language. It is not surprising that critics of globalization regard such tendencies as extensions of American global ambitions rather than as expressions of the existence of an authentic global community. The corporate embrace of globalism should perhaps not even be associated with citizenship, as it posits no accompanying global community, and hence contains no bonds of solidarity with those who are weak and disadvantaged. At the same time, those who operate in such settings see themselves as "global citizens," at home everywhere, but lacking any definitive address.

Closely related are the inhabitants of cyberspace who view the Internet as the basis for a reconstituted world that relies on self-organizing systems, disavowing regulative roles for governmental institutions on the grounds of both values and efficiency. Their citizenship is articulated in terms of "netizenship" to set it off from the bonds of commitment associated with a world of sovereign states. Netizens have their libertarian community with its own protocols of freedom and technological optimism.

Fortunately, there are more positive forms of global citizenship at the horizons of change. The human rights and environmental movements gave rise to a variety of social and activist orientations that associate identity with normative commitments without territorial content more than with traditional approaches to reform on a state or society basis (Keck and Sikkink 1998). In the first half of the 1990s these global identities were impressively networked, especially in the arenas provided by a series of UN conferences on global issues (environment, human rights, population, social welfare, women), which also served to incubate a nascent aspiration and demand for global democracy. There were many initiatives in this direction that began to assume a more coherent formation in the antiglobalization movement starting with the Seattle demonstrations against the WTO at the end of 1999, culminating in the protests directed at the Genoa meeting of the G-8 just a few months before September 11. At the same time, there was a statist backlash that reacted against allowing these forces of global civil society to be provided with such potent arenas in the future, with wide opportunities for media exposure and the opportunity to make manifest the refusal of leading governments to respond to normative (moral and legal) challenges of global scale. Such a backlash was intensified by the U.S. walkout from the 2001 UN Conference on Racism held in Durban. From the perspective of citizenship, these initiatives situated the activists in various zones related to global civil society. The sense of participation and affiliation or membership is quite complex, varying from issue to issue, and evolving over time, especially in relation to the changing global setting. For the purposes of this chapter these activists complement or supersede their Westphalian citizenship with a new connectedness to global civil society (Colas 2002; Lipschutz 1992; Anheier, Glasius, and Kaldor 2001). It is a politically engaged modality of global citizenship that is oppositional in part, reformist in part, and visionary in part. In the latter part of the 1990s these transnational energies were most effectively expressed in collaboration with a coalition of governments dedicated to shared treatymaking undertakings. The most notable successes of this "new internationalism" were the Anti-Personnel Landmines Treaty and the Rome Treaty on the Establishment of an International Criminal Court.

This orientation toward global citizenship was also exhibited in the one-time Millennium Assembly of NGO representatives held in 2000 within the halls of the United Nations. This was an initiative pushed with vigor by Kofi Annan, the secretary general, despite considerable foot-dragging by Washington. As might be expected, the participants were eager to extend their beachhead in the UN system by institutionalizing their access in the spirit of global democracy. While corporate actors have enjoyed some success in their efforts to gain a legitimizing presence within the United Nations, civil society actors have been rebuffed. In reaction, the antiglobalization movement has had increasing success in establishing its own arenas, the most notable of which so far has been the annual sessions of the World Social Forum meeting in Porto Allegre, Brazil, dialectically modeled to imitate the structure and counter the influence of the World Economic Forum. In further reaction, there is considerable advocacy around the world in support of the creation of a Global Peoples Assembly chosen by some sort of electoral process (Falk and Strauss 2001).

The general idea is to promote global or cosmopolitan democracy, building on the European experience, especially the European Court of Human Rights and the European Parliament (Archibugi and Held 1995). There is further recent encouragement for such an undertaking arising from the resolve of the African Union to adopt as a definite commitment the establishment of an African parliamentary institution.

There are also present more visionary approaches to global citizenship that draw on utopian and religious traditions. I have tried in the past to suggest such a perspective on participation and membership through the terminology of "citizen pilgrim." The citizen pilgrim is embarked upon a long journey, that of the pilgrim, but with fulfillment to be achieved at some undesignated point in the future. In this trope, the citizen pilgrim is a global citizen with a predominantly temporal identity that contrasts with that of the world federalist who is a captive of spatial identity. The consciousness of the citizen pilgrim is more closely aligned with that of the transnational activist who identifies global citizenship with an engagement in a values-driven process, promoting specific goals but necessarily rooted in present urgencies, and typically to some degree anti-utopian in relation to the adoption of any grand overarching solution, although not inherently or permanently so. If the present crises in world order lead to the eruption of major warfare, especially if nuclear or other weapons of mass destruction are used, it would not be surprising to witness the emergence of a movement dedicated to a one-world polity organized on democratic lines, and with a strong commitment to the demilitarization of global security.

I think this matrix of global citizenship was facilitated in the 1990s (Falk, forthcoming). There was a sense that globalizing trade, investment, and labor policy were redefining political space in such a way as to diminish the significance of the sovereign state. Indeed those who had earlier seen states as obstacles to humane global governance reversed course and came to regard a strong, people-oriented social democratic state as the most feasible means to promote the goals of globalization from below. The dramatic breakthroughs in European regionalism also had the effect of weakening the Westphalian grip on citizenship and loyalty, as did the absence of credible strategic conflict among major states.

At least temporarily, September 11 has reasserted the primacy of the security state, at least in the United States, and made globalization seem a secondary phenomenon, by no means rejected, but definitely subordinated to the war on global terror. More damaging in relation to the theme of global citizenship, the military focus and nationalistic climate that has been generated by September 11 has disrupted the normative revolution, at least for now. Despite the momentum of some undertakings, such as the successful moves to establish the International Criminal Court by obtaining the needed sixty ratifications in 2002, there has been introduced into patterns of global governance a single-minded preoccupation with antiterrorist actions. Of course, if this attention were to be extended to address the root causes of terrorism it could revive the normative revolution from the opposite direction. By and large, the American leadership has been unwilling to engage in the sort of self-criticism that might move along such a path, but there are glimmers of hope. The Bush administration surprisingly, given its overall hostility to governmental approaches to social issues, upped the U.S. contributions to foreign economic assistance by about $5 billion in 2002, seemingly in recognition of the connections between poverty and terrorism in the countries of the south. But such a gesture pales beside the huge increase of resources given to the military, including for developing and deploying an expensive defense shield against incoming nuclear weapons. It pales even more in relation to a new American doctrine relating to the use of nuclear weapons, which basically seems to make these instruments of war available for use in situations where important battlefield advantages would ensue. Most damaging so far has been the coupling of security with nationalistic forms of patriotism that view criticism of government policy as tantamount to disloyalty.

As suggested by the earlier discussion of the Lindh case, there is a surge of antiglobalist political feelings that have dominated the American scene since September 11. Given the leading role of the United States, this means both a retreat from global citizenship by some constituencies and a probable embrace by others, including in the form of providing the peoples of the world with an alternative future to that of an American empire imposed by force to the extent necessary. In this sense, September 11 could actually strengthen global (and regional) citizenship, to achieve countervailing power and influence to that wielded by the United States, but it may also lead to a revival of nineteenth- and twentieth-century alliance politics and rivalries shaped by Westphalian actors. In essence, the impact of September 11 is substantial, yet inconclusive, and probably not unidirectional. The most likely pattern of influence is to en-hance statism in some settings, both offensively (empire building) and defensively (avoiding hegemonic encroachments), and weaken it in others (globalization, interventionary and hegemonic statecraft).

In sum, citizenship as a dimension of world order is no longer a simple mat-ter. The Westphalian framework, although still crucial, cannot by itself provide an adequate purchase on political reality. A more complex and differentiated model is needed, one that includes different styles of traditional citizenship but also is open to regional, transnational, and global identities that make their own citizenship claims.

Notes

1. For varying perspectives see Kymlicka 1995 and Ong 1999.
2. I have explored this case, and its limits, in *The Great Terror War*. (Falk, 2003)
3. The apologists and rationalizers of this new order are receiving mainstream approval at this point, but the consensus is fraying around the issue of waging war against Iraq. Among the more perceptive presentations, see Bobbit 2002, Kaplan 2002, and Ferguson 2002. Also see the new breed of "humanitarian imperialists" most articulately depicted in the writings of Michael Ignatieff. Ignatieff is an interesting instance, as he was a forceful advocate of humanitarian intervention in the 1990s, and has now recast the argument to take account of post–September 11 realities, but with an equivalent justification for interventionary diplomacy under an American aegis. See Ignatieff 2002.
4. The structural importance of networking as subversive of territoriality is the major theme of Castels 1996–98.

11
The Repositioning of Citizenship*

SASKIA SASSEN

Most of the scholarship on citizenship has claimed a necessary connection to the national state. The transformations afoot today raise questions about this proposition insofar as they significantly alter those conditions that in the past fed that articulation between citizenship and the national state. The context for this possible alteration is defined by two major, partly interconnected conditions. One is the change in the position and institutional features of national states since the 1980s resulting from various forms of globalization. These range from economic privatization and deregulation to the increased prominence of the international human rights regime. The second is the emergence of multiple actors, groups, and communities partly strengthened by these transformations in the state and increasingly unwilling to automatically identify with a nation as represented by the state.

Addressing the question of citizenship against these transformations entails a specific stance. It is quite possible to posit that at the most abstract or formal level not much has changed over the last century in the essential features of citizenship. The theoretical ground from which I address the issue is that of the historicity and the embeddedness of both categories, citizenship and the national state, rather than their purely formal features. Each of these has been constructed in elaborate and formal ways. And each has evolved historically as a tightly packaged bundle of what were in fact often rather diverse elements. The dynamics at work today are destabilizing these particular bundlings and bringing to the fore the fact itself of that bundling and its particularity. Through their destabilizing effects, these dynamics are producing operational and rhetorical openings for the emergence of new types of political subjects and new spatialities for politics.

More broadly, the destabilizing of national state-centered hierarchies of legitimate power and allegiance has enabled a multiplication of nonformalized or only partly formalized political dynamics and actors. These signal a deterritorializing of citizenship practices and identities, and of discourses about

---

* This text is based on the keynote lecture, conference of the *Berkeley Journal of Sociology* on "Race and Ethnicity in a Global Context," held at the University of California, Berkeley (March 7, 2002), reprinted in the *Journal*.

loyalty and allegiance. Finally, specific transformations inside the national state have directly and indirectly altered particular features of the institution of citizenship. These transformations are not predicated necessarily on deterritorialization or locations for the institution outside the national state as is key to conceptions of postnational citizenship, and hence are usefully distinguished from current notions of postnational citizenship. I will refer to these as denationalized forms of citizenship.

Analytically I seek to understand how various transformations entail continuities or discontinuities in the basic institutional form. That is to say, where do we see continuities in the formal bundle of rights at the heart of the institution and where do we see movement toward postnational and/or denationalized features of citizenship? And where might as yet informal citizenship practices engender formalizations of new types of rights?

Particular attention goes to several specific issues that capture these features. One of these is the relationship between citizenship and nationality and the evolution of the latter toward something akin to "effective" nationality rather than "allegiance" to one state or exclusively formal nationality. In a later section of this chapter I examine the mix of distinct elements that actually make up the category of citizenship in today's highly developed countries. Far from being a unitary category or a mere legal status, these diverse elements of citizenship can be contradictory. One of my assumptions here is that the destabilizing impact of globalization contributes to accentuating the distinctiveness of each of these elements. A case in point is the growing tension between the legal form and the normative project toward enhanced inclusion as various minorities and disadvantaged sectors gain visibility for their claim making. Critical here is the failure in most countries to achieve "equal" citizenship—that is, not just a formal status but an enabling condition.

The remaining sections begin to theorize these issues with a view toward specifying incipient and typically not formalized developments in the institution of citizenship. Informal practices and political subjects not quite fully recognized as such can nonetheless function as part of the political landscape. Undocumented immigrants who are long-term residents engage in practices that are the same as those of formally defined citizens in the routines of daily life; this can produce an informal social contract between these undocumented immigrants and the community. Subjects who are by definition categorized as nonpolitical, such as "housewives," may actually have considerable political agency and be emergent political subjects. Insofar as citizenship is at least partly shaped by the conditions within which it is embedded, conditions that have today changed in certain very specific and also general ways, we may well be seeing a corresponding set of changes in the institution itself. These may not yet be formalized, and some may never become fully formalized. Further, social constructions that mark individuals, such as race and ethnicity, may well become destabilized by these developments in both the institution of citizenship and the nation-state. Generally, the analysis in this chapter suggests that we might see a debordering of existing types of subjects, particularly dominant ones such as the citizen-subject, the alien, and the racialized subject.

A concluding section argues that many of the these tranformations in the broader context and in the institution itself become legible in today's large cities. Perhaps the most evolved type of site for these types of transformations is the global city. In this process, the global city is reconfigured as a partly denationalized space that enables a partial reinvention of citizenship. This reinvention takes the institution away from questions of nationality narrowly defined and toward the enactment of a large array of particular interests, from protests against police brutality and globalization to sexual preference politics and house squatting by anarchists. I interpret this as a move toward citizenship practices that revolve around claiming rights to the city. These are not exclusively or necessarily urban practices. But it is especially in large cities that we see simultaneously some of the most extreme inequalities as well as conditions enabling these citizenship practices. In global cities, these practices also contain the possibility of directly engaging strategic forms of power, a fact I interpret as significant in a context where power is increasingly privatized, globalized, and elusive.

Citizenship and Nationality

In its narrowest definition, citizenship describes the legal relationship between the individual and the polity. This relation can in principle assume many forms, in good part depending on the definition of the polity. In Europe the definition of the polity was originally the city, both in ancient and in medieval times. But it is the evolution of polities along the lines of state formation that gave citizenship in the West its full institutionalized and formalized character and that made nationality a key component of citizenship.

Today the terms *citizenship* and *nationality* both refer to the national state. In a technical legal sense, while essentially the same concept, each term reflects a different legal framework. Both identify the legal status of an individual in terms of state membership. But citizenship is largely confined to the national dimension, while nationality refers to the international legal dimension in the context of an interstate system. The legal status entails the specifics of whom the state recognizes as a citizen and the formal basis for the rights and responsibilities of the individual in relation to the state. International law affirms that each state may determine who will be considered a citizen of that state. (See the Hague convention.) Domestic laws about who is a citizen vary significatnly across states, and so do the definitions of what it entails to be a citizen. Even within Europe, let alone worldwide, there are marked differences in how citizenship is articulated and hence how noncitizens are defined.

The aggressive nationalism and territorial competition among European states in the eighteenth and nineteenth centuries and well into the twentieth century made the concept of dual nationality generally undesirable, incompatible with individual loyalties and destabilizing of the international order. Absolute state authority over a territory and its nationals could not easily accommodate dual nationality. Indeed, we see the development of a series of mechanisms aimed at preventing or counteracting the common causes for dual nationality (Marrus 1985). This negative perception of dual nationality continued into the first half of the twentieth century and well into the 1960s. There were no international accords on dual nationality. The main effort by the international system remained rooting out the causes of dual nationality by means of multilateral codification of the law on the subject (Rubenstein and Adler 2000). It is probably the case that this particular form of the institution of citizenship, centered on exclusive allegiance, reached its high point in the twentieth century.

The major transformations of the 1980s and 1990s have once again brought conditions for a change in the institution of citizenship and its relation to nationality, and they have brought about changes in the legal content of nationality. Mostly minor formal and nonformal changes are beginning to dilute the particular formalization coming out of European history. The long-lasting resistance to dual or multiple nationality is shifting toward a selective acceptance. According to some legal scholars (Spiro 1997; Rubenstein and Adler 2000), in the future dual and multiple nationality will become the norm. Today, more people than ever before have dual nationality (Spiro 1997). Insofar as the importance of nationality is a function of the central role of states in the international system, it is quite possible that a decline in the importance of this role and a proliferation of other actors will affect the value of nationality.

These transformations may give citizenship yet another set of features as it continues to respond to the conditions within which it is embedded (Sassen 1996: ch. 2). The nationalizing of the institution that took place over the last several centuries may today give way to a partial denationalizing. A fundamental dynamic in this regard is the growing articulation of national economies with the global economy and the associated pressures on states to be competitive. Crucial to current notions of competitive states is withdrawal from various spheres of citizenship entitlements, with the possibility of a corresponding dilution of loyalty to the state. Citizens' loyalty may in turn be less crucial to the state today than it was at a time of frequent and people-intensive warfare, with its need for loyal citizen-soldiers (Turner 2000). Masses of troops today can be replaced by technologically intensive methods of warfare. Most important, in the highly developed world warfare has become less significant, partly due to economic globalization. Global firms and global markets do not want the rich countries to fight wars among themselves. The "international" project of the most powerful actors on the world stage today is radically different from what it was in the nineteenth century and the first half of the twentieth century.

Many of the dynamics that built economies, polities, and societies in the nineteenth and twentieth centuries contained an articulation between the national scale and the growth of entitlements for citizens. During industrialization, class formation, class struggles, and the advantages of both employers and workers tended to scale at the national level and became identified with state-produced legislation and regulations, entitlements and obligations. The state came to be seen as a key to ensuring the well-being of significant portions of both the working class and the bourgeoisie. The development of welfare states in the twentieth century became a crucial institutional domain for granting entitlements to the poor and the disadvantaged. Today, the growing weight given to notions of the "competitiveness" of states puts pressure on states to cut down on these entitlements. This in turn weakens the reciprocal relationship between the poor and the state (see Munger 2002). Finally, the growth of unemployment and the fact that many of the young are developing weak ties to the labor market, once thought of as a crucial mechanism for the socialization of young adults, will further weaken the loyalty and sense of reciprocity between these future adults and the state (Roulleau-Berger 2002).

As these trends have come together toward the end of the twentieth century they are contributing to a destabilization of the meaning of citizenship as it was forged in the nineteenth century and much of the twentieth century. Economic policies and technical developments we associate with economic globalization have strengthened the importance of cross-border dynamics and reduced that of borders. The associated emphasis on markets has brought into question the foundations of the welfare state. T. H. Marshall and many others saw and continue to see the welfare state as an important ingredient of social citizenship. Today the assumptions of the dominant model of Marshallian citizenship have been severely diluted under the impact of globalization and the ascendance of the market as the preferred mechanism for addressing these social issues. For many critics, the reliance on markets to solve political and social problems is a savage attack on the principles of citizenship. Thus Saunders (1993) argues that citizenship inscribed in the institutions of the welfare state is a buffer against the vagaries of the market and the inequalities of the class system.

The nature of citizenship has also been challenged by a proliferation of old issues that have gained new attention. Among the latter are the question of state membership of aboriginal communities, stateless people, and refugees (Knopp 2002; Sassen 1999). All of these have important implications for human rights in relation to citizenship. These social changes in the role of the state, the impact of globalization on states, and the relationship between dominant and subordinate groups also have major implications for questions of identity. "Is citizenship a useful concept for exploring the problems of belonging, identity and personality in the modern world?" (Schotter 1993: ix; see in this regard Ong's notion of flexible citizenship, 1999: chs. 1 and 4).

Can such a radical change in the conditions for citizenship leave the institution itself unchanged?

Deconstructing Citizenship

Though often talked about as a single concept and experienced as a unitary institution, citizenship actually describes a number of discrete but related aspects in the relation between the individual and the polity. Current developments are bringing to light and accentuating the distinctiveness of these various aspects, from formal rights to practices and psychological dimensions (see Ong 1999; Bosniack 2000). They make legible the tension between citizenship as a formal legal status and citizenship as a normative project or an aspiration. The formal equality granted to all citizens rarely rests on the need for substantive equality in social and even political terms. In brief, current conditions have strengthened the emphasis on rights and aspirations that go beyond the formal legal definition of rights and obligations. This is mirrored most recently in the reinvigoration of theoretical distinctions: communitarian and deliberative, republican and liberal, feminist, postnational, and cosmopolitan notions of citizenship.

Insofar as citizenship is a status that articulates legal rights and responsibilities, the mechanisms through which this articulation is shaped and implemented can be analytically distinguished from the status itself, and so can the content of the rights. In the medieval cities so admired by Max Weber (1958), it was urban residents themselves who set up the structures through which to establish and thicken their rights in the space of the city. Today it is the national state that provides these mechanisms, and it does so for national political space. But these mechanisms may well be changing once again, given globalization, the associated changes in the national state, and the ascendance of human rights. In each of these major phases, the actual content and shape of the legal rights and obligations also changed.

Some of these issues can be illustrated through the evolution of equal citizenship over the last few decades. Equal citizenship is central to the modern institution of citizenship. The expansion of equality among citizens has shaped a good part of its evolution in the twentieth century. There is debate as to what brought about the expanded inclusions over this period, most notably the granting of the vote to women. For some (for example, Karst 2000), it is (national) law itself that has been crucial in promoting recognition of exclusions and measures for their elimination.[1] For others (Young 1990; Taylor 1992), politics and identity have been essential because they provide the sense of solidarity necessary for the further development of modern citizenship in the nation-state. Either way, insofar as equality is based on membership, citizenship status forms the basis of an exclusive politics and identity (Walzer 1985; Bosniak 1996).

In a country such as the United States, the principle of equal citizenship remains unfulfilled, even after the successful struggles and legal advances of the last five decades (Karst 1997). Groups defined by race, ethnicity, religion, sex, sexual orientation, and other "identities" still face various exclusions from full participation in public life notwithstanding formal equality as citizens. Second, because full participation as a citizen rests on a material base (Marshall 1977; Handler 1995), poverty excludes large sectors of the population, and the gap is widening. Feminist and race critical scholarship have highlighted the failure of gender- and race-neutral conceptions of citizenship, such as legal status, to account for the differences of individuals within communities (Crenshaw et al. 1996; Delgado and Stefancic 1999). In brief, legal citizenship does not always bring full and equal membership rights. Citizenship is affected by the position of different groups within a nation-state.

Yet it is precisely the position of these different groups that has engendered the practices and struggles that forced changes in the institution of citizenship itself. Kenneth Karst (1997) observes that in the U.S. it was national law that "braided the strands of citizenship"—formal legal status, rights, belonging—into the principle of equal citizenship. This took place through a series of Supreme Court decisions and acts of Congress beginning with the Civil Rights Act of 1964. Karst emphasizes how important these constitutional and legislative instruments are, and that we cannot take citizenship for granted or be complacent about it.

There are two aspects here that matter for my argument. This history of interactions between differential positionings and expanded inclusions signals the possibility that the new conditions of inequality and difference evident today and the new types of claim making they produce may well bring about further transformations in the institution. Citizenship is partly produced by the practices of the excluded. Second, by expanding the formal inclusionary aspect of citizenship, the national state contributed to creating some of the conditions that eventually would facilitate key aspects of postnational citizenship. At the same time, insofar as the state itself has undergone significant transformation, notably the changes bundled under the notion of the competitive state, it may reduce the chances that state institutions will do the type of legislative and judiciary work that has led to expanded formal inclusions.

The consequence of these two developments may well be the absence of a lineal progression in the evolution of the institution. The expanding inclusions that we have seen in the United States since the 1960s may have produced conditions that make possible forms of citizenship that follow a different trajectory. And the pressures of globalization on national states may mean that claim making will increasingly be directed at other institutions as well. This is already evident in a variety of instances. One example is the decision by first-nation people to go directly to the UN and claim direct representation in international forums, rather than going through the national state. And it is evident in the increasingly institutionalized framework of the international human rights regime and the emergent possibilities for bypasing unilateral state sovereignty.

As the importance of equality in citizenship has grown and become more visible, and as the role of national law to giving presence and voice to hitherto silenced minorities has been weakened by changes in the national state, the tension between the formal status and the normative project of citizenship has grown. For many, citizenship is becoming a normative project whereby social membership becomes increasingly comprehensive and open-ended. Globalization and human rights are further enabling this tension and therewith furthering the elements of a new discourse on rights. These developments signal that the analytic terrain within which we need to place the question of rights, authority, and obligations is shifting (Sassen 1996: ch. 2; 2004).

Toward Effective Nationality and Informal Citizenship

Some of these issues can be illustrated by two contrasting cases, described below.

Unauthorized Yet Recognized

Perhaps one of the more extreme instances of a condition akin to effective as opposed to formal nationality is what has been called the informal social contract that binds undocumented immigrants to their communtiies of residence (Schuck and Smith 1985). Thus, unauthorized immigrants who demonstrate civic involvement, social deservedness, and national loyalty can argue that they merit legal residency. To make this brief examination more specific, I will focus on one case, undocumented immigrants in the United States.

Individuals, even when undocumented immigrants, can move among the multiple meanings of citizenship. The daily practices of undocumented immigrants as part of their life in the community where they reside (raising a family, schooling children, holding a job) earn them citizenship claims in the United States even as the formal status and, more narrowly, legalization may continue to evade them. There are dimensions of citizenship, such as strong community ties and participation in civic activities, that are being enacted informally through these practices. These practices produce an at least partial recognition of these people as full social beings. In many countries around the world, including the United States, long-term undocumented residents often can gain legal residence if they can document the fact of this long-term residence and "good conduct." U.S. immigration law recognizes such informal participation as grounds for granting legal residency. For instance, prior to the immigration law passed in 1996, individuals who could prove seven years of continuous presence, good moral character, and that deportation would be an extreme hardship were eligible for suspension of deportation, and thus U.S. residency. One case, NACARA, extended the eligibility of this suspension of deportation to some 300,000 Salvadorans and Guatemalans who were unauthorized residents in the United States.[2]

The case of undocumented immigrants is, in many ways, a very particular and special illustration of a condition akin to effective citizenship and nationality. One way of interpreting this dynamic in the light of the discussion in the preceding sections is to emphasize that it is the fact of the multiple dimensions of citizenship that engenders strategies for legitimizing informal or extrastate forms of membership (Soysal 1994; Coutin 2000). The practices of these undocumented immigrants are a form of citizenship practice, and their identities as members of a community of residence assume some of the features of citizenship identities. Supposedly this could hold even in the communitarian model, where the community can decide whom to admit and whom to exclude, but once an immigrant is admitted, proper civic practices earn full membership.

Further, the practices of migrants, even if undocumented, can contribute to recognition of their rights in countries of origin. During the 1981–92 civil war, Salvadoran migrants, even though citizens of Salvador, were directly and indirectly excluded from El Salvador through political violence, enormous economic hardship, and direct persecution (Mahler 1996). They could not enjoy their rights as citizens. After fleeing, many continued to provide support to their families and communities. Further, migrants' remittances became a key factor for Salvador's economy—as they are for several countries around the world. The government of Salvador actually began to support the emigrants' fight to get residency rights in the United States, even joining U.S.-based activist organizations in this effort. The Salvadoran government was thus supporting Salvadorans who were the formerly excluded citizens—they needed those remittances to keep coming and they needed the emigrants to stay out of the Salvadoran workforce, given the high unemployment in the country. Thus the participation of these undocumented migrants in cross-border community, family, and political networks has contributed to increasing recognition of their legal and political rights as Salvadoran citizens (Coutin 2000; Mahler 1996).

According to Coutin (2000) and others, movements between membership and exclusion, between different dimensions of citizenship, and between legitimacy and illegitimacy, may be as important as redefinitions of citizenship itself. Given scarce resources the possibility of negotiating the different dimensions of citizenship may well represent an important enabling condition. Undocumented immigrants develop informal, covert, often extrastate strategies and networks connecting them with communities in sending countries. Hometowns rely on their remittances and their information about jobs in the United States. Sending remittances illegally by an unauthorized immigrant can be seen as an act of patriotism, and working as an undocumented can be seen as contributing to the host economy. Multiple interdependencies are thereby established, and grounds for claims on the receiving and the originating country can be established even when the immigrants are undocumented and laws are broken (Basch et al. 1994; Cordero-Guzman et al. 2001).

Authorized Yet Unrecognized

At perhaps the other extreme of the undocumented immigrant whose practices allow her to become accepted as a member of the political community is the case of full citizens who are not recognized as political subjects. In an enormously insightful study of Japanese housewives in Tokyo, Robin LeBlanc (1999) finds precisely this combination.

Being a housewife is basically a full-time occupation in Japan and restricts Japanese women's public life in many important ways, both practical and symbolical. A "housewife" in Japan is a person whose very identity is customarily that of a particularistic, nonpolitical actor. Yet, paradoxically, it is also a condition providing these women with a unique vehicle for other forms of public participation, ones in which being a housewife is an advantage denied to those who might have the qualifications of higher-level political life. LeBlanc documents how the housewife has an advantage in the world of local politics or the political life of a local area: she can be trusted precisely because she is a housewife, she can build networks with other housewives, hers is the image of desirable public concern and of a powerful, because believable, critic of mainstream politics.

There is something extremely important in this condition that is shared with women in other cultures and vis-à-vis different issues. For instance, and in a very different register, women emerged as a specific type of political actor during the brutal dictatorships of the 1970s and 1980s in several countries of Latin America. It was precisely their condition as mothers and wives that gave them the clarity and the courage to demand justice and to demand bread and to do so confronting armed soldiers and policemen. Mothers in the barrios of Santiago during Pinochet's dictatorship, the mothers of the Plaza de Mayo in Buenos Aires, the mothers regularly demonstrating in front of the major prisons in Salvador during the civil war—all were driven to political action by their despair at the loss of children and husbands and the struggle to provide food in their homes.

Further, and in a very different type of situation, there is an interesting parallel between LeBlanc's capturing of the political in the condition of the housewife and a set of findings in some of the research on immigrant women in the United States. There is growing evidence that immigrant women's regular wage work and improved access to other public realms has an impact on their culturally specified subordinate role to men in the household. Immigrant women gain greater personal autonomy and independence, while immigrant men lose ground compared to their condition in their culture of origin. Women gain more control over budgeting and other domestic decisions, and greater leverage in requesting help from men in domestic chores. Also, their women's need to access public services and other public resources gives them a chance to become incorporated in the public domain—they are often the ones in the household who mediate in this process (e.g., Quinchilla and Hamilton 2001). It is likely that some women benefit more than others from these circumstances; we need more research to establish the impact of class, education, and income on these gendered outcomes.

Besides the relatively greater empowerment of immigrant women in the household associated with waged employment, I want to elaborate on second outcome: their greater participation in the public sphere and their possible emergence as public actors. There are two arenas in which immigrant women are active: institutions for public and private assistance, and the immigrant/ethnic community. The incorporation of women in the migration process strengthens the likelihood of settlement and contributes to greater immigrant participation in their communities and vis-à-vis the state. For instance, Pierrette Hondagneu-Sotelo (1994) found that immigrant women come to assume more active public and social roles, which further reinforces their status in the household and the settlement process. These immigrant women are more active in community building and community activism and they are positioned differently from men regarding the broader economy and the state. They are the ones who are likely to have to handle the legal vulnerability of their families in the process of seeking public and social services for their families. This greater participation by women suggests that they may emerge as more forceful and visible actors and make their role in the labor market more visible as well.[3]

These are dimensions of citizenship and citizenship practices that do not fit the indicators and categories of mainstream frameworks for understanding citizenship and political life. Women in the position of housewives and mothers do not fit the categories and indicators used to describe participation in public life. Feminist scholarship in all the social sciences has had to deal with a set of similar or equivalent difficulties and tensions in its effort to constitute its subject or to reconfigure a subject that has been flattened. The theoretical and empirical distance that has to be bridged between the recognized world of politics and the as yet unmapped experience of citizenship of the housewife—not of women as such, but of women as housewives—is a distance we encounter in many types of inquiry. Bridging this distance entails both an empirical research strategy and a theorization.

Postnational or Denationalized?

From the perspective of nation-based citizenship theory, some of these transformations might be interpreted as declines or devaluations of citizenship or, more favorably, as displacements of citizenship in the face of other forms of collective organization and affiliation, as yet unnamed (Bosniak 2000). Insofar as citizenship is theorized as necessarily national (see, for example, Himmelfarb 2001), by definition these new developments cannot be captured in the language of citizenship.[4] An alternative interpretation would be to suspend the national, as in postnational conceptions, and to posit that the issue of where citizenship is enacted is one to be determined in light of developing social practice (see, for example, Soysal 1994; Jacobson 1996; Torres 1998; Torres et al. 1999).

From where I look at these issues, there is a third possibility beyond these two. It is that citizenship even if situated in institutional settings that are "national" is a possibly changed institution if the meaning of the national itself has changed. That is to say, insofar as globalization has changed certain features of the territorial and institutional organization of the political power and authority of the state, the institution of citizenship—its formal rights, its practices, its psychological dimension—has also been transformed even when it remains centered in the national state. I have argued, for instance, that this territorial and institutional transformation of state power and authority has produced operational, conceptual, and rhetorical openings for nation-based subjects other than the national state to emerge as legitimate actors in international/global arenas that used to be exclusive to the state. (See *Indiana Journal of Global Legal Studies* 1996.)

I distinguish what I would narrowly define as denationalized from postnational citizenship, the latter the term most commonly used and the only one used in the broader debate.[5] In my reading we are dealing with two distinct dynamics rather than only the emergence of locations for citizenship outside the frame of the national state. Their difference is a question of scope and institutional embeddedness. The understanding in the scholarship is that postnational citizenship is located partly outside the confines of the national. In considering denationalization, the focus moves to the transformation of the national, including the national in its condition as foundational for citizenship. Thus it could be argued that postnationalism and denationalization represent two different trajectories. Both are viable, and they do not exclude each other.

The national, then, remains a referent in my work (Sassen 2004). But, clearly, it is a referent of a specific sort: it is, after all, its change that becomes the key theoretical feature through which it enters my specification of citizenship today. Whether this does or not devalue citizenship (compare Jacobson 1996) is not immediately evident to me at this point. Citizenship has undergone many transformations in its history precisely because it is to varying extents embedded in the specifics of each of its eras.[6] Also significant to my argument here is the fact discussed earlier about the importance of national law in the process of expanding inclusions, inclusions that today are destabilizing older notions of citizenship. This pluralized meaning of citizenship, partly produced by the formal expansions of the legal status of citizenship, is today contributing to exploding the boundaries of that legal status even further.

First, and most important in my reading, is the strengthening, including the constitutionalizing, of civil rights that allow citizens to make claims against their states and allow them to invoke a measure of autonomy in the formal political arena that can be read as a lengthening distance between the formal apparatus of the state and the institution of citizenship. The implications, both political and theoretical, of this dimension are complex and in the making: we cannot tell what practices and rhetorics might be invented.

Second, I add to this the granting, by national states, of a whole range of "rights" to foreign actors, largely and especially economic actors—foreign firms, foreign investors, international markets, foreign business people (see Sassen 1996: ch. 2). Admittedly, this is not a common way of framing the issue. It comes out of my particular perspective about the impact of globalization and denationalization on the national state, including the impact on the relation between the state and its own citizens, and the state and foreign economic actors. I see this as a significant though not much recognized development in the history of claim making. For me the question as to how citizens should handle these new concentrations of power and "legitimacy" that attach to global firms and markets is a key to the future of democracy. My efforts to detect the extent to which the global is embedded and filtered through the national (for example, the concept of the global city, see also Sassen 2000 on the temporality of the global) is one way of understanding whether therein lies a possibility for citizens, still largely confined to national institutions, to demand accountability from global economic actors through national institutional channels, rather than having to wait for a "global" state.

Citizenship in the Global City

The particular transformations in the understanding and theorization of citizenship discussed thus far bring us back to some of the earlier historical formations around questions of citizenship, most prominently the crucial role played by cities and civil society. The large city of today, most especially the global city, emerges as a strategic site for these new types of operations. It is one of the nexi where the formation of new claims materializes and assumes concrete forms. The loss of power at the national level produces the possibility for new forms of power and politics at the subnational level. The national as container of social process and power is cracked. This cracked casing opens up possibilities for a geography of politics that links subnational spaces. Cities are foremost in this new geography. One question this engenders is how and whether we are seeing the formation of new types of politics that localize in these cities.

If we consider that large cities concentrate both the leading sectors of global capital and a growing share of disadvantaged populations—immigrants, many of the disadvantaged women, people of color generally, and, in the megacities of developing countries, masses of shanty dwellers—we can see that cities have become a strategic terrain for a whole series of conflicts and contradictions (Sassen 2001). We can then think of cities also as one of the sites for the contradictions of the globalization of capital, even though, heeding Ira Katznelson's (1992) observation, the city cannot be reduced to this dynamic. Recovering cities along these lines means recovering the multiplicity of presences in this landscape. The large city of today has emerged as a strategic site for a whole range of new types of operations—political, economic, "cultural," subjective (Isin 2000; Bridges and Watson 2000; Allen et al. 1999).

While citizenship originated in cities and cities played an important role in its evolution, I do not think we can simply read some of these current developments as a return to that older historical condition. The significance of the city today as a setting for engendering new types of citizenship practices and new types of incompletely formalized political subjects does not derive from that history. Nor does current local city government have much to do with earlier notions of citizenship and democracy described for ancient and medieval cities in Europe (Isin 2000: 7). It is, rather, more connected to what Lefebvre (1991; 1995) was capturing when describing the city as oeuvre and hence the importance of agency. Where Lefebvre found this agency in the working class in the Paris of the twentieth century, I find it in two strategic actors—global corporate capital and immigration—in today's global cities. Here I would like to return to the fact of the embeddedness of the institution of citizenship.

What is being engendered today in terms of citizenship practices in the global city is quite different from what it might have been in the medieval city of Weber. In the medieval city we see a set of practices that allowed the burghers to set up systems for owning and protecting property and to implement various immunities against despots of all sorts.[7] Today's citizenship practices have to do with the production of "presence" of those without power and a politics that claims rights to the city. What the two situations share is the notion that through these practices new forms of citizenship are being constituted and that the city is a key site for this type of political work and is, indeed, partly constituted through these dynamics. After the long historical phase that saw the ascendance of the national state and the scaling of key economic dynamics at the national level, the city is today once again a scale for strategic economic and political dynamics.

In his effort to specify the ideal-typical features of what constitutes the city, Weber sought out a certain type of city—most prominently the cities of the late Middle Ages rather than the modern industrial cities of his time. Weber sought a kind of city that combined conditions and dynamics that forced its residents and leaders into creative and innovative responses and adaptations. Further, he posited that these changes produced in the context of the city signaled transformations that went beyond the city, and could institute often fundamental transformations. In that regard the city offered the possibility of understanding far-reaching changes that could, under certain conditions, eventually encompass society at large.

There are two aspects of Weber's *The City* that are of particular importance here. Weber sought to understand under what conditions cities can be positive and creative influences on peoples' lives. For Weber, cities are a set of social structures that encourage social individualitiy and innovation and hence are an instrument of historical change. There is in this intellectual project a deep sense of the historicity of these conditions. For Weber, modern urban life did not correspond to this positive and creative power of cities; Weber saw modern cities as dominated by large factories and office bureaucracies. My own reading of the Fordist city corresponds in many ways to Weber's in the sense that the strategic scale under Fordism is the national scale, and cities lose significance. It is the large Fordist factory and the mines that emerge as key sites for the political work of the disadvantaged and those without power.

For Weber, it is particularly the cities of the late Middle Ages that combine the conditions that pushed urban residents, merchants, artisans, and leaders to address them and deal with them. These transformations could make for epochal change beyond the city itself: Weber shows us how in many cities these struggles led to the creation of the elements of what we could call governance systems and citizenship. In this regard, struggles around political, economic, legal, and cultural issues that are centered in the realities of cities can become the catalysts for new transurban developments in all these institutional domains: markets, participatory governance, rights for members of the urban community regardless of lineage, judicial recourse, and cultures of engagement and deliberation.

The particular analytic element I want to extricate from this aspect of Weber's understanding and theorization of the city is the historicity of those conditions that make cities strategic sites for the enactment of important transformations in multiple institutional domains. Elsewhere (Sassen 2001) I have developed the argument that today a certain type of city—the global city—has emerged as a strategic site precisely for such innovations and transformations in multiple institutional domains. Several of the key components of economic globalization and digitization instantiate in this type of city and produce dislocations and destabilizations of existing institutional orders and legal, regulatory, and normative frames for handling urban conditions. It is the high level of concentration of these new dynamics in these cities that forces creative responses and innovations. There is, most probably, a threshold effect at work here.

The historicity of this process rests in the fact that under Keynesian policies, particularly the Fordist contract, and the dominance of mass manufacturing as the organizing economic dynamic, cities had lost strategic functions and were not the sites for creative institutional innovations. The strategic sites were the large factory and the whole process of mass manufacturing and mass consumer markets, and, second, the national government where regulatory frameworks were developed and the Fordist contract instituted. The factory and the government were the strategic sites where the crucial dynamics producing the major institutional innovations of the epoch were located. With globalization and digitization—and all the specific elements they entail—global cities emerge as such strategic sites. While the strategic transformations are sharply concentrated in global cities, many of the transformations are also enacted, besides being diffused, in cities at lower orders of national urban hierarchies. Furthermore, in my reading, particular institutions of the state also are such strategic sites even as there is an overall shrinking of state authority through deregulation and privatization.

A second analytic element I want to extricate from Weber's *The City* is the particular type of embeddedness of the transformations he describes and renders as ideal-typical features. This is not an embeddedness in what we might think of as deep structures, because the latter are precisely the ones that are being dislocated or changed and are creating openings for new fundamental arrangements to emerge. The embeddedness is, rather, in very specific conditions, opportunities, constraints, needs, interactions, contestations, interests. The aspects that matter here are the complexity, detail, and social thickness of the particular conditions and the dynamics Weber identifies as enabling change and innovation. This complexity and thickness also produce ambiguities in the meaning of the changes and innovations. It is not always clear whether they are positive—where we might interpret positive as meaning the creation or strengthening of some element, even if very partial or minor, of participatory democracy in the city—and in what time frame their positiveness would become evident. In those cities of the late Middle Ages Weber saw as being what the city is about, he finds contradictory and multivalent innovations. He dissects these innovations to understand what they can produce or launch.

The argument I derive from this particular type of embeddedness of change and innovation is that current conditions in global cities are creating not only new structurations of power but also operational and rhetorical openings for new types of political actors that may have been submerged, invisible or without voice. A key element of the argument here is that the localization of strategic components of globalization in these cities means that the disadvantaged can engage the new forms of globalized corporate power, and second that the mix of growing numbers and diversity of the disadvantaged in these cities under these conditions assumes a distinctive "presence." This entails a distinction between powerlessness and invisiblity or impotence. The disadvantaged in global cities can gain "presence" in their engagement with power but also vis-à-vis each other. This is different from the period from the 1950s to the 1970s in the United States, for instance, when white flight and the significant departure of major corporate headquarters left cities hollowed out and the disadvantaged in a condition of abandonment. Today, the localization of the global creates a set of objective conditions of engagement; for example, the struggles against gentrification that encroaches on minority and disadvantaged neighborhoods and led to growing numbers of homeless beginning in the 1980s. These struggles are different from the ghetto uprisings of the 1960s, which were short, intense eruptions confined to the ghettos and in which most of the damage was done to the neighborhoods of the disadvantaged themselves. In these ghetto uprisings there was no engagement with power.

The conditions that today mark the possibility of cities as strategic sites are basically two, and both capture major transformations that are destabilizing older systems organizing territory and politics. One of these is the rescaling of the strategic territories that articulate the new politicoeconomic system. The other is the partial unbundling or at least weakening of the national as container of social process due to the variety of dynamics encompassed by globalization and digitization. The consequences for cities of these two conditions are many: what matters here is that cities emerge as strategic sites for major economic processes and that new types of political actors can emerge. Insofar as citizenship is embedded and in turn marked by its embeddedness, these new conditions may well signal the possibility of new forms of citizenship practices and identities even when the bundle of formal rights remains largely unchanged.

There is something to be captured here—a distinction between powerlessness and the condition of being an actor even though lacking power. I use the term *presence* to name this condition. In the context of a strategic space such as the global city, the types of disadvantaged people described here are not simply marginal; they acquire presence in a broader political process that escapes the boundaries of the formal polity. This presence signals the possibility of a politics. What this politics might be will depend on the specific projects and practices of various communities. Insofar as the sense of membership of these communities is not subsumed under the national, it may well signal the possibility of a politics that while centered in concrete localities is actually transnational.

Notes

1. In Karst's interpretation of the U.S. law, aliens *are* "constitutionally entitled to most of the guarantees of equal citizenship, and the Supreme Court has accepted this idea to a modest degree" (2000: 599; see also fn.20, where he cites cases). Karst also notes that the Supreme Court has not carried this development nearly as far as he might wish.
2. NACARA is the 1997 Nicaraguan Adjustment and Central American Relief Act. It created an amnesty for Salvadorans and Guatemalans to apply for suspension of deportation. This is an immigration remedy that has been eliminated by the Illegal Immigration Reform and Immigrant Responsibility Act in 1996 (see Coutin 2000).
3. For the limits of this process see, e.g. Parreñas 2001.
4. Thus for Karst, "[i]n the US today, citizenship is inextricable from a complex legal framework that includes a widely accepted body of substantive law, strong law-making institutions, and law-enforcing institutions capable of performing their task" (2000: 600). Not recognizing the centrality of the law is, for Karst, a big mistake. Postnational citizenship lacks an institutional framework that can protect the substantive values of citizenship. Karst does acknowledge the possibility of rabid nationalism and the exclusion of aliens when legal status is made central.
5. Bosniak uses the term *denationalized* interchangeably with *postnational*. I do not.

6. In this regard, I have emphasized as significant (1996: chapter 2) the introduction in the new constitutions of South Africa, Brazil, Argentina and the Central European countries, of a provision that qualifies what had been an unqualified right (if democratically elected) of the sovereign to be the exclusive representative of its people in international fora.
7. In Russia, where the walled city did not evolve as a center for immunities and liberties, the meaning of citizenship diverges from concepts of civil society and belongs to the state, not the city.

12
Conclusion: Globalizing Citizenship?

ALISON BRYSK AND GERSHON SHAFIR

Human rights have made great strides in the centuries since the French Revolution, but to be truly effective in a globalizing era, the "rights of man and the citizen" will need to become the "universal rights of [hu]mans *as global citizens.*" How can we transform rights into a new form of global citizenship—namely, membership in one or more political communities with institutions for participation, distribution, and enforcement? Overall, our analyses suggest that globalization of migration, production, regulation, and conflict construct rights without sufficient institutions to enforce them, identities without membership, and participation for some at the expense of others.

Existing institutions are insufficient in scope, powers, membership, and participation. A key problem for rights is accountability. Global processes have blurred accountability of new or transformed political actors—although many states failed their citizens, theoretical mechanisms such as voting, strikes, and courts did propose state accountability to citizens. States are not accountable to the UN High Commission on Refugees, and no one elects multinational corporations. Furthermore, noncitizens and second-class citizens have little access to whatever levers of accountability do exist. Who does the migrant maid call when she is assaulted or exploited?

Beyond a general deficit in governance and accountability, particular types of states face specific governance challenges. Historically, different types of states have provided distinct legal regimes and practical packages of citizenship rights. Now, different types of states have experienced systematically distinct patterns of globalization (Brysk 2002).

In collapsing or "failed" states—such as in large sectors of Africa and sporadic zones of intense civil conflict—weak citizenship combines with relative isolation from world markets alongside intense interstate and transnational penetration. These states contain large numbers of noncitizen refugees and widespread second-class citizenship, but globalization often offers better prospects for rights than the thin and predatory state does. However, these zones are also the major source of violent reactionary responses to globalization and coercive attempts to build alternative membership through terrorism and denial of rights to others (Falk in this volume).

For the majority of less developed capitalist states, many of them new democracies, citizenship is more checkered and globalization more perilous. In most of Latin America, parts of Asia, and many post-Soviet states, historically limited citizenship with civic and social components has recently been extended to political rights. But these states are the most subject to global market deflation of citizenship (see Varas 1998), and consequently also become the main migration sending zones of noncitizens. The chapters by Seidman, Maher, and Brysk show the effects of this process on social rights, membership, and accountability.

In the developed European and North American heartland of citizenship, liberal capitalist democracies simultaneously expand interstate and transnational rights (discussed by Jacobson and Ruffer) while struggling to regulate global markets. In this process, noncitizen migrants and second-class citizens are caught in the citizenship gap (Sassen).

On what basis could new institutions emerge to address these insufficiencies? Lipschutz urges us to consider a radical rethinking of the basis of political community, looking beyond state structures to their purposes in realizing agency and the common good. Others believe that globalization calls for unbundling and "reconfiguring" the citizenship package of rights, responsibilities, participation, and identity (Delanty 2000: 126). Ong's chapter shows how globalizing relations of production already reconfigure some forms of membership and identity, but this is an unintended consequence—not a program for global governance.

How can we use the resources of the citizenship tradition to address the global gap?

Comprehensive global governance of the multifaceted citizenship gap requires at least three dimensions. First, new venues and forms of participation must be constructed to broaden accountability for new subjects and to manage global issues that fall between the cracks of the current system. At the same time, "people out of place" must be granted space in existing institutions and leverage in state structures. Finally, the relationship between traditional state citizenship and new forms of global community must be developed.

Models for implementing global governance range from formal global institutions to nongovernmental networks to issue-specific or sectoral regimes (Keohane and Nye 2000). Each of these modalities must be considered for its contribution to effective and inclusive delivery of universal rights—closing the citizenship gap. We will examine a series of proposals that begin with existing state structures, some of which introduce additional layers or venues of transnational authority, and close with the possibility of completely transcending state authority through global cosmopolitanism.

A Global Safety Net—Better States, More Rights

The most restricted but grounded proposal for global citizenship builds on existing state structures to broaden membership, rights, and participation.

Based on the "English school" view of an "international society" of states, this modality attempts to strengthen the governance obligations and multilateralism of state members. Rather than resting on amoral claims of sovereignty, the club of states would evict or sanction members who fail to uphold a code of conduct based in universal rights. It might result in concrete gains for humanitarian intervention in situations of acute gross rights abuses, or facilitate regulation of state-controlled "public bads" such as land mines. But even proponents note that this pragmatic humanitarianism cannot address inequities among states, and tends toward a lowest common denominator of rights (Williams 2002).

A further necessary critique is the starting premise of this volume—that many kinds of human needs have outgrown state structures in a globalizing era. For migrants, refugees, many types of second-class citizens, workers in weak states, all residents of failed states, and anyone accused of fundamental breaches such as terrorism or treason, the state system is silent.

Another rights-based approach serves to enlarge the global safety net through limited intergovernmental extensions. The emergence of new levels of agency, international law, and judicialization discussed by Jacobson and Ruffer and by Spiro might begin to build a global *right to rights* (including the right to national citizenship). Enforcement institutions for these rights are not specified, although the default mode would be the state—a kind of global subsidiarity in which issues are managed at the lowest effective level. However, regional and global institutions serve as a backup for state failure in this model, as envisaged by the new International Criminal Court for crimes against humanity. While such a model is theoretically accountable to stateless or transnational persons, no clear venue or jurisdiction is provided. Another positive but murky and complex implication of a global right to rights would be a corresponding responsibility for all international institutions to incorporate rights, not just those that serve as pressure on or supplements to state enforcement. Thus, developments like the World Bank's increasing attention to human rights in economic adjustment programs and attendant conditionality would be extended, with controversial consequences for participation, self-determination, and distribution.

Since these rights safety nets do not expand membership, they are subject to reversals and limitations. In the Roman Empire, various gradations of citizenship were granted to individuals and groups with the aim of incorporating the upper strata into the imperial institutions, though with the narrower goal of unifying the loyal supporters of the emperor. Under conditions of security threat and the globalization of conflict, Falk's chapter reminds us that we may be seeing a revival of something like a graduated, defensive international citizenship. Thus, rights can be selectively denied to some noncitizens (and even citizens, in the post–September 11 United States), at the same time that members of security and economic alliances are granted honorary membership. In response to terrorism, the United States simultaneously declares that noncitizens can be tried by military tribunals, and passes fast-track trade legislation allowing the president to negotiate binding trade agreements intensifying globalization.

Multilevel Citizenship—A Place for Everyone

One more comprehensive approach to people out of place is the creation and vesting of rights in multiple institutions, based in locales within and across state borders. In the short term, *multi-level citizenship* could provide rights on various scales: local or communal, district or urban, state, regional, and global. Bull calls this a neomedieval model, observing that it "might . . . seem fanciful to contemplate a return to the medieval world, but it is not fanciful to imagine that there might develop a modern secular counterpart of it that embodies its central characteristics: a system of overlapping authority and multiple loyalty" (Bull 1977: 254). Such multilayered political orders do not erase national and subnational identities, but allow infra- and supranational levels of loyalties to find political and legal expressions through the dilution of sovereignty (Bull 1979: 114). As Lipschutz points out, diverse citizenship may provide a positive stimulus for enhanced civic engagement (Lipschutz 1999: 227). Sassen's chapter shows that even the traditional territorial link to state identity has been disrupted by new geographies of membership, based more on markets, migration, and locality than on national boundaries. However, relocation of rights at the level of the global city opens options but does not secure accountability.

Multilevel citizenship may be particularly helpful to second-class citizens, such as women, who can appeal to levels above and below the state to enhance their access to rights. Multilevel citizenship may also provide the best hope for migrants and stateless peoples. At the same time, breaking up the universalism of the human rights tradition to ensure the provision of effective citizenship rights could easily lead to a hierarchy of citizenships. A woman working in the EU may be able to appeal to a more robust set of labor rights than her state provides (Cicchowski 2001), but a woman in Nigeria sentenced to death for adultery by a local religious court can barely appeal to her national courts—whose response is uncertain—and has no recourse to a transnational body. In addition, multilevel citizenship runs the risk of weak enforcement and neglect of enabling institutions. Euro-skeptics critique the levels of deliberation, accountability, and social rights in even the most advanced regional institution (Follesdal 2002; Miller 2002).

Segmented Citizenship—Form Follows Function

Alternatively, rights could be granted through multiple institutional venues clustered around issues (such as "international regimes"; see Krasner 1984;

Rittberger 1993), in a kind of *segmented citizenship*. For example, labor rights would be provided through the ILO, migration through Maastricht-type agreements, and protection from crimes against humanity through an international court of justice. Under such arrangements, there is the danger of the fragmentation of rights, contradictions between overlapping international regimes and issues, and gaps in between them. For example, a 2000 International Labor Organization agreement asking member states to sanction Myanmar for forced labor has foundered on World Trade Organization rules forbidding trade discrimination (Olson *New York Times* 2001). Segmented citizenship could also be selectively available to different identity groups that match regimes, such as indigenous rights or children's rights, while leaving out equally needy but less distinctive noncitizens.

A related phenomenon is the emergence of transnational market citizenship, rooted in apolitical but authoritative corporate entities. As Ong's work suggests, where corporate, ethnic, or other collectivities control rights and conditions more effectively than governments do, individuals' fates will be determined by their membership and status in these organizations. This would clearly exacerbate rather than ameliorate inequalities for people out of place. Proposals to enhance corporate social responsibility appear to be one of the few channels for enhancing market citizenship. The most institutionalized and comprehensive initiative is the Global Compact, in which more than four hundred global companies have pledged via the United Nations to honor a set of core labor, environmental, and human rights standards. Ruggie suggests that this and related developments of socially responsible investment, corporate codes of conduct, and trade certification are constructing partial but meaningful private governance, which may be a harbinger of a global "embedded liberalism" linking sustainable capitalism to accountability and perhaps participation (although not membership) (Ruggie, forthcoming).

Global Cosmopolitanism—Citizenship without Borders

Just as in the past new political entities established a commonality of fate among their members, or among those who mattered the most, through shared citizenship, so in the long term the logic of citizenship as membership in a political community would require that the now globalized human rights tradition be realized under conditions of global governance (Carter 1977; Held 1995; Archibugi 1998). *Global citizenship* would be based on membership in a global political institution.

Of course, such a goal still appears to be utopian, and, consequently, the meaning of global citizenship remains elusive. The main gap is between notions of "cosmopolitan citizenship," which is a state of mind, focused more on duties than on rights, and seems to require no political organization (Held 1995), and forms of "global citizenship," which provide "a set of positive legal and political rights to enable individuals to play a part in global institutions" (Carter 1977: 72). For example, Heater's study of Western cosmopolitan ideas leads him to focus on a world social citizenship that emphasizes compassion and the duty of the strong to help others, without anchoring that duty in a binding legal framework (Heater 1996).

The institutional variant of global citizenship would be the most comprehensive mode of incorporation for new issues and people out of place, but its feasibility and effectiveness remain unknown. Some venues for the practice of global citizenship would be a second, popularly elected, UN assembly; a new International Human Rights Court; or perhaps the extension of the International Court of Justice's jurisdiction to permit it to hear claims by individuals against governments (Carter 1977: 74). Another option would be a UN assembly of unrepresented peoples to supplement the states parties—but it is unclear whether this would include only stateless national groups, diasporic or indigenous peoples, and how membership and participation in these constituencies would be determined.

From a human rights perspective, it is also important to note a paradoxical trade-off between these questions of inclusion and effectiveness and the very rights global citizenship aspires to safeguard. Any global government would run the risk of becoming a Leviathan, all the more dangerous for the multiple powers it concentrates. Thus, Held calls for "cosmopolitan democracy"—not just global citizenship—instantiated at multiple levels (Held 1995). But even this balanced proposal leaves unclear the division of powers among states and new global entities, the relationship between global political participation and global social rights, and the potential distortion of democratic global institutions by undemocratic state members (Axtmann 2002).

Conclusion

What can we offer noncitizens and second-class citizens? What can replace the passport or polling place that some never had and others find insufficient? Only multilevel or segmented citizenship seem to offer plausible short-term alternatives, supplemented by a safety net of a global right to rights, membership, and appeal. This patchwork incrementalism seems consistent with the short-run solution to governance suggested by "globalization with a human face"—a combination of liberal free markets for economic gain and structured escape clauses for political accountability (Rodrik 2000).

In terms of policy prescriptions, this means we must continue to build global rights to rights through international law, while recognizing the difficulties of true global institutions. Multilevel citizenship may offer relief to second-class citizens of strong states and regions, but cannot provide a universal substitute for weak states and noncitizens. Segmented citizenship will be the best bet for many of the migrants, refugees, diasporas, laborers, and others at risk from globalization—because globalization is generating new norms, institutions, and pressures that permit the construction of issue-specific forms of governance. These organizations and campaigns cannot offer membership, but they can enhance rights, participation, and accountability.

In a world of nation-states, in an era of globalization, people out of place will always be at risk. While new forms of membership cannot yet grant them a place, evolving institutions can give them greater voice and protection.

Bibliography

Abraham, David. 2001. "Asylum . . . ," *American Journal of International Law* 95, no. 1 January: 204–12.

Adler, Glenn (ed.). 2000. *Engaging the State and Business: The Labor Movement and Co-determination in Contemporary South Africa*. Johannesburg: Witwatersrand University Press.

Alexander, Robin. 1999. "The UE-FAT Strategic Organizing Alliance." In *Confronting Change: Auto Labor and Lean Production in North America*, ed. Huberto Juarez and Steve Babson. Detroit: Wayne State University, and Universidad de Puebla.

Ali, Karamat. 1996. "Social Clauses and Workers in Pakistan." *New Political Economy* 1, no. 2: 269–73.

Ali, Tariq. 2002. *The Clash of Fundamentalisms: Crusades, Jihads, and Modernity*. London: Verso.

Allen, John, Doreen Massey and Michael Pryke, eds. *Unsettling Cities*. London: Routledge, 1999.

al-Najjar, Sabika. 2002. "Migrant Women Domestic Workers in Bahrain." Report of the International Labor Organization.

Althusser, Louis. 1971. "Ideology and Ideological State Apparatuses (Notes toward an Investigation)." In *Lenin and Philosophy, and Other Essays*, trans. Ben Brewster. New York: Monthly Review Press.

Altstein, Howard, and Rita J. Simon (eds.). 1991. *Intercountry Adoption: A Multinational Perspective*. New York: Praeger.

Amon, Elizabeth. 2001. "Access Denied: Children in INS Custody Have No Right to a Lawyer." *National Law Journal* 23, no. 34 (April 16).

Anderson, Bridget. 2000. *Doing the Dirty Work? The Global Politics of Domestic Labour*. London: Zed Books.

Andersson, Gunilla. 1986. "The Adopting and Adopted Swedes and Their Contemporary Society." In *Adoption in Worldwide Perspective: A Review of Programs, Policies, and Legislation in Fourteen Countries*, ed. R.A.C. Hoksbergen. Lisse: Swets and Zeitlinger.

Anheier, Helmut, Marlies Glasius, and Mary Kaldor (eds.) 2001. *The Global Civil Society Yearbook*. Oxford: Oxford University Press.

Anner, Mark. 2000. "Local and Transnational Campaigns to End Sweatshop Practices." In *Transnational Cooperation among Labor Unions*, ed. Michael Gordon and Lowell Turner. Ithaca: ILR/Cornell University Press.

Appadurai, Arjun. 1996. *Modernity at Large: Cultural Dimensions of Globalization*. Minneapolis: University of Minnesota Press.

Archdeacon, Thomas J. 1983. *Becoming American: An Ethnic History*. New York: Free Press.

Archibugi, Daniele, and David Held (eds.). 1995. *Cosmopolitan Democracy: An Agenda for a New World Order*. Cambridge: Polity.

Archibugi, Daniele, David Held, and Martin Köhler (eds.). 1998. *Re-imagining Political Community: Studies in Cosmopolitan Democracy*. Stanford, Calif.: Stanford University Press.

Arendt, Hannah. 1951. *The Origins of Totalitarianism*. New York: Harcourt, Brace, Jovanovich.

Arendt, Hannah. 1958a. *The Human Condition*, 2nd ed. Chicago: University of Chicago Press.

Arendt, Hannah. 1958b. "The Public and Private Realm." In *The Human Condition* (Chicago: University of Chicago Press, 1958).

Arendt, Hannah. 1990. *On Revolution* (London: Penguin). "Ashcroft Wants That Boy Used By Smugglers To Stay in U.S.," 2001, *New York Times*, July 24.

Avineri, Sholomo. 1972. *Hegel's Theory of the Modern State*. London: Cambridge University Press. Available at http://www.marxists.org/reference/subject/philosophy/works/avineri7.htm (accessed October 5, 2001).

Axford, Barrie. *The Global System: Economics, Politics, and Culture*. Cambridge: Polity Press.

Axtmann, Roland. 2002. "What's Wrong with Cosmopolitan Democracy?" In *Global Citizenship: A Critical Introduction*, ed. Nigel Dower and John Williams. New York: Routledge.

Baer, Ingrid. 1986. "The Development of Adoptions in the Federal Republic of Germany." In *Adoption in Worldwide Perspective: A Review of Programs, Policies, and Legislation in Fourteen Countries*, ed. R.A.C. Hoksbergen. Lisse: Swets and Zeitlinger.

Bagley, Christopher, with Loretta Young, Anne Scully. 1993. *International and Transracial Adoptions: A Mental Health Perspective.* Aldershot, England: Avebury.

Bagley, Christopher. 1986. "The Institution of Adoption: A Canadian Case Study." In *Adoption in Worldwide Perspective: A Review of Programs, Policies, and Legislation in Fourteen Countries,* ed. R.A.C. Hoksbergen. Lisse: Swets and Zeitlinger.

Bakan, Abigail B, and Daiva K. Stasiulis. 1994. "Foreign Domestic Worker Policy in Canada and the Social Boundaries of Modern Citizenship." *Science and Society* 58, no. 1: 7–33.

Bakan, Abigail B., and Daiva K. Stasiulis. 1995. "Making the Match: Domestic Placement Agencies and the Racialization of Women's Household Work." *Signs* 20, no. 21: 303–35.

Bancroft, George. 1849. Letter from George Bancroft to Lord Palmerston, January 26, 1849, reprinted in *S. Exec. Doc.* 36–38 (1850).

Barkun, Elazar. 2000. *The Moral Guilt of Nations: Restitution and Negotiating Historic Injustice.* New York: W.W. Norton.

Bar-Yaacov, Nissim. 1961. *Dual Nationality.* New York: Praeger.

Basch, Linda, Nina Glick Schiller, Cristina Blanc-Szanton. 1994. *Nations Unbound: Transnational Projects, Postcolonial Predicaments, and Deterritorialized Nation-States.* Langhorne, PA: Gordon and Breach.

Bauböck, Rainer. 1991. "Migration and Citizenship." *New Community* 18, no. 1: 27–48.

Bauer, Otto. 2000. *The Question of Nationalities and Social Democracy,* ed. Ephraim Nimni, trans. Joseph O'Donnell. Minneapolis: University of Minnesota Press.

Beetham, David. 1998. "Human Rights as a Model for Cosmopolitan Democracy." In *Re-imagining Political Community: Studies in Cosmopolitan Democracy,* ed. Daniele Archibugi, David Held, and Martin Köhler. Stanford, Calif.: Stanford University Press.

Bell, Mark. 1999. "Shifting Conceptions of Sexual Discrimination at the Court of Justice: from *P v S* to *Grant v SWT.*" *European Law Journal* 5 (1999): 1.

Benhabib, Seyla. 2002. *Democratic Equality and Cultural Diversity: Political Identities in the Global Era.* Princeton, NJ: Princeton University Press.

Benhabib, Seyla, Judith Butler, Drucilla Cornell, Nancy Fraser. 1995. *Feminist Contentions: A Philosophical Exchange.* New York, NY: Routledge.

Ben Ruffer, Galya. 2000. *Virtual Citizenship.* Unpublished diss. University of Pennsylvania.

Bergquist, Charles. 1996. *Labor and the Course of American Democracy.* London: Verso.

Berman, Marshall. 1982. *All That Is Solid Melts into Air.* New York: Simon and Schuster.

Bernault, Florence. 2001. "What Absence Is Made Of: Human Rights in Africa." In *Human Rights and Revolutions,* ed. Jeffrey N. Wasserstrom et al. Lanham, Md.: Rowman and Littlefield.

Bhabha, Jacqueline. 1999. "Belonging in Europe: Citizenship and Post-National Rights." *International Social Science Journal* 51, no. 1: 11–25.

Bhabha, Jacqueline. "Enforcing the Human Rights of Citizens and Non-citizens in the Era of Maastricht: Some Reflections on the Importance of States." *Development and Change* 29 (1998): 697–724.

Biersrecker, Thomas. 1995. "The 'Triumph' of Liberal Economic Ideas in the Developing World." In *Global Change, Regional Response: The New International Context of Development,* ed. Barbara Stallings. Cambridge: Cambridge University Press.

Block, J. E. 2001. *A Nation of Agents: The American Path to a Modern Self and Society.* Cambridge, Mass.: Harvard University Press.

Bluestone, Barry, and Bennett Harison. 1982. *The Deindustrialization of America.* New York: Basic.

Bluestone, Barry, and Irving Bluestone. 1992. *Negotiating the Future: A Labor Perspective on American Business.* New York: Basic.

Bobbitt, Philip. 2002. *The Shield of Achilles: War, Peace, and the Course of History.* New York: Alfred A. Knopf.

Bonacich, Edna, and Richard Appelbaum. 2000. *Behind the Label: Inequality in the Los Angeles Apparel Industry.* Berkeley: University of California Press.

Bonner, Raymond. 2002. "Pakistani Gang Said to Kidnap Children To Be Sold Abroad." *New York Times,* March 17.

Borchard, Edwin Montefiore. 1970. *The Diplomatic Protection of Citizens Abroad; or, the Law of International Claims.* New York: Kraus Reprint Co.

Borjas, George J. 2000 *Heaven's Door: Immigration Policy and the American Economy.* Princeton, N.J.: Princeton University Press.

Bosniak, Linda. 1996. " 'Nativism' The Concept: Some Reflections." *Immigrants Out: The New Nativism and the Anti-Immigrant Impulse in the United States.* Juan Perea, ed. New York: NYU Press.

————. 2000. "Universal Citizenship and the Problem of Alienage." *Northwestern University Law Review* 94(3): 963–984.

Bosniak, Linda S. 2002. "Multiple Nationality and the Postnational Transformation of Citizenship." *Virginia Journal of International Law* 42 (Summer 2002): 979.

Breslau, Karen. 2000. "Tomorrowland, Today." *Newsweek* (Asia), September 18, 2000, 52–53.

Bridge, Gary and Sophie Watson, eds. 2000. *A Companion to the City.* Oxford, United Kingdom: Blackwell.

Brooks, Stephen G., and William C. Wohlforth. "American Primacy in Perspective." *Foreign Affairs* 81, no. 4 (July–August 2002): 20–33.

Brown, Wendy. 2001. *Politics Out of History.* Princeton, N.J.: Princeton University Press.

Brubaker, William Rogers. 1989. "Introduction." In *Immigration and the Politics of Citizenship in Europe and North America.* Lanham, Md.: University of America Press.

Brysk, Alison (ed.). 2002. *Globalization and Human Rights.* Berkeley: University of California Press.

Brysk, Alison. 2000. *From Tribal Village to Global Village: Indian Rights and International Relations in Latin America.* Stanford, Calif.: Stanford University Press.

Buhlungu, Sakhela, and Eddie Webster. 2002. "Labor Internationalism at a Turning Point." *South African Labour Bulletin* 26, no. 1 (February): 71–82.

Buhlungu, Sakhela. 2000. "Trade Union Organization and Capacity in the 1990s: Continuities, Changes, and Challenges." In *Trade Unions and Democratization in South Africa, 1985–1997*, ed. Glenn Adler and Eddie Webster. New York: St. Martin's Press.

Bull, Hedley. 1977. *The Anarchical Society.* New York: Columbia University Press.

Bull, Hedley. 1979. "The State's Positive Role in World Affairs." *Daedalus* no. 108.

Cairns, Alan C. et al. (eds.). 1999. *Citizenship, Diversity, and Pluralism: Canadian and Comparative Perspectives.* Ithaca, N.Y.: McGill-Queens University Press.

Calavita, Kitty. 1992. *Inside the State: The Bracero Program, Immigration, and the I.N.S.*, NY: Routledge.

Caldeira, Teresa, and James Holston. "Democracy and Violence in Brazil." *Comparative Studies in Society and History* 41, no. 4 (October): 691–729.

Candland, Chris, and Rudra Sil. 2001. "The Politics of Labor in Late-Industrializing and Post-Socialist Economies: New Challenges in a Global Age." In *The Politics of Labor in a Global Age*, ed. Candland and Sil. Oxford: Oxford University Press.

Candland, Christopher. 2002. "Trading Rights: How Are International Labor Standards Established?" Paper delivered at the Havens Center, University of Wisconsin-Madison, May 7.

Carens, Joseph. 1989. "Membership and Morality." In *Immigration and the Politics of Citizenship in Europe and North America*, ed. William Rogers Brubaker. Lanham, Md.: University Press of America.

Carillo, Jorge. 1998. "Maquiladores en redes: El caso de Delphi-GM." In *Confronting Change: Auto Labor and Lean Production in North America*, ed. Huberto Juarez and Steve Babson. Detroit: Wayne State University, and Universidade de Puebla.

Carter, April. 1977. "Nationalism and Global Citizenship." *Australian Journal of Politics and History* 43, no. 1: 67–81.

Castells, Manuel. 1997. *The Power of Identity.* Oxford: Blackwell.

Castells, Manuel. 1996–98. *The Information Age: Economy, Society, and Culture*, 3 vols., esp. vol. 1, *The Rise of the Network Society.* Malden, Mass.: Blackwells.

Castles, Stephen, and Mark J. Miller. 1993. *The Age of Migration: International Population Movements in the Modern World.* New York: Guilford.

Chalmers, Damian. 2000. "A Statistical Analysis of Reported Decisions of United Kingdom Courts Invoking EU Law." Jean Monnet Chair at Harvard Law School, working paper.

Chander, Anupan. 2001. "Diaspora Bonds." 76 *New York University Law Review* 1005 (2001).

Charlesworth, Stephanie. 1993. "Ensuring the Rights of Children in Inter-country Adoption: Australian Attitudes to Access to Adoption Information." In (eds.) *Parenthood in Modern Society*, ed. J. Eekelaar and P. Sarcevic. Dordrecht, The Netherlands: Martinus Nijhoff.

Chavez, Leo. 1997. "Immigration Reform and Nativism: The Nationalist Response to the Transnationalist Challenge." In *Immigrants Out! The New Nativism and the Anti-Immigrant Impulse in the United States*, ed. Juan F. Perea. New York: New York University Press.

Chin, Christine B. N. 1998. *In Service and Servitude: Foreign Female Domestic Workers and the Malaysian Modernity Project.* New York: Columbia University Press.

Chinchilla, Norma and Nora Hamilton. 2001. *Seeking Community in the Global City: Salvadorans and Guatemalans in Los Angeles.* Philadelphia, PA: Temple University Press.

Chinkin, Christine. 1999. "Gender Inequality and International Human Rights Law." In *Inequality, Globalization, and World Politics*, ed. Andrew Hurrell and Ngaire Woods. New York: Oxford University Press.

Cichowski, Rachel. 2002. *Litigation, Mobilization, and Governance: The European Court and Transnational Activists*. Doctoral diss. University of California, Irvine.

Clark, Ian. 1999. *Globalization and International Relations Theory*. New York: Oxford University Press.

Colas, Alejandro. 2002. *International Civil Society*. Cambridge: Polity.

Colen, Shellee. 1990. "Housekeeping for the Green Card: West Indian Household Workers, the State, and Stratified Reproduction in New York." In *At Work in Homes: Household Workers in World Perspective*, ed. Roger Sanjek and Shellee Colen. Washington, D.C.: American Anthropological Association.

Colker, Ruth. 1998. *American Law in the Age of Hypercapitalism*. New York: New York University Press.

Collier, Stephen J. 2001. *Post-Socialist City: The Government of Life in Liberal Times*. Ph.D. diss., Department of Anthropology, University of California, Berkeley.

Collins, Jane L. 2001. "Flexible Specialization and the Garment Industry," *Competition and Change* 5: 165–200.

Compa, Lance, 1996. *Human Rights, Labor Rights and International Trade*, Stephen F. Diamond (eds). Philadelphia: University of Pennsylvania Press.

Constable, Nicole. 1997. *Maid to Order in Hong Kong: Stories of Filipina Workers*. Ithaca, N.Y., and London: Cornell University Press.

Copeland, Lewis C. 1993. "The Negro as a Contrast Conception." In ed. *Race Relations and the Race Problem: A Definition and an Analysis*, ed. Egar T. Thompson. Durham, N.C.: Duke University Press.

Corbett, Sara. 2001. "The Long, Long Road to Fargo," New York Times Magazine, April 1st.

Cordero-Guzmán, Héctor R., Robert C. Smith and Ramón Grosfoguel, eds. 2001. *Migration, Transnationalization, and Race in a Changing New York*. Philadelphia, PA: Temple University Press.

Coutin, Susan B. 2000. "Denationalization, Inclusion, and Exclusion: Negotiating the Boundaries of Belonging." *Indiana Journal of Global Legal Studies* 7(2): 585–594.

Cowie, Jefferson. 1999. Capital Moves: RCA's Seventy-Year Quest for Cheap Labor. Ithaca. N.Y.: Cornell University Press.

Cranston, Maurice. 1979. "What Are Human Rights?" In Chalmers Damian. 2000. "A Statistical Analysis of Reported Decisions of United Kingdom Courts Invoking EU Law." The Jean Monnet Chair at Harvard Law School, Working paper.

Crenshaw, Kimberlé, Neil Gotanda, Gary Peller, and Kendall Thomas, eds. 1996. *Critical Race Theory: The Key Writings that Formed the Movement*. New York, NY: New Press.

Dang, Janet. 1999. "High-Tech's Low Wages." *Asian Week*, December 23.

Delanty, Gerard. 2000. *Citizenship in a Global Age: Society, Culture, Politics*. Buckingham: Open University Press.

Deleuze, Gilles. 1991. "Postcript on Societies of Control." *October*, no. 59 (winter): 3–7.

Deleuze, Gilles, and Felix Guattari. 1994. *A Thousand Plateaus: Capitalism and Schizophrenia*, trans. and foreword by Brian Massumi. Minneapolis: University of Minnesota Press.

Delgado, Richard, and Jean Stefancic, eds. 2001. *Critical Race Theory: The Cutting Edge*. Philadelphia, PA: Temple University Press.

Dharmaruksa, Darawan. 1986. "Adoption in Thailand." In *Adoption in Worldwide Perspective: A Review of Programs, Policies and Legislation in Fourteen Countries*, ed. R.A.C. Hoksbergen. Lisse: Swets and Zeitlinger.

Dinan, Kinsey. 2000. *Owed Justice: That Women Trafficked into Debt Bondage in Japan*. NY: Human Rights Watch.

Donnelly, Jack. "Human Rights in the New World Order." *World Policy Journal* 9, no. 2 (spring): 249–77.

Drainville, André C. 1995. "Of Social Spaces, Citizenship, and the Nature of Power in the World Economy." *Alternatives* 20, no. 1 (January–March): 51–79.

Driscoll, Dennis J. 1979. "The Development of Human Rights in International Law." In Laqueur, Walter and Barry Rubin (eds.). *The Human Rights Reader*, New York: Meridian: 41–56.

Duncan, Julianne. 2002. "Joint Testimony of Migration and Refugee Services/U.S. Conference of Catholic Bishops and Lutheran Immigration and Refugee Service on the Unaccompanied

Alien Child Protection Act before the Senate Subcommittee on Immigration." February 28. (Available at http://www.usccb.org/mrs/duncantestimony.htm).

Dworkin, Ronald. 1977. *Taking Rights Seriously*. Cambridge, Mass.: Harvard University Press.

Emerson, Ralph Waldo. 1985. *Selected Essays*. Harmondsworth: Penguin.

Enloe, Cynthia. 1989. *Bananas, Beaches, and Bases: Making Feminist Sense of International Politics*. London: Pandora.

Evans, Peter. 2000. "Counter-Hegemonic Globalization: Transnational Networks as Political Tools for Fighting Marginalization." *Contemporary Sociology* (January).

Ewell, Miranda, and K. Oanh Ha. 1999a. "Long Nights and Low Wages" and "Agencies Probing Piecework." *San Jose Mercury News*, July 8.

Ewell, Miranda, and K. Oanh Ha. 1999b. "Multi-Billion-Dollar Industry at the Heart of Valley Growth." *San Jose Mercury News*, posted July 3, on *www.siliconvalley.com*.

Falk, Richard, and David Krieger. 2002. "Taming the Nuclear Monster." *Asahi Shimbum,* May 13.

Falk, Richard. 1997. "The Right of Self-Determination under International Law: The Coherence of Doctrine versus the Incoherence of Experience." In *Self-Determination and Self-Administration: A Sourcebook*, ed. *Wolfgang Danspreckgruber with Arthur Watts*. Boulder, Colo.: Lynne Rienner.

Falk, Richard. 1999a. *The Role of Law in an Emerging Global Village: A Post-Westphalian Perspective*. Ardsley, N.Y.: Transnational.

Falk, Richard. 2000b. "Reviving the 1990s: Trends toward Transnational Justice: Innovations and Institutions," *Journal of Human Development* 3: 167–90.

Falk, Richard. 2002. "Testing Patriotism and Citizenship in the Global Terror War." In *Worlds in Collision*, ed. Ken Booth and Tim Dunne. New York: Palgrave.

Falk, Richard, and Andrew Strauss. 2001. "Toward Global Parliament." *Foreign Affairs* 80, no. 1 (January–February).

Falk, Richard. Forthcoming. "The Unfinished Normative Revolution of the 1990s."

Falk, Richard. 1999. *Predatory Globalization—A Critique*. (Cambridge: Polity).

Falk, Richard. 2003. The Great Terror War. Northhampton MA: Interlink.

Ferguson, Kathy. 1996. "From a Kibbutz Journal: Reflections on Gender, Race, and Militarism in Israel." In *Challenging Boundaries—Global Flows, Territorial Identities*, ed. Michael J. Shapiro and Hayward R. Alker. Minneapolis: University of Minnesota Press.

Ferguson, Niall. 2002. "Clashing Civilizations or Mad Mullahs: The United States between Informal and Formal Empire." In *The Age of Terror: America and the World after September 11*, ed. Strobe Talbott and Nayan Chanda. New York: Basic.

Follesdal, Andreas. 2002. "Citizenship: European and Global." In *Global Citizenship: A Critical Introduction*, ed. Nigel Dower and John Williams. New York: Routledge.

Foucault, Michel. 1984. "Nietzsche, Genealogy, History." In *The Foucault Reader*, ed. Paul Rabinow, trans. Donald F. Bouchard and Sherry Simon. New York: Pantheon.

Frank, Dana. 1999. *Buy American: The Untold Story of Economic Nationalism*. Boston: Beacon.

Fraser, Nancy, and Linda Gordon. 1998. "Contract versus Charity: Why Is There no Social Citizenship in the United States?" In *The Citizenship Debate: A Reader*, ed. Gershon Shafir. Minneapolis: University of Minnesota Press.

Fraser, Nancy. 1997. *Justice Interruptus—Critical Reflections on the "Postsocialist" Condition*. New York: Routledge.

Fraser, Nancy. 1999. "Social Justice in the Age of Identity Politics: Redistribution, Recognition, and Participation," from a Distinguished Lecture at the Centre for Theoretical Studies, Essex University, London. Available at http://www.newschool.edu/gf/polsci/faculty/excerpts/nfexcpt.htm (accessed March 30, 2001).

Freeman, Carla. 2000. *High Tech and High Heels in the Global Economy: Women, Work, and Pink-Collar Identities in the Caribbean*. Durham, N.C. Duke University Press.

Frenkel, Stephen, and Carol Royal. 1997. "Globalization and Employment Relations." *Research in the Sociology of Work* 6: 3–41.

Freundlich, Madelyn. 1999. "Families without Borders." *UN Chronicle* 36, no. 2 (summer): 88.

Friedman, Milton, and Rose Friedman. 1980. *Free to Choose*. New York: Harcourt Brace Jovanovich.

Friedman, Milton. 1962. *Capitalism and Freedom*. Chicago: University of Chicago Press.

Fukuyama, Francis. 1995. *Trust: Social Virtues and the Creation of Prosperity*. New York: Free Press.

Fung, Archon, Dara O'Rourke, and Charles Sabel. 2001. *Can We Put an End to Sweatshops?* Boston: Beacon.

Gai, Yash. 1999. "Rights, Social Justice, and Globalization in East Asia." In *The East Asian Challenge for Human Rights*, ed. Joanne R. Bauer and Daniel A. Bell. New York: Cambridge University Press.

Garson, Barbara. 2001. *Money Makes the World Go Around*. New York: Viking.

Gereffi, Gary. 1994. "The Organization of Buyer-Driven Global Commodity Chains: How U.S. Retailers Shape Overseas Production Networks." In *Commodity Chains and Global Capitalism*, ed. Gereffi and Miguel Korzeniewicz. Westport, Conn.: Praeger.

Gill, Leslie. 1994. *Precarious Dependencies: Gender, Class, and Domestic Service in Bolivia*. New York: Columbia University Press.

Gill, Stephen. 1995. "The Global Panopticon? The Neoliberal State, Economic Life, and Democratic Surveillance." *Alternatives*, 20. no. 1 (January–March): 1–50.

Glaberson, William. 2002. "Judge Gives Children Voice in Deportation," *New York Times*, Feb. 12.

Glendon, Mary Ann. 2001. *A World Made New: Eleanor Roosevelt and the Universal Declaration of Human Rights*. NY: Random House.

Glenn, Evelyn Nakano. 1992. "From Servitude to Service Work: Historical Continuities in the Racial Division of Paid Reproductive Labor." *Signs* 18, no. 1: 1–43.

Golden, Miriam, and Jonas Pontussen (eds.). 1992. *Bargaining for Change: Union Politics in North America and Europe*. Ithaca, N.Y.: Cornell University Press.

Gooding-Williams, Robert. 1993. "Introduction: On Being Stuck." In *Reading Rodney King, Reading Urban Uprising*, ed. Robert Gooding-Williams. New York: Routledge.

Goetman, Elissa. "Visa Problems Snarl Adoptions in Vietnam," *New York Times*. Jan. 29, 2002.

Greenhouse, Steven. 2001. "Report Outlines the Abuse of Foreign Domestic Workers," *New York Times*, June 14.

Greider, William. 1997. *One World, Ready or Not: The Manic Logic of Global Capitalism*. New York: Simon and Schuster.

Grossberg, Michael. 1985. *Governing the Hearth: Law and the Family in Nineteenth-Century America*. Chapel Hill: University of North Carolina Press.

Gupta, Akhil, and James Ferguson. 1992. "Beyond 'Culture,' Space, Identity, and the Politics of Difference." *Cultural Anthropology* 7, no. 1: 6–23.

Hague Convention. 1954. Available at http://exchanges.state.gov/education/culprop/hague.html

Handler, Joel. 1995. *The Poverty of Welfare Reform*. New Haven, CT: Yale University Press.

Hardin, Garrett. 1968. "The Tragedy of the Commons." *Science* 162: 1243–48.

Hardt, Michael, and Antonio Negri. 2000. *Empire*. Cambridge, Mass.: Harvard University Press.

Harris, Nigel. 2002. *Thinking the Unthinkable—The Immigration Myth Exposed*. London: I.B. Taurus.

Harvey, Pharis, n.d. "U.S. GSP Labor Rights Conditionality: 'Aggressive Unilateralism' or a Forerunner to a Multilateral Social Clause?" Washington: International Labor Rights Fund Publication. Available at http://www.laborrights.org/.

Hassner, Pierre, "Refugees: A Special Case for Cosmopolitan Citizenship?" in Daniele Archibugi et. al., *Re-imagining Political Community: Studies in Cosmopolitan Democracy*, Stanford, Stanford University Press, 1988, pp. 273–286.

Hayes, Peter. 2000. "Deterrents to Intercountry Adoption in Britain." *Family Relations* 49, no. 4, (October) 465–72.

Heater, Derek. 1996. *World Citizenship and Government: Cosmopolitan Ideas in the History of Western Political Thought*. London: Macmillan.

Hegel, G.W.F. 1821. *Philosophy of Right*. Available at http://marxists.anu.edu.au/reference/archive/hegel/ (accessed October 5, 2001).

Held, David. 1995a. "Cosmopolitan Democracy and the Global Order: Reflections on the 200th Anniversary of Kant's 'Perpetual Peace.'" *Alternatives* 20, no. 4, October–December: 415–29.

Held, David. 1995b. *Democracy and the Global Order: From the Modern State to Cosmopolitan Governance*. Stanford, Calif.: Stanford University Press.

Held, David. 1996. *Models of Democracy*, 2nd ed. Cambridge: Polity.

Henkin, Louis. 1990. *The Age of Rights*. New York: Columbia University Press.

Hernandez, Raymond. 2001. "Children's Sexual Exploitation Underestimated, Study Finds," *New York Times*, Sept. 10.

Heyzer, Noeleen, Geertje Lycklama à Nijeholt, and Nedra Weerakoon. 1994. *The Trade in Domestic Workers: Causes, Mechanisms, and Consequences of International Migration*. Kuala Lumpur: Asian and Pacific Development Centre; and London: Zed Books.

Himmelfarb, Gertrude. 2001. *One Nation, Two Cultures: A Searching Examination of American Society in the Aftermath of Our Cultural Revolution*. New York, NY: Vintage Books.

Hirschsohn, Philip, Shane Godfrey, and Johann Maree. 2000. "Industrial Policy-Making in the Automobile and the Textile and Clothing Sectors: Labor's Strategic Ambivalence." In *Engaging the State and Business: The Labor Movement and Co-determination in South Africa*, ed. Glenn Adler. Johannesburg: Wits University Press.

Hirst, Paul, and Grahame Thompson. 1996. *Globalization in Question: The International Political Economy and Possibilities of Governance*. Cambridge: Polity.

Hochschild, Arlie Russell. 2000. "The Nanny Chain: Mothers Minding Other Mothers' Children." *American Prospect* (January 3): 32–36.

Hoksbergen, R.A.C. (ed.). 1986. *Adoption in Worldwide Perspective: A Review of Programs, Policies, and Legislation in Fourteen Countries*. Lisse: Swets and Zeitlinger.

Hoksbergen, Rene A. C. 1991. "Intercountry Adoption Coming of Age in the Netherlands: Basic Issues, Trends, and Developments." In *Intercountry Adoption: A Multinational Perspective*, ed. Howard Altstein and Rita J. Simon. New York: Praeger.

Hoksbergen, Rene A. C., and Lucile A. C. Bunjes. 1986. "Thirty Years of Adoption Practice in the Netherlands." In *Adoption in Worldwide Perspective: A Review of Programs, Policies, and Legislation in Fourteen Countries*, ed. R.A.C. Hoksbergen. Lisse: Swets and Zeitlinger.

Hollifield, James. 1992. *Immigrants, Markets, and States*. Cambridge, Mass.: Harvard University Press.

Hondagneu-Sotelo, Pierrette. 1994. *Gendered Transitions: Mexican Experiences of Immigration*. Berkeley, CA: University of California Press.

Hondagneu-Sotelo, Pierrette. 1995. "Women and Children First: New Directions in Anti-Immigrant Politics." *Socialist Review* 25, no. 1: 169–90.

Hondagneu-Sotelo, Pierrette. 1997. "'I'm here, but I'm there': The Meanings of Latina Transnational Motherhood." *Gender and Society* 11, no. 5: 548–71.

Hondagneu-Sotelo, Pierrette. 2001. *Doméstica: Immigrant Women Cleaning and Caring in the Shadows of Affluence*. Berkeley: University of California Press.

Horsman, Reginald. 1981. *Race and Manifest Destiny: The Origins of American Racial Anglo-Saxonism*. Cambridge, Mass.: Harvard University Press.

Howse, Robert. 1999. "The World Trade Organization and the Protection of Workers' Rights." *Journal of Small and Emerging Business Law* 131 (summer).

HR2909. 2000. *The Intercountry Adoption Act of 1999*. Markup before the Committee on International Relations, House of Representatives, 106th Congress, 2nd Session, March 22, Serial No. 106–157.

Hu-DeHart, Evelyn. 1999 *Across the Pacific: Asian Americans and Globalization*. Philadelphia: Temple University Press.

Hukill, Traci. 1999. "When Unions Attempt to Organize Silicon Valley's Growing Vietnamese Workforce, They Find Custom, Language, and History Stand in the Way." *Metro, Silicon Valley's Weekly Newspaper*, September 16–22.

Human Rights Watch. 2001. "Hidden in the Home: Abuse of Domestic Workers with Special Visas in the United States." New York: HRW.

Human Rights Watch. 2000. "Unfair Advantage: Workers' Freedom of Association in the United States under International Human Rights Standards." Available at http://www.hrw.org/reports/2000/uslabor/.

Human Rights Watch. 1998. *United States: Detained and Deprived of Rights—Children in the Custody of the U.S. Immigration and Naturalization Service*. New York: HRW, 1998.

Human Rights Watch/Asia. 1996. *Death by Default: A Policy of Fatal Neglect in China's State Orphanages*. New York: HRW.

Hunt, Lynn. 2001. "The Paradoxical Origins of Human Rights." In Wasserstrom, Jeffrey et al. *Human Rights and Revolutions*, Lanham, MD: Rowman and Littlefield: 3–17.

Huntington, Samuel P. 1996. *The Clash of Civilizations and the Remaking of World Order*. New York: Simon and Schuster.

Hutchings, Kimberly, and Roland Dannreuther (eds.). 1999. *Cosmopolitan Citizenship*. Houndsmill and New York: MacMillan and St. Martin's.

Hutchings, Kimberly. 1999. "Political Theory and Cosmopolitan Citizenship." In *Cosmopolitan Citizenship*, ed. Kimberly Hutchings and Roland Dannreuther. Houndsmill and New York: MacMillan and St. Martin's.

Ignatieff, Michael. 2002. "How to Keep Afghanistan from Falling Apart: The Case for a Committed American Imperialism." *New York Times Magazine*, July 28, pp. 26–31, 54.

Inda, Xavier, and Renato Rosaldo (eds.). 2002. *The Anthropology of Globalization*. New York: Blackwell.

Indonesian National Council on Social Welfare. 1986. "Adoption of Children in Indonesia." In *Adoption in Worldwide Perspective: A Review of Programs, Policies, and Legislation in Fourteen Countries*, ed. R.A.C. Hoksbergen. Lisse: Swets and Zeitlinger.

International Labor Organization. 1998a. ILO Declaration on Fundamental Principles and Rights at Work. Geneva, June 28.

International Labor Organization. 1998b. Forced Labour in Myanmar (Burma). Report of the Commission of Inquiry Appointed under Article 26 of the Constitution of the International Labour Organization to Examine the Observance by Myanmar of the Forced Labour Convention, 1930 (No. 29). Geneva, July 2.

International Labor Organization. 2001. "Gender and Migration," http://www.ilo.org/public/english/protection/migrant/projects/gender.

International Labor Organization. 2002. *International Programme on the Elimination of Child Labour (IPEC), Statistical Information and Monitoring Programme on Child Labour (SIMPOC), Every Child Counts: New Global Estimates on Child Labour*. Geneva: April (Available at www.ilo.org.)

Indiana Journal of Global Legal Studies. 1996. Special Issue: "Feminism and Globalization: The Impact of The Global Economy on Women and Feminist Theory." 4(1).

Isin, Engin. 2000. "Introduction: democracy, citizenship and the city." *Democracy, Citizenship and the Global City*, Engin Isin, ed. New York, NY: Routledge.

Jackson, Robert. 2000. *The Global Covenant*. Oxford: Oxford University Press.

Jacobson, David. 1996. *Rights Across Borders: Immigration and the Decline of Citizenship*. Baltimore, Md: Johns Hopkins Press.

Jacobson, David. 1998–99. "New Border Customs: Migration and the Changing Role of the State." *UCLA Journal of International Law and Foreign Affairs* (fall/winter): 443–558.

Jacobson, David. 2001. *Place and Belonging in America*. Baltimore, Md.: Johns Hopkins University Press.

Jaffe, Eliezer D. 1991. "Foreign Adoptions in Israel: Private Paths to Parenthood." In *Intercountry Adoption: A Multinational Perspective*, ed. Howard Altstein, and Rita J. Simon. New York: Praeger.

Jantera-Jareborg, Maarit. 1994. "Convention on Protection of Children and Cooperation in Respect of Intercountry Adoption," *Nordic Journal of International Law* 63: 185–203.

Jantera-Jareborg, Maarit. 1990. "The Procedural and Material Conditions for Intercountry Adoption in Sweden." In *Swedish National Reports to the XIIIth International Congress of Comparative Law*. Montreal ed. Stig Stromholm and Carl Hemstrom. Stockholm: Almqvist and Wiksell International.

Johansen, Bruce. 1993. "Kidnapped by 'La Migra.'" *Progressive* 57, no. 4 (April): 21.

Jonas, Susanne, and Susie Dod Thomas (eds.). 1999. *Immigration: A Civil Rights Issue for the Americas*. Scholarly Resources.

Jones, Charles. 1999. *Global Justice—Defending Cosmopolitanism*. Oxford: Oxford University Press.

Joppke, Christian. 1999. *Immigration and the Nation-State*. New York: Oxford University Press.

Juarez, Huberto, and Steve Babson (eds.). 1998. *Confronting Change: Auto Labor and Lean Production in North America*. Detroit: Wayne State University, and Benemerita Universidad Autonomia de Puebla.

Judge, Sharon Lesar. 1999. "Eastern European Adoptions: Current Status and Implications for Intervention." *Topics in Early Childhood Special Education* 19, no. 4 (winter): 244.

Jureidini, Ray. 2002. "Migrant Women Domestic Workers in Lebanon." International Labor Organization.

Kagan, Robert. 2002. "Power and Weakness: Why the United States and Europe See the World Differently." *Policy Review* no. 113: 3–28.

Kaplan, Amy. 1993. "'Left Alone with America': The Absence of Empire in the Study of American Culture." In *Cultures of United States Imperialism*, ed. A. Kaplan and D. E. Pease. Durham, N.C.: Duke University Press.

Kaplan, Robert. 2002. *Warrior Politics: Why Leadership Demands a Pagan Ethos*. New York: Random House.

Kaplinsky, Raphael. 1993. "Export-Processing Zones in the Dominican Republic: Transforming Manufactures into Commodities." *World Development* 21, no. 11: 1851–65.

Kaplinsky, Raphael. 1995. "Technique and Management: The Spread of Japanese Management Techniques to Developing Countries." *World Development* 23, no. 1: 57–71.

Kapner, Suzanne. 2000. "Britain's Legal Barriers Start to Fall: Discrimination Lawsuits Are Becoming More Commonplace." *New York Times*, October 4, W1.

Kapstein, Ethan. 1999. *Sharing the Wealth: Workers and the World Economy.* New York: Norton.

Karst, Kenneth. 1997. "The Coming Crisis of Work in Constitutional Perspective." *Cornell Law Review* 82(3): 523–571.

———. 2000. "Citizenship, Law, and the American Nation." *Indiana Journal of Global Legal Studies* 7(2): 595–601.

Kashiwazaki, Chikako. 1998. "Jus Sanguinis in Japan: The Origin of Citizenship in a Comparative Perspective." *International Journal of Comparative Sociology* 39, no. 3 (August): 278.

Katznelson, Ira. 1992. *Marxism and the City.* Oxford, United Kingdom: Clarendon.

Keck, Margaret, and Kathryn Sikkink. 1998. *Activists beyond Borders.* Ithaca, N.Y.: Cornell University Press.

Keohane, Robert O., and Joseph S. Nye Jr. 2000. "Introduction." In Joseph S. Nye Jr. and John D. Donahue, *Governance in a Globalizing World*, Washington, D.C.: Brookings Institution Press.

Khor, Martin. 1994. "The World Trade Organization and Labour Standards." Jakarta: Third World Network. Available at http://www.stile.lboro.ac.uk/~gyedb/STILE.

Kimminich, Otto. 1996. "The Conventions for the Prevention of Double Nationality and Their Meaning for Germany and Europe in an Era of Migration." *German Yearbook of International Law* 38: 224, 232.

Klusmeyer, Douglas B. 1996. *Between Consent and Descent: Conceptions of Democratic Citizenship.* Washington, D.C., Carnegie Endowment for International Peace.

Klusmeyer, Douglas. 2000. "Four Dimensions of Membership in Germany." *SAIS Review* 20, no. 1 (2000): 1–21.

Knop, Karen. 2001. "Relational Nationality: On Gender and Nationality in International Law." In *Citizenship Today: Global Perspectives and Practices*, ed. T. Alexander Aleinikoff and Douglas Klusmeyers. Washington, D.C.: Carnegie Endowment for International Peace.

Knop, Karen. 2002. *Diversity and Self-Determination in International Law.* Cambridge, United Kingdom: Cambridge University Press.

Koo, Hagen. 2000. "The Dilemmas of Empowered Labor in Korea: Korean Workers in the Face of Global Capitalism." *Asian Survey* 40, no. 2: 227–50.

Koo, Hagen. 2001. *Korean Workers: The Culture and Politics of Class Formation.* Ithaca, N.Y.: Cornell University Press.

Korten, David. 1995. *When Corporations Rule the World.* West Hartford, Conn.: Kumarian.

Koslowski, Rey. 2000. *Migrants and Citizens.* Ithaca, N.Y.: Cornell University Press.

Kotsonis, Yanni. 2001. "A European Experience: Human Rights and Citizenship in Revolutionary Russia." In Wasserstrom, Jeffrey et al., *Human Rights and Revolutions*, Lanham, MD: Rowman and Littlefield, 99–110.

Krasner, Stephen. D. (ed.). 1982. *International Regimes.* Ithaca, N.Y.: Cornell University Press.

Kuttner, Robert. 2002. "Enron: A Powerful Blow to Market Fundamentalists." *BusinessWeek*, February 4, p. 20.

Kwong, Peter. 2002. "Forbidden Workers and the U.S. Labor Movement: Fuzhounese in New York City." *Critical Asian Studies* 34, no. 1.

Kymlicka, Will. 1998. "Multicultural Citizenship." In *The Citizenship Debates*, ed. Gershon Shafir. Minneapolis: University of Minnesota Press.

Kymlicka, Will. 1995. *Multicultural Citizenship: A Liberal Theory of Minority Rights.* Oxford: Oxford University Press.

Lambert, Robert. 2000. "Globalization and the Erosion of Class Compromise in Contemporary Australia." *Politics and Society* 28, no. 1: 93–118.

Laqueur, Walter, and Barry Rubin (eds.). 1979. *The Human Rights Reader*, rev. ed. New York: Meridian.

Latouche, Serge. 1996. *The Westernization of the World: The Significance, Scope and Limits of the Drive towards Global Uniformity.* Cambridge: Cambridge University Press.

Leary, Virginia. "Citizenship, Human Rights, and Diversity," in Alan Cairns, *Citizenship Diversity and Pluralism*; Ithaca, NY: McGill-Queens University Press.

LeBlanc, Robin. 1999. *Bicycle Citizens: The Political World of the Japanese Housewife.* Berkeley, CA: University of California Press.

Lee, Ching Kwan. 1998. *Gender and the South China Miracle: Two Worlds of Factory Women.* Berkeley: University of California Press.

Lefebvre, Henri. 1991. *The Production of Space.* Cambridge, MA: Blackwell.

————. 1995. *Writing on Cities.* Cambridge, MA: Blackwell.

Lemann, Nicholas. 2002. "The Next World Order." *New Yorker*, April 1, pp. 42–48.

Linklater, Andrew. 1998. *The Transformation of Political Community.* Cambridge: Polity.

Linklater, Andrew. 1999. "Cosmopolitan Citizenship." In: *Cosmopolitan Citizenship*, ed. Kimberly Hutchings and Roland Dannreuther. Houndsmill and New York: MacMillan and St. Martin's.

Lipietz, Alain. 1987. *Mirages and Miracles: The Crisis in Global Fordism*, trans. David Macey. London: Verso.

Lipschutz, Ronnie D. 1999. "Members Only? Citizenship and Civic Virtue in a Time of Globalization." *International Politics* 36 (June): 203–33.

Lipschutz, Ronnie D. 1992. "Reconstructing World Politics: The Emergence of Global Civil Society." *Millennium: Journal of International Studies* 21: 389–420.

Lipschutz, Ronnie D. 2000. *After Authority—War, Peace, and Global Politics in the 21st Century.* Albany: SUNY Press.

Lipschutz, Ronnie D. 2001. "Regulation for the Rest of Us? Activists, Capital, States, and the Demand for Global Social Regulation." Paper presented at the International Studies Association Conference, Chicago, February 20–24. Available at http://people.ucsc.edu/~rlipsch/Regulation%20for%20the%20Rest%20of%20Us.html.

Lipschutz, Ronnie D. 2002. "Where Is the Double Movement—Or, Politics vs. Markets in the 21st Century." Paper presented at the International Studies Association Conference, New Orleans, March 24–27.

Lipschutz, Ronnie. 1996. *Global Civil Society and Global Environmental Governance.* New York: SUNY Press.

Lister, Ruth. 1997. *Citizenship: Feminist Perspectives.* London: Macmillan.

Lister, Ruth. 1998. "Dialectics of Citizenship." *Hypatia* 12, no. 4. Available at http://iupjournals.org/ hypatia/hyp12-4.html (accessed September 13, 2001).

Little, Marie-Noëlle (ed.). 2001. *The Poet and the Diplomat: The Correspondence of Dag Hammarskjöld and Alexis Leger.* Syracuse, N.Y.: Syracuse University Press.

Locke, John. 1988. *Two Treatises of Government*, ed. Peter Laslett. Cambridge: Cambridge University Press.

Locke, John. 1958. *The Reasonableness of Christianity.* ed. I.T. Ramsey. Stanford Calif.: Stanford University Press.

Loon, J.H.A. van. 1992. "Intercountry Adoption of Children: A challenge for International Cooperation to Protect Children's Rights." *Hague Yearbook of International Law* 5 (1992): 137–163.

Lubeck, Paul M. 1992. "Malaysian Industrialization, Ethnic Divisions, and the NIC Model: The Limits to Replication." In *States and Development in the Asian Pacific Rim,* ed. Richard P. Appelbaum and Jeffrey Henderson. Newbury Park, Calif.: Sage.

Lucker-Babel, Marie-Francoise. 1991. "Inter-Country Adoption and Trafficking in Children: An Initial Assessment of the Adequacy of the International Protection of Children and Their Rights." *International Review of Penal Law* 62, no. 3–4 (1991): 799–818.

Luthje, Boy. 1998. "Race and Ethnicity in 'Post-Fordist' Production Networks: Silicon Valley and the Global Information Technology Industry." Dept. of Social Sciences, University of Frankfurt, unpubl. ms.

MacFarquhar, Neil. 2001. "In Egypt, Law of Man Creates a Caste of Shunned Children," *New York Times*, May 14.

MacKay, Stephen. 2001. *Securing Commitment in an Insecure World: Power and the Social Regulation of Labor in the Philippine Electronics Industry.* Doctoral diss., University of Wisconsin-Madison.

Maher, Kristen Hill, and Silke Staab. 2003. "Identity Projects at Home and Labor from Abroad: Migrant household workers in Southern California and Santiago, Chile." Working Paper # 15, Center for Comparative Immigration Studies, San Diego.

Maher, Kristen Hill. 1999. *A Stranger in the House: American Ambivalence about Immigrant Labor.* Diss., University of California-Irvine.

Maher, Kristen Hill. 2001. "Labor Brokers and the International Maid Trade: The Commodification of 'Traditional Femininity' in a Global Market." Paper presented at the Social Science History Association Conference, Chicago, November 15–18.

Maher, Kristen Hill. 2002. "Who Has a Right to Rights? Citizenship's Exclusions in an Age of Migration." *Globalization and Human Rights*, ed. Alison Brysk. Berkeley: University of California Press.

Maher, Kristen Hill. 2004. "Good Women 'Ready To Go': Labor Brokers and the International Maid Trade," *Labor* 1, 1.

Mahler, Sarah. 1995. *American Dreaming: Immigrant Life on the Margins.* Princeton, NJ: Princeton University Press.

Malone, Scott. 2002. "Anti-Globalization Targets: Why Gap Is Number One." *Women's Wear Daily* 183, no. 139 (February 27).

Marcuse, Herbert. 1964. *One-Dimensional Man.* Boston: Beacon.

Marquez, Gustavo. 1995. "Reforming the Labor Market in a Liberalized Economy." In *Reforming the Labor Market in a Liberalized Economy*, ed. Gustavo Marquez. Washington, D.C.: Inter-American Development Bank and Johns Hopkins University Press.

Marrus, Michael R. 1985. *The Unwanted: European Refugees in the Twentieth Century.* New York, NY: Oxford University Press.

Marshall, T. H. 1950. *Citizenship and Social Class.* New York: Cambridge University Press.

Marshall, T. H. 1963. *Citizenship and Social Class.* New York: Doubleday.

Martin, Michael. 1999. "'Fortress Europe' and Third World Immigration in the Post–Cold War Global Context." *Third World Quarterly* 20, no. 4: 821–38.

Mattingly, Doreen. 2001. "The Home and the World: Domestic Service and International Networks of Caring Labor." *Annals of the Association of American Geographers* 91, no. 2: 370–86.

McPherson, C. B. 1962. *The Political Theory of Possessive Individualism.* Oxford: Oxford University Press.

Melchior, Torben. 1986. "Adoption in Denmark," in *Adoption in Worldwide Perspective: A Review of Programs, Policies, and Legislation in Fourteen Countries*, ed. R.A.C. Hoksbergen. Lisse: Swets and Zeitlinger.

Meyer, John, et al. 1997. "World Society and the Nation-State." *American Journal of Sociology* 103, no. 1: 144–81.

Milkman, Ruth. 1985. *Women, Work, and Protest: A Century of U.S. Women's Labor History.* Boston: Routledge and Kegan Paul.

Mill, John Stuart. 1962. *Essays on Politics and Culture*, ed. Gertrude Himmelfarb. New York: Doubleday.

Miller, David. 2002. "The Left, the Nation-State, and European Citizenship." In *Global Citizenship: A Critical Introduction*, ed. Nigel Dower and John Williams. New York: Routledge.

Mills, Kurt. 1998. *Human Rights in the Emerging Global Order: A New Sovereignty?* New York: St. Martin's Press.

Milotte, Mike. 1997. *Banished Babies: The Secret History of Ireland's Baby Export Business.* Dublin: New Island Books.

Minogue, Kenneth. 1979. "The History of the Idea of Human Rights." In Laqueur, Walter and Barry Rubin, *The Human Rights Reader*, New York: Meridian, 3–117.

Mohanty, Chandra Talpade, Ann Russo, and Luordes Torres. 1991. *Third World Women and the Politics of Feminism.* Bloomington: Indiana University Press.

Moody, Kim. 1997. *Workers in a lean world: Unions in the international economy.* London: Verso.

Moore, Mark. 1995. *Creating Public Value: Strategic Management in Government.* Cambridge, Mass.: Harvard University Press.

Morokvasic, Mirjana. 1984. "Birds of Passage are also Women . . ." *International Migration Review* 18, no. 4: 886–907.

Mouffe, Chantal. 1992. "Preface: Democratic Politics Today." In *Dimensions of Radical Democracy*, ed. Chantal Mouffe. London: Verso.

Munger, Frank, ed. 2002. *Laboring Under the Line.* New York, NY: Russell Sage Foundation.

Mydans, Seth, "U.S. Interrupts Cambodian Adoptions," *New York Times*; Nov. 5, 2001.

Nash, June, and Maria Patricia Fernandez-Kelly (eds.). 1983. *Women, Men, and the International Division of Labor.* Albany: SUNY Press.

Nazario, Sonya. 2002. "Enrique's Journey." Six-part series. *Los Angeles Times*, September 29–October 7.

Neuman, Gerald L. 1998. "Nationality Law in the United States and the Federal Republic of Germany." In Peter H. Schuck and Rainer Münz, eds., *Paths to Inclusion: The Integration of Migrants in the United States and Germany.* New York: Berghahn.

Newland, Kathleen, and Demetrios Papademetriou. 1998–99. "Managing International Migration." *UCLA Journal of International Law and Foreign Affairs* 3, no. 2: 637.

Novak, David A. 1978. *The Wheel of Servitude: Black Forced Labor after Slavery.* Lexington: University Press of Kentucky.

OECD (Organization for Economic Cooperation and Development). 2000. *Trends in International Migration.* Paris: OECD.

Ohmae, Kenichi. 1999. *The Borderless World.* New York: HarperBusiness.

Oishi, Nana. 2002. "Gender and Migration: An Integrative Approach." Working Paper No. 49. University of California, San Diego: Center for Comparative Immigration Studies.

Olson, Elizabeth. 2002. "50 Million Children without a Nationality." *New York Times,* June 5.

Olson, Elizabeth. "United Nations: Labor monitor to go to Myanmar." *New York Times,* March 23, 2002, A6.

Olson, Elizabeth. 2001. "Myanmar Tests Resolve of ILO on Enforcing Standards," *New York Times,* June 5.

Omi, Michael, and Howard Winant. 1986. *Racial Formation in the United States.* New York: Routledge and Kegan Paul.

Ong, Aihwa. 1987. *Spirits of Resistance and Capitalist Discipline: Factory Women in Malaysia.* Albany: SUNY Press.

Ong, Aihwa. 1997. "'Strategic Sisterhood' or Sisters in Solidarity? Questions of Communitarianism and Citizenship in Asia." *Indiana Journal of Global Legal Studies,* 4, no. 1: 107–35.

Ong Aihwa. 2003. *Buddha in Hiding: Refugees, Citizenship, and the New America.* Berkeley: University of California Press.

Ong Aihwa. Forthcoming. "The Techno-Migrants." In *Global America,* ed. Ulrich Beck, Rainer Winter, and Natan Sznaider. Liverpool: University of Liverpool Press.

Ong, Aihwa. 1999. *Flexible Citizenship: The Cultural Logic of Transnationality.* Durham, N.C.: Duke University Press.

Ong, Aihwa, and Donald Nonini (eds.). 1997. *Ungrounded Empires: The Cultural Politics of Modern Chinese Transnationalism.* New York: Routledge.

Onuf, Nicholas. 1989. *World of Our Making.* Columbia: University of South Carolina Press.

Oppenheim, L. 1928. *1 International Law,* 4th ed.

Orend, Brian. 2002. *Human Rights: Concept and Context.* Ontario: Broadview Press.

Orentlicher, Diane. 1998. "Citizenship and National Identity." In David Wippman, ed., *International Law and Ethnic Conflict.* Ithaca, N.Y.: Cornell University Press.

Pahz, James A. 1988. *Adopting from Latin America: An AGENCY Perspective.* Springfield: Ill. Charles C. Thomas.

Painter, Joe. 2000. "Citizenship, Diversity, and Critical Geography." Paper presented to the Second International Conference of Critical Geography, Taegu, South Korea, August 9–13. Available at http://econgeog.misc.hit-u.ac.jp/icgg/intl_mtgs/JPainter.pdf (accessed October 5, 2001).

Pandit, Nirmala. 1993. "Inter-Country Adoption: The Indian View." In J. Eekelaar and P. Sarcevic (eds.) *Parenthood in Modern Society.* Dordrecht, The Netherlands: Martinus Nijhoff Publishers.

Parreñas, Rhacel Salazar. 2001. *Servants of Globalization: Women, Migration, and Domestic Work.* Stanford, Calif.: Stanford University Press.

Pateman, Carole. 1988. *The Sexual Contract.* Cambridge: Polity.

Pettman, Jan Jindy. 1996. *Worlding Women: A Feminist International Politics.* London and New York: Routledge.

Pettman, Jan Jindy. 1999. "Globalization and the Gendered Politics of Citizenship." In *Women, Citizenship, and Difference,* ed. Nira Yuval-Davis and Pnina Werbner. London: Zed Books.

Picton, Cliff. 1986. "Adoption in Australia." In Hoksbergen, R.A.C. (ed.) *Adoption in Worldwide Perspective: A review of programs, policies and legislation in fourteen countries.* Lisse: Swets and Zeitlinger.

Pocock, J.G.A. "The Ideal of Citizenship since Classical Times." *Queen's Quarterly* 99: 1.

Polyani, Karl. 1944. *The Great Transformation.* Boston: Farrar and Rinehart.

Portes, Alejandro. 1996. "Global Villagers: The Rise of Transnational Communities." *American Prospect* 7(25).

Portes, Alejandro, and Rubén G. Rumbaut. 1996. *Immigrant America—A Portrait,* 2nd ed. Berkeley: University of California Press.

Posthuma, Anne. 1995. "Japanese techniques in Africa? Human resources and industrial restructuring in Zimbabwe." *World Development*, 23, no. 1: 103–16.

Pratt, Geraldine. 1997. "Stereotypes and Ambivalence: The Construction of Domestic Workers in Vancouver, British Columbia." *Gender, Place, and Culture* 4, no. 2: 159–77.

Preuss, Ulrich K. 1998. "Citizenship in the European Union: A Paradigm for Transnational Democracy?" In Archibugi, Daniele, David Held, and Martin Kohler, *Reimaging Political Community*, Stanford: Stanford University Press, 138–151.

Przeworski, Adam. 1985. *Capitalism and social democracy*. Cambridge: Cambridge University Press.

Putnam, Robert. 2000. *Bowling Alone: The Collapse and Revival of American Community*. New York: Touchstone.

Rabkin, Jeremy. "Children adrift." *American Spectator* 33, no. 5 (March): 44.

Reich, Robert. 1991. *The Work of Nations*. New York: Vintage.

Rich, Ruby. 2000. "Ming has two mommies." *Advocate*, July 18, 45.

Risse, Thomas, and Kathryn Sikkink. 1999. "The Socialization of International Human Rights Norms into Domestic Practices: Introduction." In *The Power of Human Rights: International Norms and Domestic Change*, ed. Risse et al. Cambridge: Cambridge University Press.

Rittberger, Volker (ed.). 1993. *States and International Regimes*. Oxford: Clarendon.

Rodrik, Dani. 2000. "Governance of Economic Globalization." In Joseph S. Nye and John D. Donahue, *Governance in a Globalizing World*. Washington, D.C.: Brookings Institution Press.

Roediger, D. 1991. *The Wages of Whiteness: Race and the Making of the American Working Class*. London: Verso.

Rofel, Lisa. 2001. "Discrepant Modernities and Their Discontents." *Positions* 9, no. 3: 637–49.

Rollins, Judith. 1985. *Between Women: Domestics and Their Employers*. Philadelphia: Temple University Press.

Rosaldo, Renato 1997. "Cultural Citizenship, Inequality, and Multiculturalism." In *Latino Cultural Citizenship: Claiming Identity, Space, and Politics*, ed. William V. Flores and Rina Benmayor. Boston: Beacon.

Ross, Andrew (ed.). 1997. *No sweat: Fashion, free trade, and the rights of garment workers*. London: Verso.

Roulleau-Berger, Laurence, ed. 2002. *Youth and Work in the Postindustrial Cities of North America and Europe*. Leiden, Netherlands: Brill.

Rubbo, Anna, and Michael Taussig. 1978. "Up off Their Knees: Servanthood in Southwest Colombia." In *Female Servants and Economic Development*, ed. Louise Tilly, et al. Michigan Occasional Paper No. I. Ann Arbor: University of Michigan.

Rubenstein, Kim and Daniel Adler. 2000. "International Citizenship: The Future of Nationality in a Globalized World." *Indiana Journal of Global Legal Studies* 7(2): 519–548.

Rubio-Marin, Ruth. 2000. *Immigration as a Democratic Challenge: Citizenship and Inclusion in Germany and the United States*. Cambridge and New York: Cambridge University Press.

Rueschemeyer, Deitrich, Evelyne Huber Stephens, and John D. Stephens, 1992. *Capitalist development and democracy*. Chicago: University of Chicago Press.

Ruffer, Galya, Benarch. 2000. *Virtual Citizenship*. Unpublished diss., University of Pennsylvania.

Ruggie, John. 1998. *Constructing the World Polity*. New York: Routledge.

Ruggie, John Gerard. 2003. "Taking Embedded Liberalism Global: The Corporate Connection." In *Taming globalization: frontiers of governance*, ed. David Held and Mathias Koenig-Archibugi. Cambridge: Polity.

Sacks, Karen. 1994. "How Did Jews Become White Folks?" In *Race*, ed. Steven Gregory and Roger Sanjek. New Brunswick, N.J.: Rutgers University Press.

Sarat, Autsin, and Thomas R. Kearns. 2001. "The Unsettled Status of Human Rights: An Introduction." In *Human Rights: Concepts, Contests, Contingencies*, ed. Sarat and Kearns. Ann Arbor: University of Michigan Press.

Sassen, Saskia. 1996. *Losing Control? Sovereignty in an Age of Globalization*. New York: Columbia University Press.

Sassen, Saskia. 1994. *Cities in a World Economy*. Thousand Oaks, Calif.: Pine Forge Press.

Sassen, Saskia. 1998. *Globalization and its discontents: Essays on the mobility of people and money*. New York: New Press.

Sassen, Saskia. 1999. *Guests and Aliens*. New York: New Press.

———. 2000. "Spatialities and Temporalities of the Global: Elements for a Theorization." *Public Culture* 12(1): 215–232.

———. 2001. *The Global City: New York, London, Tokyo.* Second edition. Princeton, NJ: Princeton University Press.

———. 2003. *Denationalization: Territory, Authority, and Rights in a Global Digital Age.* Princeton, NJ: Princeton University Press (Under Contract).

Saunders, Peter. 1993. "Citizenship in a Liberal Society." *Citizenship and Social Theory,* Bryan Turner, ed. London: Sage.

Saxenian, AnnaLee. 1999. *Silicon Valley's New Immigrant Entrepreneurs.* San Francisco: Public Policy Institute of California.

Scanlan, Shivaun. Forthcoming. "Report on Trafficking from Moldova: Irregular labour markets and restrictive migration policies in Western Europe." International Labor Organization, Migrant Branch.

Scheper-Hughes, Nancy. 1998. "Truth and rumor on the organ trail." *Natural History* 107, no. 8 (October): 48.

Schiek, Dagmar. 1998. "Sex Equality Law after Kalanke an Marschall." *European Law Journal* 4, no. 2: 152.

Schmitt, Eric. 2001. "Children Adopted Abroad Win Automatic Citizenship." *New York Times,* February 27.

Schmitt, Eric. 2001. "INS Both Jailer and Parent To a Child Without a Nation." *New York Times,* June 24.

Schoenberger, Karl. 2000. *Levi's children: Coming to terms with human rights in the Global marketplace.* New York: Atlantic Monthly Press.

Schuck, Peter, and Rogers Smith. 1996. *Citizenship without Consent.* New Haven, Conn.: Yale University Press.

Schwarzenburger, Georg. 1967. *A Manual of International Law,* 5th ed. Milton, England: Professional Books.

Scott, James C. 1976. *The Moral Economy of the Peasant.* New Haven, Conn.: Yale University Press.

Scott, Joan. 1992. "'Experience.'" In Judith Butler and Joan Scott (eds.). *Feminists Theorize the Political.* London: Routledge.

Seckler-Hudson, Catheryn. 1934. *Statelessness, with Special Reference to the United States.* Washington, D.C.: Digest Press.

Seidman, Gay. 1994. *Manufacturing militance: Workers' movements in Brazil and South Africa, 1970–1985.* Berkeley: University of California Press.

Seidman, Gay. 1997. "Restructuring gold mines, redesigning lives: Confronting globalization in the context of apartheid's legacies." In *Research in the Sociology of Work,* vol. 6, 199–221.

Sellers, Patricia. 2000. "The 50 Most Powerful Women in Business," *Fortune,* October 16, p. 34.

Sengupta, Somini, 2002. "Child Traffickers Prey on Bangladesh," *New York Times,* April 29.

Shafir, Gershon (ed.). 1998. *The Citizenship Debates.* Minneapolis: University of Minnesota Press.

Shaiken, Harley. 1995. "Lean production in a Mexican context." In *Lean work: Empowerment and exploitation in the global auto industry.* Detroit: Wayne State University Press.

Shapiro, Michael J. 1997. *Violent Cartographies—Mapping Cultures of War.* Minneapolis: University of Minnesota Press.

Shklar, Judith N. 1991. *American Citizenship: The Quest for Inclusion.* Cambridge, Mass.: Harvard University Press.

Shotter, John. 1993. "Psychology and Citizenship: Identity and Belonging." *Citizenship and Social Theory,* Bryan Turner, ed. London: Sage.

Silverman, Victor. 2000. *Imagining internationalism in American and British labor, 1939–49.* Urbana: University of Illinois Press.

Simon, Rita J., and Howard Altstein. 1991. "Intercountry Adoptions: Experiences of Families in the United States." In Altstein, Howard and Rita J. Simon (eds.). *Intercountry Adoption: A Multinational Perspective.* New York: Praeger.

Simon, Rita J., and Howard Altstein. 2000. *Adoption across Borders: Serving the Children in Transracial and Intercountry Adoptions.* Lanham, Md.: Rowman and Littlefield.

Simons, Lisa. 1999. "Mail Order Brides: The Legal Framework and Possibilities for Change." In *Gender and Immigration,* ed. Gregory A. Kelson and Debra L. DeLaet. New York: New York University Press.

Sinke, Suzanne. 2001. "Gender Ideology Crossing Borders: Finding a 'traditional' spouse in the U.S. international migration context." Paper presented at the Social Science History Association Conference, Chicago, November 15–18.

Small, Cathy. 1997. *Voyages: From Tongan Villages to American Suburbs*. Ithaca, N.Y.: Cornell University Press.

Smith, Lucy. 1993. "Children, Parents, and the European Human Rights Convention." In J. Eekelaar and P. Sarcevic (eds.) *Parenthood in Modern Society*. Dordrecht, The Netherlands: Martinus Nijhoff.

Solinger, Dorothy. 1995. "China's Urban Transients in the Transition from Socialism." *Comparative Politics* 27, no. 2 (January): 127–46.

Solomon, Alisa. 2002. "The Gatekeeper: Watch on the INS—Kids in Captivity." *Village Voice*, February 27–March 5.

Soysal, Yasemin N. 1994. *The Limits of Citizenship: Migrants and Postnational Membership in Europe*. Chicago: University of Chicago Press.

Spiro, Peter J. 1997. "Dual Nationality and the Meaning of Citizenship." *Emory Law Journal* 46: 1411.

Stahler-Sholk, Richard. 1994. "El Salvador's Negotiated Transition: From low-intensity conflict to low-intensity democracy." *Journal of Inter-American Studies and World Affairs* 36, no. 4 (winter): 1–58.

Stallings, Barbara. 1995. "The new international context of development." In *Global change, regional response: the new international context of development*, ed. Barbara Stallings. Cambridge: Cambridge University Press.

Stanley, Amy Dru. 1998. *From Bondage to Contract—Wage Labor, Marriage, and the Market in the Age of Slave Emancipation*. Cambridge: Cambridge University Press.

Stark, David. 2001. "Values, Values, and Valuation: Work and Worth in the New Economy." Paper prepared for the Social Science Research Council Conference on "The New Economy." Emory University, Atlanta, April 13–14.

Stolcke, Verena. 1999. "New Rhetorics of Exclusion in Europe." *International Social Science Journal* 51, no. 1: 25–36.

Stone, Alec. 1997. "The European Court and the National Courts: A Statistical Analysis of Preliminary References, 1961–1995." The Jean Monnet Chair at Harvard Law School, Working Paper.

Storey, Hugo. 1998. "Implications of Incorporation of the European Convention of Human Rights in the Immigration and Asylum Context." *European Human Rights Law Review* 4: 452–75.

Strange, Susan. 1998. *The Retreat of the State: The Diffusion of Power in the World Economy*. Cambridge: Cambridge University Press.

Strauss, Andrew L. 2002. "Overcoming the Dysfunction of the Bifurcated Global System: The Promise of a Peoples Assembly." In Richard Falk, Lester Ruiz, and R.B.J. Walker (eds.), *Reframing the International—Law, Culture(s), Politics*. New York: Routledge.

Symonides, Janusz (ed.). 1998. *Human Rights: New Dimensions and Challenges*. Aldershot: Ashgate.

Tahk, Youn-Taek. 1986. "Intercountry Adoption Program in Korea: Policy, Law and Services." In Hoksbergen, R.A.C. (ed.) *Adoption in Worldwide Perspective: A review of programs, policies and legislation in 14 countries*. Lisse: Swets and Zeitlinger.

Takaki, Ron. 1990. *Iron Cages: Race and Culture in 19th-Century America*. New York: Oxford University Press.

Taylor, Charles. 1994. "The Politics of Recognition," in *Multiculturalism*, ed. Amy Gutmann. Princeton. N.J.: Princeton University Press.

Tilly, Charles (ed.). 1995. "Citizenship, Identity, and Social History." *International Review of Social History*, supplement 3.

Tilly, Charles (ed.). 1996. *Citizenship, Identity, and Social History*. Cambridge: Cambridge University Press.

Tinsman, Heidi. 1992. "The Indispensible Service of Sisters: Considering Domestic Service in Latin America and the United States." *Journal of Women's History* 4, no. 1: 37–59.

Torpey, John. 2000. "'Making Whole What Has Been Smashed': Reflections on Reparations." *Journal of Modern History*, no. 73 (June): 333–58.

Torres, Maria de los Ángeles. 1998. "Transnational Political and Cultural Identities: Crossing Theoretical Borders." *Borderless Borders*, Frank Bonilla, Edwin Mélendez, Rebecca Morales, and Maria de los Ángeles Torres, eds. Philadelphia, PA: Temple University Press.

Torres, Rudy D., L. F. Miron, and J. Xavier Inda (eds.). 1999. *Race, Identity, and Citizenship*. London: Blackwell.

Truong, Thanh-Dam. 1996. "Gender, International Migration, and Social Reproduction: Implications for theory, policy, research, and networking." *Asian and Pacific Migration Journal* 5, no. 1: 27–52.

Turner, Bryan. 2000. "Cosmopolitan Virtue: Loyalty and the City." *Democracy, Citizenship and the Global City*, Engin Isin, ed. New York, NY: Routledge.

UN General Assembly. Resolution 2625, "Resolution on Friendly Relations among States."

United Nations Children's Fund. 2001. *A Decade of Transition*. November 30.

United Nations Children's Fund. *Newsline—summarizing the Progress of Nations 1998*. July 8. Available at www.unicef.org.

United Nations General Assembly. 2000. Resolution 54/263. Optional Protocols to the Convention on the Rights of the Child on the Involvement of Children in Armed Conflict and on the Sale of Children, Child Prostitution, and Child Pornography. 54th Session, Agenda Item 116(a). June 26.

United Nations High Commission on Refugees. *Trends in Unaccompanied and Separated Children Seeking Asylum in Europe, 2000*. Geneva: UNHCR, 2001.

United Nations High Commission on Refugees. 2000. *The State of the World's Refugees 2000*. New York: Oxford University Press.

United Nations. 2000. *The World's Women 2000: Trends and Statistics*. Social Statistics and Indicators, Series K, No. 16. New York: United Nations.

United States Department of Justice. *Immigration of Adopted and Prospective Adoptive Children*. M-249. n.d. pamphlet series.

Varas, Augusto. 1998. "Democratization in Latin America: A Citizen Responsibility." In Felipe Aguero and Jeffrey Stark (eds.), *Fault Lines of Democracy in Post-Transition Latin America*. Miami: North-South Center/University of Miami.

Vidal, Gore. 2002. *Perpetual War for Perpetual Peace: How We Got to Be so Hated*. New York: Thunder's Mouth Press/Nation Books.

von Holdt, Karl. 2000. "From the politics of resistance to the politics or reconstruction? The union and 'ungovernability' in the workplace." In *Trade unions and democratization in South Africa, 1985–1997*, ed. Glenn Adler and Eddie Webster. New York: St. Martin's Press.

Vonk, M. Elizabeth, Peggy J. Sims, and Larry Nackerud. 1999. "Political and Personal Aspects of Intercountry Adoption of Chinese Children in the United States." *Families in Society: The Journal of Contemporary Human Services* 80, no. 5 (September): 496.

Walker, R.B.J. 1998. *One World, Many Worlds*. Boulder, Colo.: L. Rienner.

Walker, R.B.J. 1999. "Citizenship after the Modern Subject." In Kimberly Hutchings and Roland Dannreuther (eds.), *Cosmopolitan Citizenship*. Houndsmill and New York: MacMillan and St. Martin's.

Walzer, Michael. 1983. *Spheres of Justice*. New York: Basic.

Wapner, Paul. 1996. *Environmental Activism and World Civic Politics*. Albany: SUNY Press.

Wasserstrom, Jeffrey N., et al. (eds.). 2001. *Human Rights and Revolutions*. Lanham, Md.: Rowman and Littlefield.

Weber, Max. 1958. *The City*, New York, NY: Free Press.

Weber, Max. 1981. *General Economic History*. New Brunswick, N.J.: Transaction.

Webster, Eddie, and Glenn Adler. 2000. "Consolidating democracy in a liberalizing world: Trade unions and democratization in South Africa." In *Trade unions and democratization in South Africa, 1985–1997*, ed. Glenn Adler and Eddie Webster. New York: St. Martin's Press.

Weil, Patrick. 2001. *Access to Citizenship: A Comparison of Twenty-Five Nationality Laws*. In T. Alexander Aleinikoff and Douglas Klusmeyers, eds., *Citizenship Today: Global Perspectives and Practices*. Washington, D.C.: Carnegie Endowment for International Peace.

Weiler, Joseph. 1999. "The European Union: Enlargment, Constitutionalism, and Democracy." Talk presented at the Humbolt University, Berlin, Germany, November 29. Available at http://www.rewi.hu-berlin.de/WHI/deutsch/fce/fce799/weiler.htm.

Weis, P. 1979. *Nationality and Statelessness in International Law*, 2nd ed. London: Stevens Press.

Wells, Don. 1999. "Building transnational coordinative unionism." In *Confronting change: Auto labor and lean production in North America*, ed. Huberto Juarez and Steve Babson. Detroit: Wayne State University, and Universidade de Puebla.

Werbner, Pnina, and Nira Yuval-Davis. 1999. "Women and the New Discourse of Citizenship." In *Women, Citizenship, and Difference*, ed. Nira Yuval-Davis and Pnina Werbner. London: Zed Books.

Whitaker, Barbara. 2001. "Judge Hearing Custody Fight Would Keep Thai Boy in U.S." *New York Times*, June 5.

Wijers, Marjan and Lin Lap-Chew. 1997. *Trafficking in Women*. Utrecht, Netherlands: Foundation against Trafficking in Women.

Williams, Brackette. 1995. "The Symbolics of Ethnic Historical Traditions and 'Suffering': Some Implications for the Doctrine of Equal Citizenship in the United States." Unpublished paper (October).

Williams, Heather. 2000. "Of labor tragedy and legal farce: The Han Young factory struggle in Tijuana, Mexico." Paper presented at "Human Rights and Globalization: When Transnational Civil Society Networks Hit the Ground." University of California, Santa Cruz, December 1–2.

Williams, John. 2002. "Good International Citizenship." In Nigel Dower and John Williams (eds.), *Global Citizenship: A Critical Introduction*. New York: Routledge.

Williams, Oliver (ed.). 2000. *Global codes of conduct: An idea whose time has come*. Notre Dame, Ind.: Notre Dame University Press.

Wilson, Jim. 2000. "From 'solidarity' to convergence: International trade union cooperation in the media sector." In *Transnational cooperation among labor unions*, ed. Michael Gordon and Lowell Turner. Ithaca, N.Y.: ILR/Cornell.

Wintersberger, Helmut. 2000. "Family Citizenship or Citizenship for Children? Childhood Perspectives and Policies." In Henry Cavanna (ed.), *The New Citizenship of the Family*. Aldershot: Ashgate.

Wolin, Sheldon. 1996. "Fugitive Democracy." In Seyla Benhabib (ed.), *Democracy and Difference*. Princeton, N.J.: Princeton University Press.

World Bank. 1996. *World Development Report 1995: Workers in an integrating world*. Oxford: Oxford University Press, for the World Bank.

World Trade Organization. 1996. Draft Singapore Ministerial Conference, Ministerial Conference, Singapore, December 9–13. Available at www.wto.org.

Wrigley, Julia. 1995. *Other People's Children: An Intimate Account of the Dilemmas Facing Middle-Class Parents and the Women They Hire to Raise Their Children*. New York: Basic.

Young, Iris Marion. 1989. "Polity and group difference: A critique of the ideal of universal citizenship." *Ethics* 99, no. 2: 250–74.

Young, Iris Marion. 1990. *Justice and the Politics of Difference*. Princeton, N.J.: Princeton University Press.

Yu Zhou and Yen-Fen Tseng. 2001. "Regrounding the 'Ungrounded Empires': Geographic Conditions of Transnationalism." *Global Networks*, no. 2.

Zhao, Yilu. 2002. "Foreign-Born Adoptees Explore Their Cultural Roots." *New York Times*, April 9.

Zinn, Kenneth. 2000. "Solidarity across borders: The UMWA's corporate campaign against Peabody and Hanson PLC." In *Transnational Cooperation among Labor Unions*, ed. Michael Gordon and Lowell Turner. Ithaca, N.Y. ILR/Cornell.

Contributors

Alison Brysk is Professor of Political Science and International Studies at the University of California, Irvine. She is the author of *The Politics of Human Rights in Argentina* (1994) and *From Tribal Village to Global Village: Indian Rights and International Relations in Latin America* (2000), and the editor of *Globalization and Human Rights* (2002). Her forthcoming book, *Human Rights and Private Wrongs*, will be part of Routledge's Human Rights Horizons series.

Richard Falk has been a Visiting Professor in Global Studies at the UCSB since 2002. Prior to that he was Milbank Professor of International Law at Princeton University where he was a member of the faculty for forty years. He is currently Chair of the Board of the Nuclear Age Peace Foundation and a member of the Editorial Board of The Nation. His most recent books are *The Great Terror War* (2003) and *Unlocking the Middle East* (2003). He is also the author of *Human Rights Horizons: The Pursuit of Justice in a Globalizing World* (2000).

David Jacobson is Professor of Sociology at Arizona State University. His research is in political sociology from a global, comparative and legal perspective, with a particular interest in international institutions, immigration and citizenship. Jacobson, who was born in South Africa, was educated at the Hebrew University, the London School of Economics and Princeton University. He is the author of *Rights Across Borders: Immigration and the Decline of Citizenship* (Johns Hopkins University Press, 1996) and *Place and Belonging in America* (Johns Hopkins University Press, 2002), and is editor of *Identities, Borders and Orders: New Perspectives in International Relations* (University of Minnesota Press, 2001, with Mathias Albert and Yosef Lapid); *The Immigration Reader: America in Multidisciplinary Perspective* (Blackwell, 1998); and *Old Nations, New World: Conceptions of the World Order* (Westview Press, 1994), among other publications. Jacobson is a member of the Cycladic Academy for Europe in Athens and Tinos, Greece.

Ronnie D. Lipschutz is Professor of Politics and Associate Director of the Center for Global, International and Regional Studies at the University of California, Santa Cruz. He has written widely on national security, global environmental politics, the crisis of the modern state, and Cold War film and fiction. His most recent books are *After Authority—War, Peace and Global Politics in the 21st Century* (2000), *Cold War Fantasies: Film, Fiction and Foreign Policy* (2001) and *Global Environmental Politics: Power, Perspectives and Practice* (2003). He is currently completing a book tentatively titled *Regulation for the Rest of Us? Globalization, Governmentality and Global Politics.*

Kristen Hill Maher is an Assistant Professor of Political Science at San Diego State University, also affiliated with the Center for Comparative Immigration Studies at the University of California, San Diego. She has published work on the rights of migrant workers as well as on the immigrant-based service economy in Southern California, most recently in *Urban Affairs Review.* This year, she expanded her research in a comparative direction with new fieldwork on Peruvian domestic workers in Santiago, Chile, and has also begun a project on "gendered migrations," or the transnational migration of women filling traditional women's roles in more developed states.

Aihwa Ong is Professor at the Department of Anthropology and the Department of South and Southeast Asian Studies at the University of California, Berkeley. She is the author of the now-classic *Spirits of Resistance and Capitalist Discipline* (1987); and the award-winning *Flexible Citizenship: The Cultural Logistics of Transnationality* (1999), and co-editor of *Ungrounded Empires: The Cultural Struggles of Modern Chinese Transnationalism* (1997). Her most recent works are *Buddha is Hiding: Refugees, Citizenship, the New America* (2003), and (co-edited with Stephen Collier) *Global Assemblages: Technology, Politics, and Ethics as Anthropological Questions* (forthcoming).

Galya Benarieh Ruffer is Visiting Assistant Professor of International Studies and Political Science at DePaul University, Chicago. She is co-author of "Courts Across Borders: The Implications of Judicial Agency for Human Rights and Democracy," *Human Rights Quarterly* 25 (2003). She holds a J.D. from Northwestern University and has recently completed a doctorate in Political Science from the University of Pennsylvania. Her work focuses on constitutional democracy, the construction of citizenship and the exclusion of "undesireables." As an immigration attorney, she has specialized in political asylum.

Saskia Sassen is the Ralph Lewis Professor of Sociology at the University of Chicago, and Centennial Visiting Professor at the London School of Economics. She is currently completing her forthcoming book *Denationalization : Territory, Authority and Rights in a Global Digital Age* (Under contract with Princeton University Press 2003) based on her five year project on governance and accountability in a global economy. She has also just completed for UNESCO a five-year project on sustainable human settlement for which she set up a network of researchers and activists in over 50 countries. Her most recent books are *Guests and Aliens* (New Press 1999) and the edited *Global Networks, Linked Cities* (New York and London: Routledge 2002). *The Global City* is out in a new fully updated edition in 2001. Her books are translated into fourteen languages. She serves on several editorial boards and is an advisor to several international bodies. She is a Member of the National Academy of Sciences Panel on Cities, a Member of the Council on Foreign Relations, and Chair of the new Information Technology, International Cooperation and Global Security Committee of the Social Science Research Council (USA).

Gay W. Seidman is Professor of Sociology at the University of Wisconsin-Madison. In addition to *Manufacturing Militance: Workers' Movements in Brazil and South Africa, 1970–1985* (1994), she has published widely on labor, gender and democratization in South Africa. She is currently writing a comparative study of transnational labor monitoring schemes.

Gershon Shafir is Professor of Sociology at the University of California, San Diego. He is the author of *Land, Labor, and the Origins of the Israeli-Palestinian Conflict, 1882–1914* (1989, and updated edition 1996), *Immigrants and Nationalists* (1995), the editor of *The Citizenship Debates* (1998), and co-editor of *The New Israel: Peace and Socio-Economic Transformation* (2000). His most recent book, co-authored with Yoav Peled, is *Being Israeli: The Dynamics of Multiple Citizenship,* and it was the winner of the Middle Eastern Studies Association's Albert Hourani Award for outstanding book in 2002.

Peter J. Spiro is Professor of Law at Hofstra University Law School in Hempstead, N.Y. In 1998–99, he studied the law of U.S. citizenship as an Open Society Institute Individual Project Fellow. His book on the subject is forthcoming from Oxford University Press.

INDEX

(ʻnʼ indicates a note)

A

Abdulaziz case, ECHR, 80
Accountability, global human rights, 209
Adoption, 155, 165. *See also* Transnational adoption
"Adoption triangle," 165
Aerospace industry, venture capital, 58
Affirmative action, 94
African-American Civil Rights, 54
African Commission on Human and People's Rights, 22
African Union, 187
Agency
    definition, 73
    and immigration, 83
    institutional mechanisms, 73, 78–83
    international instruments, 80–81
    and judicial rights, 77
Al Qaeda network, 181
Ali, Karamat, 123
Alsace-Lorraine, struggle for, 36
American Bar Association, Office of Children's Services bill, 160–161
American Bill of Rights, 4, 13
American citizenship, meanings of, 53
American Citizenship, 64
American Civil Liberties Union, 160–161
Amnesty International
    Office of Children's Services bill, 160–161
    on social and economic rights, 20
Amuur case, ECHR, 84
"Anarchiacal Fallacies," 21
Anderson, Bridget, 155
Annan, Kofi, 187
Anti-Personnel Landmines Treaty, 187
Anti-Slavery International, children's rights, 158
Appadurai, Arjun, 54
Apparel industry, labor codes, 125, 126
Arendt, Hannah,, 23, 48, 51nn.13, 16, 92
Asians
    entrepreneur networks, 57–58
    middle class immigration, 57

Assembly piecework, electronics, 59, 60
"Asset ambiguity," 57
Association, core right, 109, 111–112
Asylum and Immigration Appeals Act, 80
Asylum laws, interpretations, 83
Autonomy, and rights, 155
Axford, Barrie, 5
"Axis of evil," 181

B

Bahrain, domestic workers, 137
Bakan, Abigail B., domestic labor hierarchy, 141, 142
Bancroft, George, 104n.4
Bancroft treaties, nationality transfer, 90
Bangladesh, child trafficking, 160
Bar-Yaacov, Nissim, 104n.5
Baubök, Rainer, 136
Belgium, citizenship claims, 156
Bentham, Jeremy, 21
Bhutan, childhood registration, 157
Bin Laden, Osama, 181, 182–183, 185
Borjas, George J. 63
Boys, child trafficking, 160
Brazil, workforce development, 117–118
Burke, Edmund, 20
Bush, George W., policies of, 183–189

C

California, as West of East, 56
Canada
    domestic guest workers, 144
    INTERCEDE, 150
    live-in caregiver recruitment, 141–142
    nanny agencies, 145
Capital flight, 24
    and labor rights, 111–112, 114
Capitalism
    and citizenship, 33
    and social citizenship, 14
    neoliberal philosophy, 55
Captive Daughters, children's rights, 158
Cardoso, Fernando Henrique, 111
Categorical Imperative, 42
Catholic Conference of Bishops, juvenile refugee placement, 161

People Out of Place

Globalization, Human Rights, and the Citizenship Gap